P9-CLQ-943

DO FACTS MATTER?

THE JULIAN J. ROTHBAUM DISTINGUISHED LECTURE SERIES

THE MORE YOU KNOW, THE HARDER IT IS TO TAKE DECISIVE ACTION.

ONCE YOU BECOME INFORMED, YOU START SEEING COMPLEXITIES AND SHADES OF GRAY.

© 1993 Watterson/Dist. by Universal Press Syndicate

YOU REALIZE THAT NOTHING IS AS CLEAR AND SIMPLE AS IT FIRST APPEARS. ULTIMATELY, KNOWLEDGE IS PARALYZING.

BEING A MAN OF ACTION, I CAN'T AFFORD TO TAKE THAT RISK.

YOU'RE IGNORANT, BUT AT LEAST YOU ACT ON IT.

DO FACTS MATTER?

Information and Misinformation in American Politics

JENNIFER L. HOCHSCHILD
and
KATHERINE LEVINE EINSTEIN

UNIVERSITY OF OKLAHOMA PRESS : NORMAN

Frontispiece: CALVIN AND HOBBES © 1993 Watterson. Reprinted with permission of UNIVERSAL UCLICK. All rights reserved.
Figures 2.1, 6.2: DOONESBURY © 2012 G. B. Trudeau. Reprinted with permission of UNIVERSAL UCLICK. All rights reserved.

This book is published with the generous assistance of The Kerr Foundation.

Library of Congress Cataloging-in-Publication Data

Hochschild, Jennifer L., 1950–
    Do facts matter? : misinformation and American politics / Jennifer L. Hochschild and Katherine Levine Einstein.
      pages cm
    Includes bibliographical references and index.
    ISBN 978-0-8061-4686-7 (cloth)
    ISBN 978-0-8061-5590-6 (paper)
    1. Political participation—United States. 2. Democracy—United States. 3. Judgment—Political aspects. 4. Decision making—Political aspects. I. Einstein, Katherine Levine. II. Title.
    JK1764.B76 2015
    323'.0420973—dc23
                        2014027612

Do Facts Matter? Information and Misinformation in American Politics is Volume 13 in The Julian J. Rothbaum Distinguished Lecture Series.

The paper in this book meets the guidelines for permanence and durability of the Committee on Production Guidelines for Book Longevity of the Council on Library Resources, Inc. ∞

Copyright © 2015 by the University of Oklahoma Press, Norman, Publishing Division of the University. Paperback published 2016. Manufactured in the U.S.A.

All rights reserved. No part of this publication may be reproduced, stored in a retrieval system, or transmitted, in any form or by any means, electronic, mechanical, photocopying, recording, or otherwise—except as permitted under Section 107 or 108 of the United States Copyright Act—without the prior permission of the University of Oklahoma Press.

Jennifer Hochschild dedicates this book to her beloved sister Melissa, too soon gone but always remembered.

Katherine Einstein dedicates this book to her daughter, Elise, the most wonderful writing distraction.

Widespread education not only creates the conditions within which broad-based participation in political affairs is possible, but also enhances the quality of that participation.

Mission statement for the Julian J. Rothbaum
Distinguished Lecture Series

It isn't what we don't know that gives us trouble, it's what we know that ain't so.

Variously attributed to Will Rogers,
Mark Twain, and Satchel Paige

Politics and facts don't belong in the same room.

Attributed to Lee Atwater

CONTENTS

ILLUSTRATIONS

TABLES

FOREWORD

AMONG THE MANY good things that have happened to me in my life, there is none in which I take more pride than the establishment of the Carl Albert Congressional Research and Studies Center at the University of Oklahoma, and none in which I take more satisfaction than the Center's presentation of the Julian J. Rothbaum Distinguished Lecture Series. The series is a perpetually endowed program of the University of Oklahoma, created in honor of Julian J. Rothbaum by his wife, Irene, and son, Joel Jankowsky.

Julian J. Rothbaum, my close friend since our childhood days in southeastern Oklahoma, was a longtime leader in Oklahoma in civic affairs. He served as a regent of the University of Oklahoma for two terms and as a state regent for higher education. In 1974 he was awarded the university's highest honor, the Distinguished Service Citation, and in 1986 he was inducted into the Oklahoma Hall of Fame.

The Rothbaum Lecture Series is devoted to the themes of representative government, democracy and education, and citizen participation in public affairs, values to which Julian J. Rothbaum was committed throughout his life. His lifelong dedication to the University of Oklahoma, the state, and his country is a tribute to the ideals to which the Rothbaum Lecture Series is dedicated. The books in the series make an enduring contribution to an understanding of American democracy.

Carl B. Albert
Forty-sixth Speaker of the
United States House of Representatives

ACKNOWLEDGMENTS

JENNIFER HOCHSCHILD THANKS Joel Jankowsky and Irene Rothbaum for envisioning and endowing the Julian J. Rothbaum Distinguished Lectures in Representative Government in honor of Julian Rothbaum. Mr. Rothbaum's family had the wisdom to point the lecture series in the direction of "the importance of the relationship between education and public service in a representative democracy and the importance of participation by private citizens in public affairs." These are essential features of a would-be liberal democracy, and they deserve and need a great deal of careful, sustained attention.

Hochschild also offers deep thanks to everyone who made her trip to the University of Oklahoma to deliver the Rothbaum Lectures so pleasant and fruitful. The lectures provided her the opportunity to think systematically about a topic on which she had long ruminated. President David Boren, the faculty and staff of the Carl Albert Congressional Research and Studies Center, and the graduate fellows were hospitable hosts doing important work. Questions and comments at the lectures and in conversations helped greatly to sharpen the nascent arguments. Special thanks to Cindy Rosenthal, Ronald Peters, and Ladonna Sullivan for all of their hospitality—including picking her up before the crack of dawn to go to the gym—as well as their substantive comments on the lectures and manuscript. And Hochschild will always cherish the T-shirt from the undergraduate rowing team; she hopes to row with them soon.

Our thanks to Tom Silver, of the invaluable *Polling Report,* for his work over many years and in particular for retrieving surveys on Clarence Thomas from his files. Similar thanks go to Lydia Saad of the Gallup Organization for her generous help in plumbing Gallup data. We received excellent research assistance from Andrew Benitez, Sheldon Bond, Jay Lundy, and especially Richard Coffin, who heroically stuck with this project even while holding the much more exciting position of White House intern.

The John W. Kluge Center at the Library of Congress provided an excellent facility in which to work out some of the analysis. Hochschild thanks Carolyn Brown, Joanne Kitching, Mary Lou Reker, and her fellow Fellows for their help and companionship. Over a longer period the Center for American Political Studies at Harvard University has offered a wonderful setting in which to teach, write, complain, start over, and do all of the other things that constitute the life of an academic. Hochschild and Einstein both thank Daniel Carpenter and Lilia Halpern-Smith for maintaining such a congenial setting. Hochschild finished her share of the writing at the Straus Institute for the Advanced Study of Law and Justice at the New York University School of Law; a more pleasant environment, and one more conducive to getting work done, would be hard to imagine. Einstein finished her share of the writing at the equally pleasant environment of Boston University's Department of Political Science, and she thanks her colleagues for many valued conversations.

Along the way, participants in Harvard University's Political Psychology and Behavior Workshop provided helpful comments on the lectures, the ideas, or the manuscript, as did a terrific set of colleagues: Larry Bartels, David Chappell, Michael Fortner, Martin Gilens, David Glick, Douglas Kriner, Arthur Lupia and his perspicacious students, David Mayhew, Brendan Nyhan, John Sides, and two insightful reviewers for the University of Oklahoma Press. Anthony King read and commented on the whole manuscript, to its great benefit. These people saved us from errors large and small, pushed us to clarify and deepen (or abandon) arguments, and disagreed with one or another part of the analysis or evidence. All of that made our task much more difficult and the book much better. Others in the invisible academy were also invaluable—responding quickly to urgent requests for a citation, or a crosstab, or an idea. We won't try to list them all for fear of missing some, but they both benefited the book and made us ever more appreciative of the collegiality among scholars.

Einstein thanks Nathan Einstein for his tireless research assistance. We also thank our careful and insightful manuscript editor, John Thomas, as well as Charles Rankin, Steven Baker, Carol Zuber-Mallison, and others at the University of Oklahoma Press. Their love of books and their dedication to the complex task of improving them shone through in all of our dealings.

Katherine Levine Einstein started as a research assistant but rose quickly to coauthor. The ideas, arguments, and evidence are shared equally between the authors; put better, perhaps, the ideas, arguments, and evidence were so jointly developed that it would be impossible to parcel out shares for which each author was primarily responsible.

Jennifer L. Hochschild
Katherine Levine Einstein

DO FACTS MATTER?

CHAPTER 1

WHAT DO PEOPLE KNOW AND WHY DOES IT MATTER?

Misinformation on the part of the public makes for bad lawmaking on the part of the government.

Joe Keohane in the *Boston Globe*, 2010

The other thing about the Tea Party . . . is educate, is exposure. If you look into a lot of the bills, we American people have no idea what is in some of those bills. If you follow the Tea Party and they're getting more and more organized in taking on issues and really diving into them and informing the public. . . . I think this . . . motivation and stuff will really help get people . . . to band together and start pushing back.

Tea Party advocate, 2010

WAS BARACK *Hussein* OBAMA born outside the United States, so that his presidency and all laws passed under it are unconstitutional? Are two out of every five Americans black? Did the crime rate rise during the first decade of the twenty-first century? These are questions of factual information, to which there are correct answers—respectively, no, no, and no. Knowing the right answer to each question is important for making appropriate political choices and policy decisions. And yet in opinion polls, mainstream media, and general public discourse, many sensible and educated Americans have answered yes to each of these queries. They are wrong, and their views are likely to be associated with—may even contribute to—consequential and problematic political actions or public policies.

Consider another set of questions: Do higher taxes reduce car owners' consumption of gasoline? Do more Americans vote in local elections, where their vote has a much greater impact, than in state or national elections, where their vote may be substantively trivial? Can intensive tutoring improve reading and math skills of inner-city students? These are slightly more complicated questions of fact since they involve causal links. But they too have correct, or at least generally consensual, answers —respectively, yes, no, and yes. Many Americans would concur with these answers and support the implied policy or political goals—and yet do not select the actions that would seem to follow directly from them.

Almost every serious thinker who has considered how to make democratic governance stable and effective has emphasized the need for a knowledgeable citizenry that uses relevant information to inform public choices. Let us allow Thomas Jefferson, in his "Bill for the More General Diffusion of Knowledge," to speak for the many:

> Even under the best forms [of government], those entrusted with power have, in time, and by slow operations, perverted it into tyranny; and it is believed that the most effectual means of preventing this would be, to illuminate, as far as practicable, the minds of the people at large, and more especially to give them knowledge of those facts, which history exhibiteth, that . . . they may be enabled to know ambition under all its shapes, and prompt to exert their natural powers to defeat its purposes. (Jefferson 1779)

Conservative opponents of expanding the franchise in the nineteenth century stood Jefferson's argument on its head, proposing literacy tests for voting on the grounds that "persons wholly destitute of education do not possess sufficient intelligence to enable them to exercise the right of suffrage beneficially to the public" (Samuel Jones, 1842, quoted in Keyssar 2000: 66; see also Scalia 1999). Jefferson would have approved of the answer to the conservatives:

> The provision already made for the establishment of common schools, will, in a very few years, extend the benefit of education

to all our citizens. The universal diffusion of information will forever distinguish our population from that of Europe. Virtue and intelligence are the true basis on which every republican government must rest. When these are lost, freedom will no longer exist. The diffusion of education is the only sure means of establishing these pillars of freedom. . . . Our common school fund will . . . be consecrated by a constitutional provision; and I feel no apprehension, for myself, or my posterity, in confiding the right of suffrage to the great mass of such a population as I believe ours will always be. (David Buel Jr. of New York, 1821, quoted in Peterson 1966: 203)

And, indeed, most American state constitutions do include provisions requiring public schooling and its funding, following a logic similar to that found in the Texas constitution: "A general diffusion of knowledge being essential to the preservation of the liberties and rights of the people, it shall be the duty of the Legislature of the State to establish and make suitable provision for the support and maintenance of an efficient system of public free schools" (Article 7. Education, Sec. 1).

Much more recently, Michael Delli Carpini and Scott Keeter (1996: 3, 5) made the same point in their authoritative study of the role of knowledge in a democracy:

Factual knowledge about politics is a critical component of citizenship, one that is essential if citizens are to discern their real interests and take effective advantage of the civic opportunities afforded them. . . . Knowledge is a keystone to other civic requisites. In the absence of adequate information neither passion nor reason is likely to lead to decisions that reflect the real interests of the public. And democratic principles must be understood to be accepted and acted on in any meaningful way.

Most simply—and most important, given the speaker's position—a member of Congress declared to Richard Fenno: "I have the best platform from which to educate of anyone in the country. To me, there's no difference between leadership and education. . . . What is politics if it's not teaching?" (Fenno 1978: 162). President Obama agrees that "an informed and educated citizenry is essential to the functioning of our modern democratic society," though he deflects responsibility to others: "I encourage educational and community institutions across the country to help Americans find and evaluate the information they seek, in all its forms" (Oct. 1, 2009).[1]

Almost no one disputes, in short, that citizens should acquire and use appropriate and correct information when making political and policy choices (see, most generally, the essays in Friedman and Friedman 2012). Schooling is helpful; in one canonical study, for example, high school graduates correctly answered an average of 3.7 out of eight questions probing political knowledge, whereas those with a postgraduate degree correctly answered 6.1 on average (Verba et al. 1995; see also Popkin et al. 1999; Jerit et al. 2006).[2] Nevertheless, even well-educated people frequently use incorrect information in the public arena; in fact, as we show in this book, the well educated may be especially inclined to absorb and use error-laden information.[3] Other people know the facts but do not use them politically.

Do Facts Matter? addresses the political and policy implications, broadly defined, of these three conditions. The starting point is Jefferson's ideal of knowing and using correct information to make policy or political choices. However, we pay more attention to two deviations: knowing but ignoring correct information, and believing and using incorrect information. Our goal is not, as Jefferson's bill was, to design a system of public education that enables every "person, whom nature hath endowed with genius and virtue . . . to guard the sacred deposit of the rights and liberties of their fellow citizens, . . . without regard to wealth, birth or other accidental condition or circumstance." We are less ambitious than he; we seek to explicate these three relationships between facts and politics so that residents of the United States are better able to pursue Jefferson's ideal and ward off the risks he points to. But we are like Jefferson in being motivated by both hope and fear—hope that Americans can and want to use accurate information to make good decisions, and fear that the temptation to use misinformation can deeply damage the fragile system of democratic decision making.

LINKING KNOWLEDGE AND ITS USE

To introduce the basic logic of our argument and its terminology, we begin with four vignettes.

Reports of the Surgeons General

The surgeon general of the United States first issued a report on the harmful effects of smoking in 1964. It was followed by similar reports from his successors three more times in the 1960s, eight times in the 1970s, ten times in the 1980s, four times in the 1990s, and six times in the 2000s—that is, almost annually for four decades. Cigarette packages received their first warning labels in 1965, and Congress prohibited cigarette ads on television and radio in 1969.

Cigarette consumption in the United States had risen steadily since 1900, peaking in 1963 at 4,345 per capita annually among adults, at which point it started a steady decline. Adults' per-capita consumption fell to just over 3,000 in 1988 (the level in 1944), to just over 2,000 in 2001 (the level in 1940), and to 1,200 in 2011 (lower than the level of 1930). Heavy smokers, who consume more than twenty cigarettes per day, declined from 23 percent of the population in 1965 to under 7 percent in 2007 (Pierce et al. 2011). The decline has been steepest among the best educated. The proportion of young adults who have never smoked rose from just under half in 1965 to almost three-quarters in 2008 (American Lung Association 2010). As of 2012, only 17.3 percent of adults age 18–24 smoked cigarettes, according to the Centers for Disease Control and Prevention (CDC 2014).

Survey data suggest that the reports and the behavioral changes are linked. In 1958 and 1960, no more than half of the respondents to Gallup polls agreed that cigarette smoking is "one of the causes of cancer of the lung"; three in ten said it was not, and about a quarter did not know. In 1969, 1971, and 1972, however, the proportion of respondents who denied any link between cancer and smoking had declined by half and the number with no opinion had also diminished somewhat.

By 1977 and 1981, the deniers were down to 10 percent of the population, the same as the "don't knows." In 1990, both combined were only 6 percent of respondents, and that is roughly where the numbers have stayed. In short, from 1960 to 1990 the links between cancer and smoking strengthened in the public's mind from an equal division between yes and no to almost unanimity.[4]

Although the path is by no means linear, substantial policy changes have emerged from the reports and Americans' acceptance of the new knowledge. According to the American Nonsmokers' Rights Foundation, 3,876 municipalities and thirty-six states have laws or ordinances that specify locations where smoking is prohibited. Over four-fifths of the U.S. population live in places with smoking bans in some or all workplaces, restaurants, bars, or outdoor recreation areas. All three levels of government tax cigarettes, litigation by the National Association of Attorneys General and others have generated various judicial controls, and cigarette advertising is banned in particular times and places. In a move that even public health experts find excessive, a few employers are refusing to hire people who smoke (Walton 2013).

We cannot here parse the exact impact of new knowledge as distinguished from policy or cultural changes, but that is not essential; the role of facts in politics can be just as important if knowledge operates indirectly or as a reinforcement to some other causal mechanism. What matters is that the proportion of smokers declined, heavy smoking decreased, fewer young adults started to smoke, cigarette consumption reversed its upward trend, and the federal government limited advertisements, promulgated regulations, and raised taxes—all within a few years after the government began to publicize widely the association with lung cancer and other health risks (Pennock 2007).

People who have knowledge of relevant facts and make choices that accord with it are, at least in this aspect of their lives, ideal denizens of a Jeffersonian democracy. In our analysis we label them the "active" or "engaged informed" (or, sometimes, Jeffersonian citizens). Their distinctiveness becomes clearer when we compare them with three other groups.

"Yes, but . . .": School Desegregation

Surveys show that large majorities of Americans agree that racially desegregated schools benefit both blacks and whites, that they would like their child to attend school with students of different races, that public schools should serve the public interest as well as help individuals to learn, and that communities are substantially segregated and unlikely to change in the foreseeable future. But pluralities or majorities also reject every proposed government policy to mandate or promote school or neighborhood racial desegregation (Hochschild and Herk 1990).

The General Social Survey (GSS) provides one strand of evidence on this complicated conflict among norms, knowledge, and policy preferences.[5] Normatively, 89 percent of the almost 8,700 white respondents who were asked this question from 1972 through 2012 agreed that black and white children should attend the same school. Over 80 percent would not object if their child attended a school in which a few or half of the students were black. Factually, however, almost half of the GSS whites reported that no blacks lived in their neighborhood. So how do whites propose to reconcile facts and norms?

Not, it turns out, through reassignment and mandatory transportation. The GSS asked 20,000 whites over the past forty years whether they supported interdistrict busing: four-fifths were opposed. Moreover, a whopping 85 percent of white respondents who both endorse desegregation and live in all-white neighborhoods opposed busing.

These conflicted whites similarly opposed reconciling facts and their norms through residential integration, a policy alternative that would obviate the need for busing. A third of white respondents to the GSS who both endorsed school desegregation and lived in all-white neighborhoods believed that whites have the right to keep blacks out of their neighborhoods. Only 10 percent of similarly situated white respondents agreed that suburban governments should "encourage black people to buy homes in the [white] suburbs."

Perhaps most striking, many of these respondents were reluctant to support even a nongovernmental resolution to their conflicting norms and facts. In 1977, among the 1,200 whites asked both questions on the GSS, 57 percent of those who agreed that blacks and whites should attend the same schools opposed "voluntary programs" organized by "religious and business groups" to "integrate white suburbs." Among those who both lived in segregated neighborhoods and endorsed integrated schooling, three out of five nonetheless opposed even voluntary desegregative efforts. Overall, most whites were reluctant to use their knowledge in forging policy judgments, even when the proposed solution was voluntary, nongovernmental, and in accord with their stated norms.

The GSS did not ask respondents who live in all-white communities, approve of school desegregation, but oppose policies or programs to integrate neighborhoods or schools what strategy, if any, they would support to achieve their norm. Perhaps there is such a strategy, but no one has yet found it on a large scale. As Richard Kahlenberg (2001: 42) puts it, "Today a bipartisan consensus holds that integrated schools are a good thing but we shouldn't do much of anything to promote them" (see also Hochschild and Herk 1990; Frankenberg and Jacobsen 2011).

We call the set of people whose policy preferences or political engagement do not accord with their knowledge on a particular topic the "inactive" or "disengaged informed." This term has all the defects of a shorthand label; it ignores activity in other realms, it says nothing about motivations or justifications for the relevant inactivity, and it says nothing about whether such inactivity is appropriate or not. We address those issues in later chapters; for now, the central point is to contrast inaction or disengagement with action, as shown previously in the vignette of the surgeon general reports.

The Relative Status of Black Americans

A 1995 survey asked an unusual battery of questions, focusing on substantive knowledge about the well-being of different groups of Americans. Respondents were asked if African Americans were at least as well off as the average white in six domains of life—income, housing, education, health care, jobs, and risk of job loss. The empirical evidence on all of these points is clear; the correct answer is no for each.

Many respondents were, however, factually mistaken in answering these questions. Roughly three in five whites agreed that African Americans are as well off or better off than whites with regard to their jobs or risk of job loss, access to health care, and education; more than two in five said the same with regard to income and housing (only 14–32 percent of African Americans, depending on the arena in question, were similarly misinformed).[6] Overall, 81 percent of white respondents mistakenly agreed that blacks are as well off as whites on at least one item; 42 percent mistakenly saw racial equality on five or all six items. Only a quarter correctly perceived racial inequality on five or all six items (*Washington Post* et al. 1995: 54–60; see also Kaplowitz et al. 2003).

Misinformation was systematically associated with a distinctive policy stance. Compared to those with correct information, white respondents who were misinformed on at least one item were more likely to favor a balanced federal budget, cuts in personal income taxes, tax breaks for businesses, limits on abortion, and limits to affirmative action; there was no difference between the two groups on welfare reform and reforming Medicare. Overall, misinformed white respondents supported policies that were racially and fiscally more conservative than were the policy views of the correctly informed.[7]

In short, some Americans hold incorrect "knowledge" that is associated with distinctive involvement with the public arena. We label this third group the "active" or "engaged misinformed." Here, too, the label only begins to identify a group around whom questions swirl: Why do they hold misinformation? Are their mistaken opinions causally linked, in either direction, to their distinctive political and policy views or activities? Can they be taught the facts, and is it worth the effort? How and how much does their activity affect democratic decision making? We address these questions in later chapters; for now, the crucial point is to see how they resemble and differ from the two groups already described, the active informed and the inactive informed.

The Illogical, Inactive, Misinformed

Our conceptual scheme using the three vignettes above suggests a fourth category: individuals who are misinformed but politically inactive with regard to that misinformation—that is, the "inactive misinformed." Unlike the previous three categories, this one plays little role in democratic decision making because of the relatively illogical and politically unimportant nature of its subscribers. We describe it here for the sake of completeness but pay no attention to it in the rest of the book.

Two of our vignettes, the surgeon general's reports and the relative status of black Americans, illustrate both the unlikelihood of belonging to the inactive misinformed and its public insignificance. With regard to smoking, a person in this category would mistakenly believe that smoking is good for one's health, despite the government's repeated warnings. She would not act on this factual mistake, however; instead, she would not smoke. In other words, despite being misinformed she would behave identically to members of the active informed—our democratic ideal—by not smoking.

With regard to the relative status of African Americans, an inactive misinformed person would similarly subscribe to falsehoods; he would believe that blacks' status was equal or superior to that of whites across an array of economic and social categories. He would not, however, associate this knowledge with opposition to racially or socially redistributive policies as the active misinformed do. Instead, he would either have no policy views in this arena or oppose tax breaks for businesses and support affirmative action, just as the active informed did in the 1995 survey described in the vignette.

These two illustrations illustrate why from now on we ignore the inactive misinformed; one must struggle to discern any political relevance in a person who both believes that smoking is not harmful and nonetheless chooses not to smoke. There is a good theoretical reason for the infrequency of the inactive misinformed in the public arena. As we show over the next few chapters, misinformation is usually associated with identification with a group, commitment to particular partisan views, or instigation by politicians. All three of these sources would spur an individual to not only acquire but also use misinformation, thus rendering him a member of the active misinformed. If an individual acquires misguided information but chooses not to use it, his behavior has an ironic political outcome: though hardly taking the Jeffersonian path to democratic participation, his publicly relevant behaviors turn out to be the same as those of the active informed, who embody the Jeffersonian ideal. Thus, although we include the category of the inactive misinformed in our basic framework, it plays no role in this book.

LINKING THE VIGNETTES

The surgeon general's reports exemplify Jefferson's model of how knowledge of the facts ought to work in the public realm: people acquire new information from a presumably authoritative source, which is associated with (or perhaps even "causes") significant changes in political behavior or views and even in policy outcomes. The case of school desegregation exemplifies the first half of Jefferson's vision: people possess correct information. But it fails on the second half among those who do not use that information when voting or making policy choices about racial mixing in schools. In contrast, the vignette on whites' misinformation about blacks' socioeconomic status exemplifies the second half of the Jeffersonian vision since the misinformed are making policy choices that accord with their supposed knowledge. But it violates the first half, since

Figure 1.1. Relating facts and politics: placing the vignettes.

Are facts associated with distinctive political actions or policy choices?

		Yes	No
Nature of factual knowledge	*Correct*	Active Informed: Surgeon general's report	Inactive Informed: School desegregation
	Incorrect	Active Misinformed: Black Americans' well-being	Inactive Misinformed: Nonsmokers who see cigarettes as healthy

their supposed knowledge is wrong. Finally, the set of people in the category of inactive misinformed fails on both halves of the Jeffersonian ideal since they are both factually wrong and fail to apply this misinformation in relevant political or policy choices.

Thus, facts and politics can be linked in four ways. Citizens can be informed and active, informed and inactive, misinformed and active, or misinformed and inactive.[8] Figure 1.1 shows the relationships among these possibilities. With this typology in place, we can articulate the central claim of this book: people's unwillingness or inability to use relevant facts in their political choices may be frustrating, but people's willingness to use mistaken factual claims in their voting and public engagement is actually dangerous to a democratic polity. Errors of commission cause more problems than errors of omission; as Will Rogers (or someone else) put it in the comment that helped to inspire this book, "It isn't what we don't know that gives us trouble, it's what we know [and act on] that ain't so."

OUTLINE OF THIS VOLUME

Our claim about the dangers of the engaged misinformed rests on three pillars. First, although it is hard to move any set of people, it is generally more difficult to move the active misinformed than the inactive informed onto the Jeffersonian pathway of actively using factual knowledge. Second, the consequences of having a large number of people in the category of engaged misinformed can be severe, even life threatening, as we show in chapter 5. Finally, politicians who benefit from keeping individuals acting on misinformation have stronger incentives than do politicians who would benefit from moving people toward the Jeffersonian ideal. The rest of *Do Facts Matter?* develops these points and their implications.

Chapter 2 lays out the logic of our analysis more explicitly and fully. Chapter 3 addresses the inactive informed by examining two cases in detail to show why people do not act politically on their relevant knowledge. It begins the discussion of when or how they can and should be galvanized into moving into the category of active informed. Chapter 4 parallels chapter 3, explicating two cases in which people misunderstand the facts and use these errors in making political judgments or taking political action. Chapter 5 adds two additional cases to the category of active misinformed, in order to sharpen the claim that use of misinformation is dangerous to a democratic polity and its members. Chapter 6 asks why, given that danger, public actors do not do more to teach people correct information and encourage them to use it as they vote or take similar actions. It shifts the focus from description to analysis, examining asymmetry between politicians' incentives to move people into the category of correctly informed out of the category of disengaged informed versus that of engaged misinformed. Finally, chapter 7 examines policy levers and political actions that leaders and citizens could use to increase relevant knowledge, connect information to action, and correct or compensate for the use of mistaken information. It lays blame on some actors and suggests reforms, both plausible and unlikely. If any or all of those things could be done, policy making would be better and democracy in America would be improved.

CHAPTER 2

DEVELOPING THE ARGUMENT

This is a wonderfully straightforward and illustrated explanation of the debt issue. Now if we could just get the population of our country to actually care more about facts than Fox, maybe the information could enlighten the US electorate.

Message on Facebook, August 2012

THE VIGNETTES IN chapter 1 present our typology and the central argument of *Do Facts Matter?* intuitively and descriptively. We now turn to the task of making the core argument analytically sharper and deeper. We begin by clearing away some underbrush, that is, by briefly describing what is outside the boundaries of our project. We then motivate readers to continue by presenting reasons to believe that facts matter, though also recognizing that facts are not the only things that matter in decision making for a community or nation. We conclude with some necessary clarifications of the terms of our argument.

CLEARING THE UNDERBRUSH

First, the goal of *Do Facts Matter?* is not to skewer the public or politicians for their ignorance. Depicting "America the Clueless" (Bruni 2013) is all too easy, as the following examples demonstrate:

- In 1915, the first major study of the American public's knowledge found that many students in Texas could not distinguish Thomas Jefferson from Jefferson Davis or could not identify what happened in 1492 rather than 1776 (Paumgarten 2011).

- Near the end of the twentieth century, fewer than one-third of American high school students knew that the Civil War occurred between 1850 and 1900, and only two-thirds could find France on a map (Ravitch and Finn 1988).

- A poll of more than two thousand adult Americans found that a fifth of them believed that the sun revolves around the earth; another 7 percent did not know which object made the revolutions (Halpern 1997; for comparisons across countries, see Crabtree 1999).

- A third of Americans reported in 2009 that no terrorist incidents had occurred in the United States since the attacks of September 11, 2001. The most authoritative source reports thirteen (Shambaugh 2013).

- In the 2000 GSS, four of five whites and nine of ten blacks did not know that blacks comprise between 5 and 15 percent of the U.S. population; most respondents of both races dramatically overestimated the proportion of the population that is African American. Similarly, almost two-thirds of whites and seven in ten blacks did not know that whites comprised between 60 and 80 percent of the population (authors' analysis; see also Alba et al. 2005: 905; Wong 2007; Sigelman and Niemi 2001).

A long string of studies has shown that Americans think that the Bill of Rights was written recently by communists, that 40 percent do not know the name of the vice president, that few can name their own representative in Congress, and so on. Magazines are full of quizzes and exhortations; the sidebar offers one example. It is not hard, in short, to demonstrate that the United States is a "dunce-cap nation," as *Newsweek* put it (Braiker 2007).[1]

Many scholars have examined what Americans (and residents of other countries) do not know that might matter politically. This is a crucial issue, and we use some of that evidence throughout this book. But it is not our central concern, for two reasons.

For one thing, it is difficult to define meaningful political ignorance; what people need to know to be effective citizens is not obvious. As the columnist Gene Weingarten (1996) pointed

Don't Know Much about History?

Find out how you stack up in a quiz given by the American Revolution Center. (Hint: most of those who took it failed.)

You'll find the answers below, along with the percentage of Americans who answered each correctly. Good luck!

1. Who wrote the influential pamphlet called *Common Sense,* which advocated independence from Britain?
   - A. Patrick Henry
   - B. Edmund Burke
   - C. Paul Revere
   - D. Thomas Paine
   - E. Don't know

2. Which side of the American War of Independence did American Indians support?
   - A. British
   - B. American
   - C. Both
   - D. Neither
   - E. Don't know

3. The last major military action of the American Revolution was at:
   - A. Bunker Hill
   - B. Trenton
   - C. Saratoga
   - D. Yorktown
   - E. Don't know

4. Which of the following conflicts most directly led to the Stamp Act?
   - A. The War of the Roses
   - B. The War of 1812
   - C. The Mexican-American War
   - D. The French and Indian War (aka the Seven Years' War)
   - E. Don't know

5. Which of the following events came *before* the Declaration of Independence?
   - A. Founding of Jamestown, Virginia
   - B. The Civil War
   - C. The Emancipation Proclamation
   - D. The War of 1812
   - E. Don't know

How did you do? Surprisingly, the average respondent answered only 44 percent of the 27 questions correctly. Paradoxically, 90 percent of those taking the test indicated that learning the principles and history of the Revolution was essential.

"This survey revealed an alarming disparity between our desire to know and our failure to understand," said the center's president and CEO, Bruce Cole, also a board member of *American Heritage.* "Our society, our very existence as a free people, rests on our success in ensuring that all Americans understand our history, rights, and responsibilities, and pass this knowledge on to rising generations."

For more information, visit www.americanrevolutioncenter.org. The American Revolution Center is a nonprofit educational organization dedicated to increasing awareness of this time period and building the first national museum devoted to the Revolution.

ANSWERS [percent of surveyed subjects who selected the correct answer]:
1. D [50%]; 2. C [20%]; 3. D [33%]; 4. D [26%]; 5. A [49%]

out, 40 percent of adult Americans may be unable to name the vice president but "72 percent of the residents of greater Helena, Mont., were able to identify, on one of those creepy diagrams, every known slice of cow"—and the vice president probably cannot do that. People learn the facts they need to run their lives but do not bother to learn facts that seem valueless in their particular circumstances. Putting it more formally, "Elitism undermines much writing on voter competence. . . . Most political-knowledge questions are not derived from a replicable or transparent logic about how their answers bear on a voter's ability to make decisions of a particular quality in the voting booth. Instead, the questions test information that academics, journalists, and politicos value" (Lupia 2006: 217, 219; see also Downs 1957 and his many successors; Lodge and Taber 2013).[2]

We evade the problem of determining what counts as meaningful political ignorance in two ways: by focusing on facts about society or the polity that are salient in highly visible public debates, and by focusing on what people *do* know and how they use that knowledge. The latter choice points to a second reason that we set aside political ignorance. The existing scholarship on the subject is rich, extensive, and sophisticated,[3] and we have no comparative advantage in adding to it. However, it focuses mainly on causes,[4] whereas our interest lies mainly in consequences. We believe that failure to use correct information may be more troubling for democracy than simple political ignorance, and that the active use of misinformation in the public arena almost certainly is. Political ignorance is often associated with disengagement from democratic decision making; this is of concern normatively but poses less of a threat to a polity than does engagement in accord with misinformation. The impact of the active misinformed draws attention to the troubling fact that, although the widely shared goal of encouraging political participation is admirable, it is incomplete and can be problematic. Although the question of whether the inactive informed cause anything more than frustration to their cobelievers is more complex and case-specific, it too reveals that the links between knowledge and participation need much more attention.

A second bit of underbrush that we seek to clear away—or rather, sidestep—is a challenge to the very concept of a fact. According to one important epistemology, we cannot get away with simply asserting that some people are misinformed about the components of the Patient Protection and Affordable Care Act (ACA) or the black share of the American population, or any similar statement. In this view, except for trivial or superficial observations, claims about who knows what rest on the mistaken assumption that there is a real, valid, externally created world that we can more or less accurately discover, count, and know. In place of that assumption, analysis must accommodate the insight that all important facts are invented by humans, who embody a mental structure of cognitions and affects that create categories, boundaries, associations, contrasts, and everything else that separates a "fact" from something else, or a correct statement of fact from an incorrect one. In this view, who counts as being black, how we understand the concept of causation in the link between smoking and lung cancer, and how consensus is reached on that sort of claim are the important issues. As a prominent scholar of science and technology studies puts it, "Science itself is an object of representation, and *mis*-representation. . . . Understanding how particular representations arise, and the constellations of power and capital that produce them, is key" (Jasanoff 2013: 4). Most broadly, instead of focusing on whether people hold information or misinformation and how they use information as they engage publicly, we should analyze how and why people believe that there is such a thing as an objective fact and how they determine which things are to be called objective facts (Fish 1982; Lyotard 1984; Fadiman 1998).

Like the claim about the "dunce-cap nation," the postmodernist warning about the facticity of a "fact" is salutary. If nothing else, it reminds us that one person's critically important piece of information may be denied by, reinterpreted by, or simply invisible to another. Garry Trudeau's *Doonesbury* (figure 2.1) makes the same point in fewer words.

We intend to avoid the thickets of constructivism as much as the tendentiousness of "dunce-cap nation" by focusing on

DOONESBURY
by G.B. Trudeau

21

the sorts of factual knowledge that most people would agree are genuinely important for political judgment and reasonably straightforward depictions of something real in the world. That self-imposed constraint will neither satisfy the strong postmodernist nor reassure those concerned about political ignorance. But it permits us to move forward to explore the contrast between knowledge and misinformation, and between using and not using information, as those terms are understood by most Americans most of the time.

A third section of underbrush is more problematic. As one of our reviewers put it, "Shrewd voters will probe past the wording of any proposed statute into the likely foreseeable effects of enacting the statute. The scopable effects are more important, and are often far from certain given the propensities of judges, bureaucrats, and future Congresses. That is probably especially the case where considerable delegation of authority is involved." In other words, a factual claim that seems straightforward and clear on the surface may contain hidden depths that modulate or even contradict the surface assertion.

We recognize this complication, and it plays an important role in several cases examined in later chapters. To foreshadow: voters' judgments of the accusation of perjury against President Bill Clinton may have been influenced more by whether they thought he was being treated fairly than by any understanding of or concern about the legal meaning of perjury. Some Americans who wrongly believed that the proposed ACA legislation included government-sponsored death panels may have genuinely worried about the eventual likelihood of medical personnel's pressure on vulnerable family members in end-of-life consultations.

Nevertheless, we resist going too far into this thicket, for two reasons. First, the "shrewd voters" who can see past legislative language to the plausible reality beneath are in most cases too few to be captured in public opinion polls, since the ability to infer intent or likely outcome beneath an explicit factual statement requires considerable political or policy sophistication. So the point is mostly relevant to advocacy groups, legislators, candidates for office, scholarly experts, perhaps regulators or judges—but not the bulk of the American public on whom *Do Facts Matter?* focuses.

Our other reason for not pursuing this point is that it leads to a slippery slope that needs much fuller consideration than we can offer here. Almost any piece of legislation or public statement can be interpreted in ways that are wrong but have a plausible kernel of almost-truth—in which case there is ultimately no such thing as misinformation except in long-term hindsight and depending on how the politics of an issue develop over time. It might turn out in a few decades, for example, that there really are death panels, and someone might be able at that point to trace a link back to the 2009 ACA bill—but that does not mean that assertions that the health care bill included death panels were factually accurate when they were made. In short, the issue of real complexity below an apparent statement of fact is important for elite-level politics and raises fascinating questions about historical contingency, but it is relevant to this book only occasionally.

Thus, *Do Facts Matter?* pays relatively little attention to political ignorance, skirts the question of whether there is such a thing as a fact, and seldom delves into whether an apparently simple statement of fact covers over a complicated or even contradictory reality. Our focus is less subtle but no less important: do Americans have the factual knowledge they need, and do they use it appropriately, to be effective participants in a Jeffersonian democracy? That our answer is frequently *no* presents urgent questions for politics and policy making to which we hope to draw readers' attention.

THE ROLE OF FACTS IN POLITICS

Does Factual Knowledge Matter in Politics?

Perhaps our claim that using knowledge of the facts matters for the quality of democratic decision making is overdrawn. After all, citizens are often able to use group identity (Dawson

1994; Kinder and Sanders 1996); partisanship (Green et al. 2004; Druckman et al. 2013; Lewis-Beck et al. 2008), cues from trusted leaders (Zaller 1992; Popkin 1993), retrospective judgments (Fiorina 1981), or their perceptions of the society around them (Kinder and Kiewiet 1981) in lieu of factual information to vote in keeping with their preferences (more generally, see Lupia and McCubbins 1998; Elkin and Soltan 1999; Friedman 2006b). Citizens may recognize and pursue their preferences more through emotions such as loyalty, fear, or anger (Dawson 1994; Marcus et al. 2000; Valentino et al. 2008; Kam and Ramos 2008), or even through images and music (Brader 2005; Westen 2008), than through information or rational calculation. The information that citizens do absorb and use may result from loyalty and partisanship, or from fear and anger, rather than from cognitions or evaluations (Kuklinski and Quirk 2000; Goren 2005; Druckman and Bolsen 2011; Highton and Kam 2011). Or perhaps individuals simply do not care about or cannot use correct information even when provided to them (Sides and Citrin 2007; de Osuna et al. 2004), except on the rare occasion that new information startles them out of their prior views (Kuklinski et al. 2000; Lawrence and Sides 2014).

Researchers have, however, challenged the effectiveness of all of the presumed workarounds as well as the view that knowledge is mostly emotion by another name. Some argue, in short, that however acquired, knowledge matters. People who obtain and use new information make different choices than before, or than others. We have already provided two vignettes —the reports of the surgeons general on smoking, and black Americans' well-being—showing that true or false supposed knowledge was associated with different behaviors or views. These examples are not unique.

A cluster of studies focus on fiscal choices. In one, better-informed people were more willing to pay for increased government services and for deficit reduction than were those less well informed (Althaus 1998: 553). In another, levels of information mattered little to conservative and Republican support for the Bush tax cuts of 2001, but knowledgeable liberals and

Democrats showed less support than did people with similar party loyalty but less information (Lupia et al. 2007). Giving survey respondents correct information about the federal budget "significantly alters budget preferences—leading people to favor more spending on Social Security and less on defense, foreign aid, and Medicaid"; information in this study had the most impact on those who were most misinformed about budgetary expenditures (Lawrence and Sides 2009: abstract). Survey experiments in 2007 and again in 2008 found that "correct information about who actually pays the estate tax does increase support for the estate tax" as much as moral arguments on its behalf did. Unlike in the study of the 2001 Bush tax cuts, Republicans and conservatives (especially those who were relatively poor) showed the greatest changes in views (Sides 2011: abstract).[5]

Almost all of the fiscal choices just described showed more liberal policy views among those provided with correct information. But that is not always the case. If California's voters were fully informed about the targets of state expenditures and the sources of state revenues, that knowledge would "weaken support for government spending.... It may be that voters who know where the money comes from and where it is going better understand the difficult trade-offs involved in the budget process, and become more willing to accept spending cuts as a result" (McGhee 2010: 7, 10–11). Thus, although more knowledgeable respondents tend to be more liberal across most fiscal issues, they are more conservative on "issues pitting the free market against government control" (Gilens 2001: 384; see also Althaus 1998). In a different arena, survey respondents who are told the average annual salary for teachers in their state are less likely than those not given that information to support higher pay, with up to a 20 percentage point difference in some cases (Howell et al. 2011). Most generally and importantly, having a fully informed electorate would reduce incumbent presidents' vote share by almost five percentage points, and a Democratic presidential candidate's vote share by almost two percentage points—enough to swing some elections.[6]

A few studies focus on policy content. Providing new knowledge about foreign aid and changes in the crime rate in a survey experiment led to changes in policy preferences (Gilens 2001). Another set of researchers determined respondents' knowledge of fair housing law by their assessment of the legality of ten scenarios describing rental or home purchasing situations. Respondents were also asked whether they approved of each of ten actions or decisions. Compared to respondents with low levels of knowledge, those with high levels were significantly more likely to endorse fair housing protections. Furthermore, "Three-fourths of those who know the most about fair housing law favor prohibiting homeowners from refusing to sell their homes on the basis of race, religion, or nationality while only slightly over one-half of those who know the least about fair housing law favor such a prohibition." The more knowledgeable were twice as likely to claim that they had experienced housing discrimination and were almost three times as likely to have done something in response to the treatment they received (Abravanel 2002: 493–98). Causation may well run in both directions here, but the association between knowledge and activism is nonetheless clear.[7]

As with the topic of costs, substantive policy arenas also sometimes show that the knowledgeable are more conservative.[8] In 1995, respondents who knew that air quality had improved in the United States over the previous few decades were less likely to support further government spending on environmental protection than were those who failed to see progress (Keeter 1996). A 1998 survey similarly enabled comparisons between people with low and high levels of information about the environment. The more knowledgeable would endorse economic development over environmental protection if a choice were necessary. They were also more likely to think that regulation of air or water pollution had gone far enough, and that regulations to protect endangered species were going too far; they were less concerned about an environmental catastrophe in the next decade (Coyle 1998).

Information may not only be associated with distinct views but may also on occasion replace partisan cues, emotions, or other detours around factual knowledge typically used to make political or policy judgments. This stronger claim is more contested, but some evidence supports it. Campaigns can give new knowledge to voters that affects their vote choice (Nadeau et al. 2008; Gelman and King 1993). More dramatic, when people have appropriate information about policies, "their attitudes seem to be affected at least as much by that information as by cues from party elites. . . . Party cues do not inhibit . . . thinking . . . about policy" (Bullock 2011: 496; see also Druckman 2012; Bechtel et al., forthcoming; Gerber and Green 1999). If experimental subjects receive "explicit inducements to form 'accurate' decisions," they are less responsive to partisan cues regarding support for an energy law (Druckman et al. 2012). In a rare panel study of public opinion, in this case during debate about and passage of the ACA, Democrats became slightly more opposed whereas people (especially strong Republicans) who worried about paying their medical bills became less opposed. Both movements showed that, "while not resistant to elite influence, partisan identifiers do not blindly follow the rhetoric of party leaders" (Henderson and Hillygus 2011: 946). Thus, information may offset motivated reasoning or partisan framing rather than being put to their service, as most of the research literature suggests (see discussion in chapter 4).

Weighing Facts and Values

Despite the fact that almost two-fifths of the American public agree that government should use "scientific methods" to solve important problems (2012 American National Election Study [ANES]), we see few conditions in which information is all that matters in democratic decision making.[9] Emotions, commitments, imagination, and moral judgment almost inevitably come into play, as they should. That raises the large issue of how much factual knowledge should matter in decision making when balanced against commitments, emotions, or moral judgments. We cannot answer that broad normative question here, but we can address two slightly narrower questions.

First, do people make better, not just different, choices when correct information is a major element of their decision making?

The hope that knowledge not only changes but improves political choices is what motivated Jefferson's design for universal (white male!) primary public education and what continues to motivate civics teachers, political science professors, authors of books about facts in politics, and the Rothbaum lecture series. Elected officials ostensibly hold the same goals, as Fenno's member of Congress quoted in chapter 1 pointed out. Is this hope merely naïve?

The conviction that people make better choices if they possess more correct information lies behind a good deal of public policy. Federal and state laws and regulations require truth in advertising and marketing in many circumstances and forbid not only active deception but also deception through failure to include materially important facts. "Right to know" laws operate under the same principle in the arenas of environmental and workplace hazards. Even more broadly, mandates for transparency in schools, highway safety, food preparation, and mortgage financing, along with the drive to make student test scores, pharmaceutical companies' drug trials, and police departments' stop-and-frisk records public, all operate on the belief that, if correct information is made available, members of the public will use it to improve decision making and commerce. As the authors of *Full Disclosure* put it, "The idea was not just that the public deserved better information. It was that the power of information would create a chain reaction of new incentives. Armed with new rollover ratings, buyers would choose safer cars. Confronted with declining sales of the most top-heavy SUVs, auto companies would improve design. Safer design would save lives and prevent injuries. The new law thus made transparency into a precise policy tool" (Fung et al. 2007: 2; see also McDonnell 2004).

Some evidence shows that this aspiration can be fulfilled; people can on occasion make better, not just different, decisions when they use correct information. The surgeon general's reports are one instance. The unlikely setting of congressional testimony similarly illustrates how new information changes behavior for the better, in our view. Federal District Court Judge James B. McMillan presided over the multiyear school desegregation case in Charlotte-Mecklenburg, North Carolina, after which he informed members of Congress about its impact on him and on constitutional adjudication:

> I grew up . . . accepting the segregated life which was the way of America for its first 300 years. . . . I hoped that we would be forever saved from the folly of transporting children from one school to another for the purpose of maintaining a racial balance of students in each school. . . . I first said, 'What's wrong in Charlotte?". . . . I set the case for hearing reluctantly. I heard it reluctantly, at first unbelievingly. After . . . I began to deal in terms of facts and information instead of in terms of my natural-born raising, I began to realize . . . that something should be done. . . . I have had to spend some thousands of hours studying the subject . . . and have been brought by pressure of information to a different conclusion. . . . Charlotte—and I suspect that is true of most cities—is segregated by Government action. We need to be reminded, also, as I did remind myself in 1969, that the issue is one of constitutional law, not politics; and constitutional rights should not be swept away by temporary majorities. (McMillan 1981)

This is an extraordinary confession from a powerful public actor.

As a final example of improved decision making as a result of learning new facts, consider a deliberative poll with real consequences. A randomly selected sample of residents of a neighborhood in Athens, Greece, were given information about a set of candidates for mayor, and after a day of deliberation about and with the competitors they held a binding vote. The person initially least known won the nomination, arguably because of his substantive knowledge and positions. As a reporter described the events, "The questions which came [from citizens to candidates, after deliberation] . . . were sharp and detailed, demanding good answers to be convincing. And because they were so precise, it became clear very soon which of the candidates were themselves knowledgeable on the issues, and which were not." The scholar reporting this incident emphasizes that, "as in other Deliberative Polls, it was the people who became more informed who also changed their views" (Fishkin 2009: 10).[10]

We also engage the question of how to balance factual knowledge and other values or commitments by recognizing that there may be good reasons for the inactive informed to stay inactive on a given issue. Other values, or other factual information, may mediate between knowledge and the political action or policy view that it seems to imply. Jury nullification is an extreme example of choosing on moral grounds not to use specific knowledge. It is a judicially legitimate assertion that juries can judge both law and fact; they may disregard evidence or the judge's instructions, generally in order to find a defendant not guilty of a crime that he or she may have committed in what the jurors determine to be exonerating circumstances. Jury nullification is legally and morally controversial, but a milder form of the same idea lies in the use of mitigating or aggravating factors for sentencing: "Wise and successful sentencing advocacy may be found in the full exposition of all the factors in the defendant's life which brought him or her to the point at which the crime was committed" (*Sentencing Project* 2003).

Members of the public as well as elite actors may engage in something analogous to jury nullification when they ignore faults of leaders because they admire their virtues and want their leadership. Examples are legion. The media did not report President John Kennedy's many sexual affairs; residents of Chicago ignored Harold Washington's many years of tax evasion when they elected him mayor; the Watergate scandal was already percolating in public view when Richard Nixon was reelected as president. (Norms change with regard to what may legitimately be known and ignored, as a comparison between Kennedy and Bill Clinton makes clear.) The broad questions of how to judge facts against values and why the American public change their views on that question lie beyond the scope of this book. Nevertheless, our exploration of the Clinton-Lewinsky scandal in chapter 3 may usefully encourage research on that topic.

In contrast to the occasional legitimacy of remaining in the inactive informed, we know of few instances in which the active use of misinformation represents a benign value judgment.

Perhaps some individuals should be misled into believing that their cancer is less serious than is actually the case, or perhaps some prisoners of war should be misled about how much food remains in the storeroom. But these are unusual cases and are themselves contestable. For the reasons outlined in chapters 4, 5, and 6—the misinformed are difficult to move, the active use of misinformation can have devastating consequences, and some politicians have an incentive to *keep* people active but misinformed—in almost all circumstances the engaged misinformed present serious challenges to the Jeffersonian ideal.

Moral commitments, personal and partisan loyalties, emotions, and intuition will, as they should, continue to affect political and policy choices. But ignorance and false information are seldom if ever better starting points than knowledge from which to make public decisions.[11] The difficulties all lie in more subtle questions: Which facts are relevant? How should one balance facts against commitments, loyalties, emotions, or other facts when taking action? What counts as misinformation? When and why are the active misinformed dangerous for a democratic polity rather than merely unfortunate? The next few chapters probe these questions through a series of cases.

CASE SELECTION

Although not selected either at random or through some other systematic sampling procedure, the cases in *Do Facts Matter?* encompass a wide array of policy arenas, ranging from foreign policy to health care to sex scandals. We hope that their breadth shows that the phenomena we discuss are critical to understanding a large swath of American politics.

Although political partisanship is crucial in our analysis, we sought to be nonpartisan in our framework by choosing cases that reveal failings and virtues of both liberals and conservatives. To some degree, we have succeeded. Overall, however, we found that conservatives tend to traffic more in misinformation than do liberals. We are not alone in that judgment; as Adam Berinsky puts it with regard to his own research on false rumors, "This group of rumors is obviously not balanced, in large part because it was extremely difficult to find rumors that were endorsed by the political left" (Berinsky 2012b: n19). He also found a partisan asymmetry in willingness to accept misinformation. Knowledgeable Democrats tended to reject rumors coming from partisans on both sides more than did Democrats with little knowledge, as one would hope. In contrast, compared to Republicans with little knowledge, knowledgeable Republicans were more likely to accept rumors that defamed or embarrassed Democrats.

Five items on the 2012 ANES confirm both that Democrats as well as Republicans traffic in dramatic rumors and that more Republicans do, if these items are roughly parallel. On three Republican-oriented rumors (the ACA authorizes government panels to make end-of-life decisions for Medicare patients; Obama was born outside the United States; and the Obama administration's policies favor blacks over whites), an average of 49 percent of Republicans and 15 percent of Democrats found the rumors to be true or probable. Conversely, on two Democrat-oriented rumors (federal officials knew about the 9/11 attacks beforehand; and the federal government intentionally flooded poor neighborhoods in Hurricane Katrina), an average of 31 percent of Democrats and 24 percent of Republicans concurred. Thus, Republicans are more rumor prone than Democrats, and proportionally more prone to rumors that reinforce their views than Democrats are to rumors that favor *their* views.

We offer three explanations for conservatives' greater vulnerability to misinformation and its use in the government arena. The first echoes the long string of experiments by psychologists showing liberals to be more comfortable with ambiguity than are conservatives. As one authoritative summary puts it, "Liberals did appear to be more open, tolerant, creative, curious, expressive, enthusiastic, and drawn to novelty and diversity in comparison with conservatives, who appeared to be more conventional, orderly, organized, neat, clean, withdrawn, reserved and rigid" (Carney et al. 2008: 834; see citations therein for the history of this argument). Tolerance of ambiguity apparently renders liberals more willing to accept facts that contradict their political beliefs and assumptions, whereas conservatives may, on average, focus more fixedly on factual claims, true or not, that reinforce their values.

Carney and associates, however, also note that "most of the differences we observed were of small or moderate magnitude" (835), so personality traits only partly explain liberals' and conservatives' differences in acquiring and using misinformation (Xu et al. 2013). A second reason is that in the current era Republicans are more passionately partisan than Democrats. Survey experiments show an "intensity gap," such that Republicans are more psychologically committed to and identified with their party than are Democrats, and strong Republicans are more likely to engage in biased processing of undesirable information than are comparable Democrats (Theodoridis 2012). Aggregate data reinforce these individual-level results. Two longtime, sober scholars find that partisan polarization and intransigence—especially among Republicans—is "even worse than it looks." The Republican party is "unpersuaded by conventional understanding of facts, evidence, and science" (Mann and Ornstein 2013: subtitle, xiv).[12] An analysis of the party means on a liberal-conservative scale does not show susceptibility to misinformation, but it does reinforce the image of the Republican Party becoming unprecedentedly ideological during the 2000s (figure 2.2). As the analysts put it, "Partisan polarization has dramatically increased in the 112th Congress in both chambers. . . . This phenomenon has been asymmetric: contemporary polarization of the parties is almost entirely due to the movement of congressional Republicans to the right" (*Voteview* 2013). And if the research on motivated reasoning is correct (see chapter 3, note 14), the more ideologically committed a person or party is, the more prone to accept and use misinformation.

Our substantive focus may be a final reason that Republicans are more prone to active use of misinformation. We have not tested this assertion, but we are reasonably confident that focusing on misinformation related to the government makes

Figure 2.2. Ideological polarization in the U.S. House of Representatives, 1879–2013.

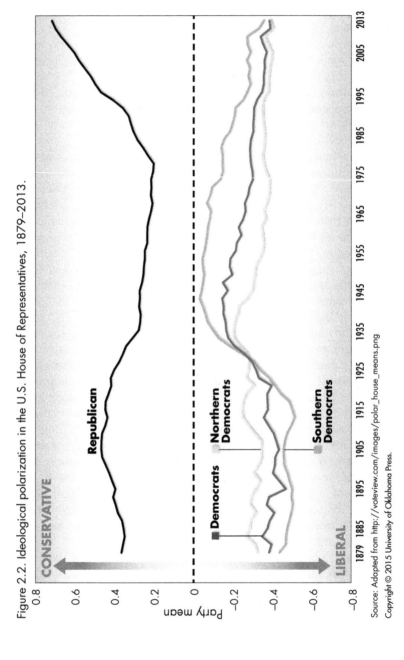

Source: Adapted from http://voteview.com/images/polar_house_means.png
Copyright © 2015 University of Oklahoma Press.

it easier to find conservatives than liberals in the category of misinformed actives. Conservatives' stronger hostility to government renders them more susceptible to false or exaggerated knowledge claims about politics and policy issues than liberals, who want to believe that governments are usually benign and effective. If *Do Facts Matter?* had focused on corporations or the market, rather than politics, we expect that we would have found much more, perhaps a disproportionate share, of liberal mobilization around misinformation. Examples might include unwarranted concern about the dangers of genetically modified food, false reports of the malign role of multinational corporations in small countries, or the claim that scientists deliberately spread the HIV virus in black communities in order to decimate them.

CLARIFICATIONS

Several issues remain to be clarified before we can plunge directly into the cases at the core of our analysis.

What Is a Fact?

Early in this chapter, we set aside three possible ways of addressing factual knowledge—measuring political ignorance, revealing the power dynamics underlying assertions of what is a fact, and exploring the possibility that beneath an apparent fact lies something different or even contradictory. But we have not yet specified what we do mean by a "fact."

To keep the analysis as simple as possible, most of the time we mean what one reviewer of the book manuscript identified as "a state of affairs that given a suitable mobilization of evidence can be said to exist." Was Obama born in the United States? Did the ACA bill propose health care coverage for undocumented immigrants? Has the earth been getting warmer over the past century? As these examples suggest, even asserting the truth of a discrete "state of affairs" can be contentious, and *Do Facts Matter?* addresses disputes on these items and others. But sometimes a fact in our analysis is something intrinsically more complex—a causal relation. Does smoking lead to cancer? Do vaccinations induce autism? Do human activities speed up climate change? With some exceptions, statements of causal fact are even more contentious than statements about a state of affairs. Since we do not intend to enter into substantive debates over causation, we try to limit our engagement with causal facts to causal statements that have strong empirical support (or no empirical support), as determined by nearly unanimous agreement among experts who have relatively little ideological or partisan motivation.

Causation and Association

A more vexing issue is our own causal theory. Some survey or field experiments permit causal statements, for example, when a difference in the information provided to two randomly selected sets of respondents leads to a significant difference in expressed policy views between the two sets. Similarly, some links between policy or practice and outcome are sufficiently tight that one can plausibly claim that the policy caused the outcome (e.g., as in clinical drug trials or some field experiments). Where possible, we report such casual links between facts and politics. In the public arena in which most important cases lie, however, we lack compelling systematic grounds for asserting that belief in a particular factual claim (true or false) leads people to make a particular political or policy choice. Indeed, as we discuss, considerable evidence shows the opposite causal logic—that having a particular political or policy view leads people to think they know a particular (true or false) statement of fact.

Whether attitudes lead to knowledge or vice versa is generally beside the point in this book; people do not think, feel, and act in any sort of one-at-a-time linear path. Instead, cognitions, emotions, and actions are mutually causal, and mutually reinforcing unless some (usually exogenous) force breaks the cycle. Public actors know that very well, and their persuasive efforts almost always mix factual claims (true or not) with emotional or partisan appeals and actions already taken or available to take. So we are generally careful to avoid explicit causal language; instead, we use terms such as "associated" or "linked" (as in "belief that human activity is making the earth warmer is associated with Democratic partisanship").

Nevertheless, in a broader and looser sense, we do have a causal view that provides the underlying motivation for this book. We believe, along with Thomas Jefferson and his many successors, that if ordinary people had more knowledge of states of affairs and a more accurate understanding of provable causal relationships, and if they used that knowledge and understanding, they would on balance make better political and policy choices and their polity would function more fairly and effectively. Conversely, we believe that the use of misinformation (whether states of affairs or causal relations) in making political and policy choices is dangerous to individuals and their polity. In an indeterminate but profound way, that is, citizens' level of knowledge and their deployment of it contribute to the quality of democratic governance. How to reconcile that broad conviction with the difficulty of making precise causal statements in a given instance remains a tension within our arguments—as in political discourse at large.

Typology or Continuum

The logic of the remaining chapters revolves around the typology illustrated in figure 1.1. It is a classic two-by-two table with clear boundaries between discrete and mutually exclusive cells. But little in politics is sharply bounded and entirely discrete—never mind clear or exclusive. So one must ask, as one reviewer did, whether the categories are ends of a quantitative continuum rather than qualitatively distinct entities. Our answer is both yes and no. On the one hand, the distinction between the active informed and the inactive informed is blurry and easily crossed. In more common parlance, people who hold a salient piece of information can be politically mobilized or demobilized and back again; their policy views can shift into and out of consistency with what they know.

On the other hand, the distinction between the active informed and the active misinformed is a genuine boundary. Regardless of whether a purported fact describes a state of affairs (the share of the population that is African American) or claims a causal relationship (smoking causes cancer), we label it as either correct or incorrect. With one crucial exception that we discuss in the final few pages, the argument of *Do Facts Matter?* is based on this premise of a sharp and important divide between individuals who know the facts and those who believe something else.

SO WHAT?

Most writing on facts in politics focuses on citizens' ignorance about policies, candidates, or government structures—but this book addresses presumed knowledge and its use or lack of use. In parallel fashion, most writing on facts in politics focuses on causes of variation in individuals' knowledge—but this book focuses on consequences of that variation. In short, explaining the psychology of individual political actors or the practices of intermediaries such as political parties or the media is not our agenda; our primary interest lies in democratic governance. Since we ask "so what?" and "what next?" rather than "why?," we explore the failure to use information or the use of misinformation mainly from the perspective of a policy maker or politician.

Can policy makers or politicians realistically aspire to move more than a minority of people into correctly informed activity? Walter Lippmann (1955: 20) famously observed that "the public opinion of the masses cannot be counted upon to apprehend regularly and promptly the reality of things." But another wise student of public opinion pointed out more recently that "opinion is not infinitely malleable. When people are feeling prosperous, you can't convince them that they should be depressed. When depressed, messages of economic good cheer fall flat. Facts matter" (Stimson 2004: 108). *Do Facts Matter?* is based on agreement that facts matter; we turn now to describing ways in which they are used, misused, or ignored before analyzing how and why they affect government outcomes.

CHAPTER 3

IGNORING CORRECT INFORMATION IN MAKING POLITICAL JUDGMENTS

There are climate facts—and facts are stubborn things.

Economist, October 2013

Facts speak for themselves.

James Ceaser, "The Great Repudiation," 2010

FACTS MAY INDEED BE stubborn things but, as chapter 1 suggests, they do not speak for themselves. Even James Ceaser (2010: 8) points out later in his essay that "political actors' . . . job is to offer explanations that serve their party's (or their own) future political prospects. It is only by coincidence that their accounts resemble the truth." The question for this chapter is how to understand occasions when a given set of facts not only do not speak for themselves but do not speak at all even when highly pertinent. In other words, chapter 3 explores cases in which people hold correct and relevant information but do not use it in their policy judgments or political actions. They are the inactive informed.

As we note in chapter 2, we do not aim to explain why a given individual knows a particular fact or, conditional on that knowledge, does not use the fact politically. Rather, our cases explore at the aggregate level the characteristics of those who are informed but are inactive with regard to that information, and the role of their choices in the public arena. For example, how do we make sense of the fact that white Americans who live in all-white neighborhoods but want their children to attend desegregated schools reject all proffered policies or organizational activity aimed at reconciling their knowledge and their values? In this and our other cases, the central answer revolves around group membership, variously understood in different contexts. A perspective on the world as filtered through attachment to a particular group best explains the process through which people choose not to use their factual knowledge in forging political or policy judgments.

Our two main case studies suggest the range of situations in which the inactive informed are extensive and important. The first is the scandal surrounding President Bill Clinton's extramarital affair with an intern, Monica Lewinsky. We trace through survey data how most Americans ignored their extraordinary level of knowledge about Clinton's sexual behavior and dealings with the judicial system, choosing—contrary to politicians' and the media's expectations and even exhortations—not to use those facts in judging his presidency. The second case is global warming. Again we use survey data to make sense of Americans who agree that the world's climate is changing dangerously and that individuals and governments can and should take action to mitigate this change, and who also ignore that knowledge in expressing preferences for environmental policies.

In both cases, the form of group membership most closely associated with the decision not to use correct factual information is political partisanship. Group membership need not revolve around political party identification; as we show later, the central axis may be race, gender, religion, or some other strong identity. But for Clinton/Lewinsky and climate change, party loyalty matters more than other group identity and more than individual characteristics such as education or income.

The power of partisanship comes as no surprise to political scientists or to politicians, but its role in impeding good democratic decision making nonetheless warrants further exploration. The cases differ, however, on exactly that dimension, which is one of the reasons we chose them. In both cases, the inactivity of the well informed is intensely frustrating to political actors trying to mobilize people to act in accord with their knowledge. We share that frustration on the issue of global warming, because failure to act may have dire consequences not only for democratic polities but for the whole earth. We have a different view about the Clinton case; ignoring knowledge of his sexual activity and even of his subsequent perjury was, at a minimum, a less severe flaw and, at a maximum, the right choice from the perspective of democratic governance. In short, one must examine what information people hold, why they are inactive with regard to it, and how their (non)behavior affects the polity in order to decide if political actors' frustration with the inactive informed is well warranted or merely an amusing sideshow in the circus of politics.

MONICA LEWINSKY

On January 19, 1998, a news report described an alleged affair between President Bill Clinton and the former Pentagon intern Monica Lewinsky, with information emerging out of a special prosecutor's probe of possible perjury and obstruction of justice in other issues involving Clinton.[1] Both alleged participants denied any sexual relationship. A series of legal negotiations and a grand jury investigation ensued, including testimony by both Lewinsky and Clinton in August 1998. The House of Representatives released independent counsel Kenneth Starr's 450-page report in September (Starr Commission and Starr 1998) along with Clinton's grand jury testimony. After hearings in the Judiciary Committee, the House of Representatives voted in December 1998 to impeach Clinton for perjury and obstruction of justice. The Senate held a trial in January 1999, and Clinton was acquitted on February 12, 1999.

Supporting the President

From our vantage point, the most intriguing element in this bizarre series of events is that most Americans did not take them into consideration when evaluating Clinton's presidency.

John Zaller was the first scholar to focus on this phenomenon. Examining all media-based polls soon after revelation of the alleged affair, he found that public support for the president fell in the first two days, after sharp criticism from elites and the media. But Clinton's approval rating steadily rose thereafter, increasing from about 60 percent before the initial news reports to 70 percent, as "the president, his wife, and their allies fought back" and as media coverage became more evenly balanced. Because Americans were pleased with Clinton's record of achievement in office—"peace, prosperity, and moderation"—most were willing to ignore an unsavory but not illegal sexual adventure. In considerable tension with his own earlier research, Zaller (1998: 184, 185, 186) concluded that "the majority of voters can stay . . . relentlessly . . . focused on the bottom line. . . . It is possible for public opinion and media opinion to go marching off in opposing directions."

The story changed little over the next year. The media and many elites focused obsessively on the mesmerizing Lewinsky story; the public was almost as engaged and disapproved of Clinton's actions, but a majority continued to approve of his presidency and reject his removal from office. As one person observed, "He's running the country well. He's just not running his life very well"; according to another, "This country seems to be doing very well, and I don't see that a personal problem has anything to do with running the country. The stock market is doing well. There are more jobs for people. Basically, I think the American people are happier than they've been in many years" (Berke and Elder 1998).

An extensive string of polls shows the pattern. Between January 22 and October 13, 1998, CBS or the *New York Times* (or both together) asked respondents thirty-one times (with minor wording variations), "If it turns out that President Clinton obstructed justice [or committed perjury] by encouraging Monica Lewinsky to lie under oath, or by lying under oath himself, what do you think should happen?" Answer alternatives were usually "no action" or "drop it," "apologize," "censure" and/or "fine," "resign," "impeach," and "don't know" or "no answer" (again with minor variations). The results are clear. Regardless of what new states of affairs they were learning about through these ten months, in every survey roughly one in five Americans —with the proportion rising through the period—thought that nothing should happen to Clinton even if the wrongdoing alleged in a given survey turned out to be true. Roughly another third, with more variation around that point, thought Clinton should apologize. Fewer than a fifth supported impeachment, with some decline by the end of the period despite continued revelations and accusations of perjury.

In short, most Americans knew the facts, with facts understood here as states of affairs.[2] But they largely disregarded the rising torrent of information, which eventually included testimony by other women directly or indirectly involved with the president, leaked grand jury testimony, Clinton's public apology for misleading the country, and, above all, Starr's detailed report ostensibly about perjury and obstruction of justice but also revealing Clinton's "sexual proclivities and fantasies, his taste in women, his favorite erotic poetry, the size and topography of his reproductive organ and yes, his instinct to dissemble when his secret passions are revealed" (Talbot 1998). Or rather, they took in the information and disregarded its potential implications for their vote and support. Clinton's average first-term presidential job approval rating was 50 percent; his average second-term approval rating was 61 percent (Gallup Poll 2013).

Americans similarly retained their views of Clinton himself. In August 1998, 45 percent of respondents agreed that, "even if all the charges are true, . . . [they] would still support Clinton," and 25 percent did "not support Clinton and would not support him even if all the allegations were proven to be false." Only a quarter thought that their "opinion of Clinton may depend on the final results of the current investigation." Even that number was too high; a week later, after Clinton admitted to an "inappropriate relationship" with Lewinsky, only one-tenth "used to support Clinton but no longer do."[3] By that time, most people were sick of the issue; 61 percent wished that they "knew less than . . . [they] currently know" (Gallup/CNN/*USA Today*, Aug. 10–12 and Aug. 18).

Ignoring Elite Cues

The public's consistent support for Clinton dumbfounded elites. It was not due to inattention or dispute over the actual state of affairs. "Media coverage of the scandal dominated the news every month in 1998 from the time the story broke in late January. The three major network news programs . . . devoted one-seventh of all of their air time to the events leading up to the presidential impeachment" (Owen 2000: 169). The major newspapers all carried twenty or more separate articles about Lewinsky on each of the first few days after the scandal broke (Kalb 2001). The new media of talk radio, television cable networks, and Internet-based websites and chat rooms reveled in the affair.

Even beyond the fact that any coverage could not help but make the president look bad, from January through September 1998 "Clinton's evaluations on network news averaged 63 percent negative to only 37 percent positive (N=1,364)" (Just and Crigler 2000: 188). And that calculation does not account for the new forms of media—for example, the 15 percent of the public who regularly listened to conservative commentator Rush Limbaugh (Owen 2000). Political elites almost universally predicted Clinton's downfall. The first four days after the news broke included such comments from reporters as these (Kalb 2001: 143, 149, 160, 164, 166, 187, 190, 203, 226):

- If Clinton "lied . . . and obstructed justice, he's going to have to leave town in disgrace."
- If the president "is not telling the truth, he's cooked."
- "Lewinsky's age and the talk of extramarital relations in the White House threaten to turn the public against the president in a way other cases haven't."
- If the reports are accurate, "his presidency will be in ruins."
- "His presidency is now worth, uh, zip."
- "He's got to maintain his credibility as a leader, and if most of the public doesn't believe him on this . . . it's going to be very difficult, if not impossible, for him to do that."

- "We all thought he might be finished."
- "Can he survive? Can he recover?" (opening question on a talk show)
- "So what does President Gore do?" (next question on the same talk show)

And these are only the brief expressions of that view; we have not quoted more extended television conversations or wordier newspaper commentaries. *Salon* captured the common view: "Ever since Clinton's Aug. 17 confession, the media have been thrashing around the White House like sharks smelling blood in the water. Now that Starr has 'got' Clinton on Lewinsky, it's become an article of faith among the opinion elite that the prosecutor's unlimited probe has been completely vindicated and that any attempt to impugn him is folly. The only question allowed for debate in the national Clinton deathwatch is when the president will walk the plank" (Talbot 1998).

The media even proposed a resolution to the purported crisis: "The solution, obvious and with very clear precedent: Clinton resigns and his successor immediately pardons him for all Starr-related crimes" (Krauthammer 1998). One Democratic member of Congress did in fact call for Clinton's resignation as early as August 1998 (Busby 2001: 108); Republicans followed suit frequently thereafter.

Reporters and commentators could not figure out why the public was not following their lead; as a puzzled *Washington Post* writer put it, the president's standing in the polls is "in defiance of the laws of physics" (Balz 1998). In a nice demonstration of postmodern self-referencing, the media reported on their own failure to understand why the public did not share the media's views. National Public Radio's Cokie Roberts could only suggest that "the polls were underestimating the negative sentiment against Clinton. . . . The national polls were dominated by East and West coast people who are more favorable toward Clinton whereas the people in the Midwest, who she claimed were largely in favor of impeachment, were underrepresented in national polls" (Miller 1999: 724). A poll even asked respondents why respondents to other polls had not changed their level of approval for Clinton despite their belief that he had had an affair with Lewinsky (NBC/*Wall Street Journal*, Mar. 1, 1998).

Americans put their votes where their poll responses were. The Republican Party lost five seats to Democrats in the November 1998 election of the House of Representatives, despite the fact that the party of the president almost always loses seats in a midterm election. In fact, not since 1922 had the presidential party gained House seats in the sixth-year election. Republicans also gained no ground in the Senate.

In short, Americans absorbed a great deal of correct and arguably relevant information about President Clinton over roughly a year of continual reportage culminating in an almost unprecedented impeachment and trial—and most did not use that information in judging Clinton's presidency or voting for congressional candidates in the middle of the scandal period. They remained informed but inactive with regard to Lewinsky.

GLOBAL WARMING

The Intergovernmental Panel on Climate Change, created in 1988 by the World Meteorological Organization and the United Nations Environmental Programme, concluded in 2001 that "human activities . . . are modifying the concentration of atmospheric constituents . . . that absorb or scatter radiant energy. . . . Most of the observed warming over the last 50 years is likely to have been due to the increase in greenhouse gas concentrations" (McCarthy et al. 2001: 21; see also Nordhaus 2013). A few years later, the U.S. National Academy of Sciences consensus report began, "Greenhouse gases are accumulating in Earth's atmosphere as a result of human activities, causing surface air temperatures and subsurface ocean temperatures to rise" (National Academy of Sciences Committee on the Science of Climate Change 2001: 5).[4] In 2012, the sober-sided *Economist* (2012: 4) observed, "It's hard to exaggerate how dramatic this [the Arctic's amplified warming] is. Perhaps not since the felling of America's vast forests in the 19th century, or possibly since the razing of China's and western Europe's great forests a thousand years before that, has the world seen such a spectacular environmental change. The consequences for Arctic ecosystems will be swingeing."[5]

Scientific consensus has been wrong before: the sun does not revolve around the earth, diseases are not caused by an imbalance of the four humors of the body. But absent another Galileo or Paracelsus, we take it as given that the earth is warming dangerously, largely because of human activity.

Recognizing the Problem?

Many Americans accept the scientists' view of the climatological state of affairs: global warming is occurring and endangers the earth's inhabitants. In 2007, 60 percent of Gallup Poll respondents agreed that "the effects of global warming . . . have already begun to happen," despite being offered four alternatives that posited its start increasingly far into the future (Gallup Organization 2007; *Newsweek*, Aug. 1–2, 2007, has similar responses). Many also accept the crucial causal fact about that state of affairs; in both 1994 and 2000, more than 60 percent of Americans agreed correctly that humans' coal or gas use contributed substantially to the greenhouse effect (GSS data, in Nisbet and Myers 2007). In the survey with the most concurrence, three-quarters of respondents said in 2010 that the earth's temperature had, in all likelihood, heated up over the past century; the same proportion viewed human behavior as at least partially responsible for this warming (Krosnick 2010; Yeager et al. 2011).[6]

Nevertheless, as scientific evidence on climate change grew in the late 2000s, Americans' acceptance of both types of facts—its existence, immediacy, or importance; and its causes—declined. The 2007 Gallup poll just cited was, in fact, near the high point of Gallup respondents' agreement on the fact of global warming.[7] In 1998 (the first year the question was asked), 48 percent agreed that its effects have begun; agreement rose to 61 percent in 2008, declined back to 49 percent in 2011, and rose slightly to 54 percent in 2013. The Pew Research Center shows the same pattern of rise and fall in Americans' recognition of both the state of affairs and the causes of climate change. From 2006 through 2013, Pew asked respondents if "there is solid evidence that the average temperature on earth has been getting warmer over the past few decades, or not?" If they said yes, they were asked if warming occurs "mostly because of human activity such as burning fossil fuels" or "mostly because of natural patterns on the earth's environment." Two-fifths of respondents answered both questions correctly in 2006; that proportion rose to almost half in 2008, dropped to just over a third in 2009 and 2010, and returned to two-fifths in 2013.[8] In short, as of 2013, somewhere between 40 and 80 percent of the American public belonged—by correctly answering one of two sets of factual questions on global warming—in either the active or inactive informed groups on the question of climate change.

Becoming informed in this case is not a straightforward result of absorbing elites' messages. An analysis of President Obama's and Governor Mitt Romney's major policy statements, press releases since 2007, and 2012 campaign speeches found that both engaged with the problem of climate change in 2007, when public concurrence was indeed at its peak. Through 2010, Obama promised to address it substantively. But by the 2012 election Obama's policy proposals had disappeared, his references to climate change had decreased, and candidate Romney was mocking the whole issue: "President Obama promised to begin to slow the rise of the oceans and heal the planet. *My* promise . . . is to help you and your family" (*Climate Silence* 2012). Thus, the most prominent elites varied both in their level of attention to climate change and in their message about it—not a condition in which individuals can receive and absorb consistent cues.

Ignoring Scientists' Proposals for Action

Because this chapter focuses on the inactive informed, the set of people who hold correct information but do not act on it in the public arena, we now set aside both environmental activists and individuals who deny that the earth is warming at a dangerous rate. That is the same logic that led us in the discussion above to pay little attention to people who were unaware of

Clinton's extramarital affair or sought his removal from office. In other words, just as we focused on Americans who knew that Clinton had had an affair and had arguably committed perjury but did not want him to leave office, we focus in the case of global warming on Americans who know about climate change but reject proposed strong policies to alleviate it.

By this logic, many Americans belong in the category of the disengaged informed. The 2007 Gallup Poll asked respondents not only if global warming is occurring and is caused by human actions but also what steps should be taken to alleviate it. Among the three-fifths with factual knowledge, an average of 28 percent did not endorse seven proposed actions that individuals could take to reduce energy use.[9] That is 17 percent of all respondents, a small but not trivial proportion. Even more knowledgeable respondents, an average of 41 percent, opposed the six steps proposed for government action.[10] That is a quarter of all respondents. Thus, a substantial proportion of Americans who knew about a serious national and global problem did not want the government to take actions to solve it, and a smaller proportion did not even want to take any actions themselves.[11]

The 2007 *Newsweek* poll (with fewer policy arenas) echoed these Gallup results, but it may be that 2007 produced an exceptionally large crop of inactive informed. To guard against inferring too much from a possibly unusual year, we analyzed a similar Gallup poll from 2012. We classified respondents as correctly informed if they agreed both that global warming is occurring and that human action is a substantial cause. By this definition, only a third of respondents were correctly informed—a reduced proportion compared with 2007.[12] Perhaps because they are a more distinctive set of people, a smaller share of the correctly informed—23 percent on average—did not endorse the eight policy proposals on offer in the survey. Thus, 8 percent of the full 2012 sample can be classified as disengaged informed (while a quarter were engaged as well as informed, both knowing about climate change and supporting an array of policy proposals to combat it).

CHARACTERISTICS OF THE INACTIVE INFORMED

Who are the Americans expressing concern about global warming but rejecting government or individual actions to address it? Which Americans repudiated Clinton's extramarital affair and perjury but did not endorse efforts to remove him from office?

One canonical analysis identifies three primary drivers of public opinion: material interests, attitudes toward particular social groups, and beliefs about political principles (Kinder 1998: 800). Scholars argue over how to define interests, groups, and beliefs, and over which is primary and how they reinforce or conflict with one another—but what matters for our purposes is that all three drivers, especially group identities and partisanship, are "sticky." Each may be acquired before adulthood, routine activities tend to reinforce more than challenge all three, and people seldom encounter an incentive strong enough to lead them to change their understanding of or commitment to their interests, group identity, or core political beliefs. All three factors are linked to membership in the category of the inactive informed, although their relative importance varies across cases.

Clinton and Lewinsky

John Zaller's initial analysis captures the essential logic of those who ignored Clinton's confession, Lewinsky's testimony, her friend Linda Tripp's disclosure of The Dress (one of Lewinsky's dresses, stained with Clinton's semen), DNA testing, Starr's prurient report, charges of perjury and obstruction of justice, and even the impeachment and Senate trial. Many Americans instead viewed the Clinton presidency through the lens of prosperity, peace, and moderation, all highly valued.[13] Dozens of poll questions asked, in effect, if the Lewinsky affair made Clinton's presidency ineffective or even harmful—and the consistent answer was no. A few examples from mid-1998, when the most dramatic revelations were occurring and impeachment was in the offing, make the point clear. In four polls in August and September, between 60 and 66 percent agreed that they were "unhappy about Clinton's behavior in the Lewinsky affair, but it has nothing to do with his doing his job as president" (ABC, Aug. 19, 23, 1998; Sept. 9, 14, 1998). Conversely, about a third agreed with the direct statement that the issue greatly "damaged Clinton's ability to serve effectively as president" (ABC, Aug. 19 and 23, 1998; Sept. 9, 1998). Also in August, two-thirds reported that Clinton's "inappropriate relationship" with Lewinsky did not affect their confidence in his ability "to perform his job as president"; the affair even gave another 3 percent "more confidence" (*Los Angeles Times*, Aug. 18–19, 1998).

Clinton enjoyed about 60 percent job approval in January 1998 before the scandal broke. With slight deviations, this rating remained in the mid-60s throughout the months of "all Lewinsky all the time" (Just and Crigler 2000: 185). Three-fifths to two-thirds continued to agree through the long fifteen months that, as one poll put it, "political leaders should be judged on their performance in office rather than on their personal life" (NBC/*Wall Street Journal*, Feb. 26–Mar. 1, 1998). Peace, prosperity, and moderation went a long way to blunt outrage.

Although it plays a smaller role than interests do in defining the inactive informed in this case, group membership (other than political partisanship—see below) nonetheless matters. Since Kinder's "attitudes toward social groups" seem largely irrelevant in this instance, we widen the scope of inquiry to include one's own group identity, or at least one's group membership. Regression analyses of an April 1998 survey show that, with other variables held at their means, women were eight percentage points less likely than men, and the religious were ten points more likely than the less religious or nonreligious, to agree that the president should be impeached or resign if he obstructed justice in the Lewinsky investigation.

This survey also, unusually, included an oversample of Jews and questions about respondents' religious commitments and American policies in the Middle East, thereby permitting us to look more closely at religious identification. The sample included 183 Jews who agreed that Israel "has always been a

special place." Among those who thought Israel is special but
disapproved of Clinton's Israel policy, two-thirds supported impeachment or resignation if Clinton obstructed justice in the
Lewinsky case. Conversely, among those who believed that Israel is special but *approved* of Clinton's Israel policy, only one-
fifth endorsed impeachment or resignation. The cell sizes are
tiny here, so the comparison is only suggestive. But these data
do support the claim that a strong social identity can partly
explain membership in the inactive informed, even with regard
to issues wholly unrelated to that identity.

Finally and most important, Kinder's third shaper of public
opinion, beliefs about political principles, is crucial for membership in the disengaged informed for the Clinton/Lewin-
sky imbroglio. We include within Kinder's phrase "political
principles" both party affiliation and political ideology; the
overlap is imperfect but close enough for our purposes. Research shows partisanship to be central to any politically relevant views; party loyalty typically develops early in life and
is strong and stable (Lewis-Beck et al. 2008; Green et al. 2004).
People may even start with party affiliation and then acquire
or retain only factual knowledge that fits comfortably within
it rather than follow the classic democratic ideal of choosing
the party that best exemplifies their values or matches their
understanding of how the world works (Goren 2005; Bartels
2002). Research demonstrating the tenacity of motivated reasoning is flourishing, so it comes as no surprise that party
loyalty distinguishes the inactive informed more clearly than
does any other characteristic such as material interests or
group identity.[14]

Partisanship would be at its strongest if Clinton's supporters claimed to care more about peace, prosperity, and moderation than about private morals or charges of perjury but really
cared only that Democrats beat Republicans. The obverse partisanship would occur if opponents claimed to care more about
morals and obstruction of justice or perjury than about the state
of the economy but really cared only about Republicans beating Democrats. People with these characteristics would be in

the category of inactive informed, not because they shy away from or fail to understand the implications of their knowledge, but because they do not want to be active in the sense of using knowledge of Clinton's malfeasance (for Democrats) or of the polity's excellent condition (for Republicans) to determine their views. Party affiliation trumps the Jeffersonian ideal of using facts to shape political choices.

We cannot directly test whether partisanship trumped any other motivation in defining Clinton's supporters and opponents. But it surely mattered intensely; figure 3.1 is unambiguous. Given media saturation, not to say obsession, on this issue, adherents of all sides presumably knew the same facts about the Lewinsky case. But they clearly differed on whether Clinton should leave office if he lied or encouraged Lewinsky to lie in a courtroom. Although party loyalists varied a little over time, almost always in parallel, the lines never crossed or converged.[15] Republicans (and independents, not shown) ended up almost exactly where they started, and Democrats ended up somewhat *more* supportive of Clinton than when the scandal broke. Partisanship mattered more than gender or religiosity; regression analyses of the April 1998 survey show that, even with other variables held at their means, Democrats were 27 percentage points less likely than all others to agree that Clinton should be impeached or resign if he impeded the Lewinsky investigation.

The views of the inactive informed are reinforced if partisanship and material interests are combined. Figure 3.2 shows how Democrats and Republicans differed over the year in their views of Clinton's effectiveness as president. Interpretation is easy: most Democrats persistently agreed that Clinton remained an effective president; most Republicans did not. So Democrats had two interacting reasons to remain disengaged despite being informed—partisanship and material interests— and Republicans had the same two interacting reasons to become informed and engaged (i.e., to believe that Clinton had obstructed justice or committed perjury, and to argue that as a result he should leave office).

Figure 3.1. Agreement that Clinton should resign or be impeached if he committed perjury or obstructed justice, by party identification, 1998.

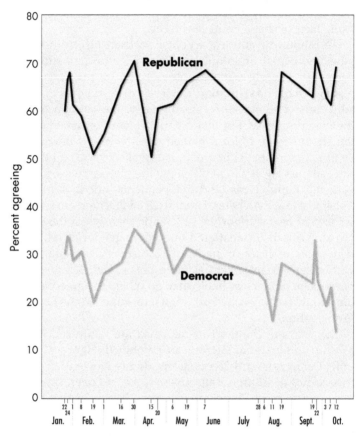

Source: CBS, *New York Times*, or CBS/*New York Times* polls, Jan.–Oct. 1998
Question (with slight variation in wording on occasion): "If it turns out that President (Bill) Clinton committed perjury/lied under oath or encouraged Monica Lewinsky to commit perjury/lie under oath, what do you think should happen? Clinton should admit his mistakes and apologize. He should resign. Congress should censure Clinton. Congress should impeach President Clinton. The matter should be dropped."

Copyright © 2015 University of Oklahoma Press.

Figure 3.2. Agreement that the Lewinsky scandal does not interfere
with Clinton's job effectiveness, by party identification, 1998–1999.

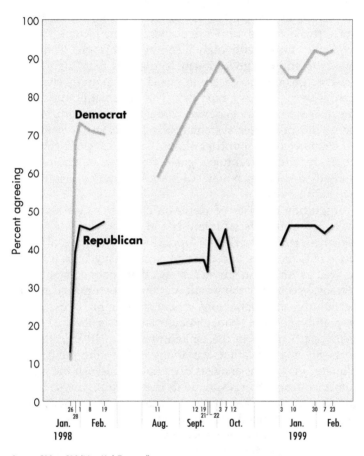

Source: CBS or CBS/New York Times polls
Question (with slight variation of wording on occasion): "Do you think this situation (the alleged
Monica Lewinsky affair) will interfere/has interfered with President (Bill) Clinton's ability to effectively
do his job as president or not?" (Jan. 24–Feb. 19, 1998); "Do you think Bill Clinton can still be
effective as president or not?" (Aug. 11, 1998–Feb. 12, 1999).

Copyright © 2015 University of Oklahoma Press.

Global Warming

The same two of Kinder's three factors also enable us to make
sense of who is informed but inactive with regard to government policies to mitigate global warming. First, material interests sometimes play a role.[16] In a 2009 poll, among the 327
correctly informed respondents for whom income data are
available, those with high incomes were more likely than
others to endorse government regulations that "significantly
lowered greenhouse gases but raised your monthly energy expenses by 10 dollars a month."[17] The same pattern held when
the increased energy expenses would be $25 a month. Respon-
dents did not differ systematically by income, however, on
whether wealthy countries should subsidize poor countries'
efforts to reduce greenhouse gases. Collective expenditures apparently do not touch material interests as much as individual
expenditures can.

Aggregate analyses of views on climate change also show
links between material interests and policy views. As unemployment rises, Americans' support for environmental protections falls (Scruggs and Benegal 2012). Analysis of European
as well as American surveys shows that "poor economic conditions, specifically the recent economic downturn, can better
account for the fluctuations, extent, and timing of the decline
in popular concern about climate change over the past several
years, particularly in the United States . . . [than] other factors—ideology, weather, variations in how the media cover
climate" (505). This analysis does not distinguish the inactive
informed from other respondents in a given survey, so it is not
ideal for our purposes. But it does confirm that material interests, broadly defined, matter in beliefs about global warming,
as they mattered for views about Clinton's presidency.

An even broader understanding of material interests also
helps to explain why people who know that human actions are
making dangerous global warming even worse nonetheless
oppose policy steps to mitigate it. Humans are poor at making
choices now that will shape their circumstances later, especially

if "later" is decades away. The author of the seminal work on the link between discount rates and views on global warming concludes that "lay people and climate scientists aren't concerned with whether greenhouse gases are going to reduce gross world product by 1 percent or 3 percent in a few decades. Existing models are really good at answering that uninteresting question, but only economists care" (Rehmeyer 2010). In our terminology, current concerns and interests lead people to make choices other than endorsing policies to mitigate climate change even when they know better; they are disengaged despite being informed.

Group membership or identity (again other than partisanship —see below) is not clearly associated with the inactive informed's mix of knowledge about global warming and disavowal of policies to alleviate it. Some surveys show women, the young, the well educated, and nonwhites to be more concerned about climate change than their opposites—but other surveys do not (Pew Research Center 2011; Borick and Rabe 2012; Center for Climate Change Communication 2008; Dunlap and McCright 2008; McCright and Dunlap 2011). Being inactive despite awareness of the serious problem, a source of considerable frustration to environmental activists, seems not to be consistently the property of any particular group of Americans.

Political partisanship is again the form of group membership most strongly associated with disengagement among the informed. It is apparent in two kinds of measures. For one, unlike the broad concurrence on the facts that we saw in most Clinton/Lewinsky surveys, a majority of Democrats accept scientists' consensus about global warming but a majority of Republicans do not. In the 2012 Gallup survey, for example, 52 percent of Democrats answered the two factual questions correctly, compared with only 20 percent of Republicans.[18]

Partisan gaps in correct information are recent. "In 2011, it may be easy to forget that the original Earth Day in 1970 was a bipartisan event, and that President Nixon worked with Democrats to enact many of the country's most significant environmental laws, including the creation of the Environmental

Protection Agency" (Rolfe-Redding et al. 2012). A generation
later, Earth Day is no longer bipartisan. In one survey, as scholars of motivated reasoning would predict, Republicans who
claimed the *most* knowledge about climate change were also
those expressing *least* concern about it (Krosnick et al. 2006). A
few years later, "those Republicans who had recently discussed
climate change with their social networks were marginally *less*
likely to support climate mitigation policies, all else equal"
(Rolfe-Redding et al. 2012: 28–29, emphasis added).

Even more worrisome is the fact that partisan gaps with regard to misinformation may be growing. The proportion of
respondents who agree that news reports exaggerate the seriousness of global warming rose from 31 percent in 1998 to a
high point of 48 percent in 2010, then returned to 42 percent
in 2014. Most of that rise occurred among Republicans and
has not been reversed, as figure 3.3 shows. The proportion of
Democrats who think the media exaggerate the dangers of climate change began and ended at about one in five, with a slight
decline in recent years. But the share of skeptical Republicans
doubled, from 35 to 68 percent over the same period. (As usual,
independents fall between the two partisan groups—with a rise
in skepticism but less than that of Republicans.) Thus, if one ac-
cepts the premise that the media accurately report scientists'
increasing alarm about the pace and impact of global warming,[19] there is a partisan slant with regard to migration out of
eligibility for the categories of inactive and active informed and
into eligibility for the category of active misinformed.[20]

Partisanship influences even the set of people who know
the state of affairs about climate change and know its human
causes. Among the 2007 *Newsweek* respondents with correct information, even with controls for gender and age, a regression
analysis shows statistically and substantively significant associations between ideology or partisanship and the view that
global warming is the most important environmental issue.
Thus, it is not surprising that Republicans tended to reject measures to conserve energy use. Again looking only at the knowledgeable, Democrats were more likely than Republicans to

Figure 3.3. Agreement that news reports exaggerate the seriousness of global warming, by party identification, 1998–2014.

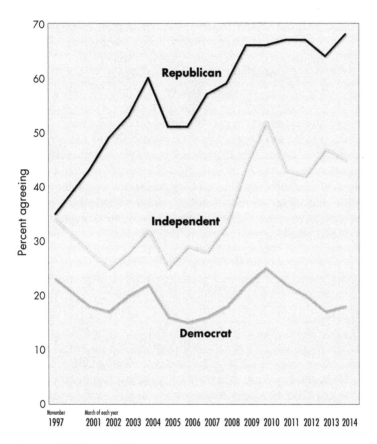

Source: Saad (2013), Dugan (2014)

Question: "Thinking about what is said in the news, in your view is the seriousness of global warming generally exaggerated, generally correct, or is it generally underestimated?"

Copyright © 2015 University of Oklahoma Press.

support ten of twelve strategies proposed by *Newsweek* to mitigate climate change. Differences ranged from a few percentage
points (people should ride mass transit whenever possible) to
almost twice as much Democratic as Republican support (for
banning vehicles with low gas mileage). Only one of the twelve
policy proposals (support for construction of nuclear plants
nearby) received greater support among knowledgeable Republicans than among knowledgeable Democrats.

The 2012 Gallup poll had slightly different policy options but
analogous partisan divides. Among the correctly informed, Republicans supported two mitigation proposals—increasing the
use of nuclear energy and (especially) oil exploration on federal
land—more than Democrats. In contrast, Democrats preferred
six other policies more than Republicans. To put the same point
in a way that focuses on informed inactivity, between 6 and 62
percent of informed Democrats opposed one or another policy,
with an average of 21 percent opposition. Between 19 and 46
percent of informed Republicans opposed one or another activity, with an average of 26 percent opposition.[21]

Interim Conclusions

In the cases of Lewinsky and global warming, both simple
crosstabs and regression analyses show that perceived interests
or actual circumstances matter, but matter less than attachment
to a group in understanding why people choose not to use correct and arguably relevant information.[22] As a consequence,
and as we discuss in later chapters, activists are more likely to
reach for group-linked political or policy levers than to try to
change perceptions of interests or material circumstances when
encouraging people to stay in or move out of a given category
in our taxonomy.

Even if politically less useful, however, interests remain analytically important because they point us toward two different
ambiguities in the relationship between the active and inactive informed. First, the global warming case reminds us that
the apparent dichotomy between active informed and inactive
informed may sometimes be a continuum for which we have

identified the end points; that is, there is no precise moment when the disengaged informed decide that they have enough resources to become engaged with regard to global warming and thus move out of one category into another. Rather, as their resources increase, those who are aware of global warming become more willing to be mobilized out of inactivity into support for policies to mitigate human causes of climate change. The converse would be true as well: as they lose income or security, those who know the facts in this arena are increasingly likely to deem climate change mitigation a luxury that they or the nation cannot afford. Or so we expect; full confirmation awaits investigation with panel data.

Attention to material interests also points toward possible ambiguity in what counts as relevant information. In the Lewinsky case, we characterize as inactive misinformed the people who ignored Clinton's sexual misbehavior and purported perjury in judging his presidency. One could, however, classify that set of people as active *informed;* they held correct factual information about the positive state of the polity and economy under Clinton's presidency, and they chose to act on that information in deciding how to vote. Either perspective makes sense; we focus on knowledge of facts about Lewinsky rather than about the economy because of the extraordinary and unprecedented attention the affair received from virtually every elite medium for almost fifteen months. That so much attention had such little impact is what needs explanation.

IMPLICATIONS OF THE INACTIVE INFORMED
FOR DEMOCRACY

Frustration and Instability

The status of informed inactivity is distressing to teachers, policy advocates, advocacy groups, and others trying to persuade people to act in accord with relevant knowledge. From the perspective of the frustrated teacher or advocate, the inactive informed miss the Jeffersonian ideal not because of insufficient or

wrong education—which teachers or advocates can correct—
but because of laziness, human frailty, or a tolerance for cognitive dissonance shared with like-minded others—which only
the inactives themselves can control.

Frustration can take one of two forms, each illustrated by
one of our cases. In the Lewinsky case, Republicans and much
of the media could not understand why most Americans did
not support Clinton's impeachment or resignation despite
awareness of his unsavory sexual affair and even perjury or
incitement to obstruct justice. Republicans staked their chances
in the 1998 midterm congressional elections on the assumption that they could persuade Americans to vote in accord with
their knowledge—but they did not, and the Republican Party
almost unprecedentedly lost seats in that election. This is an
instance in which the state of being informed but inactive was
surprisingly stable, to the annoyance of Republican partisans.

The case of global warming is an instance in which the state
of being informed but inactive is relatively unstable, which is
differently frustrating from the vantage point of an activist.
Americans' agreement that global warming is occurring as a
result of human activity has risen, then fallen, and may again
be rising. More important here, even among the (changing)
proportion who are correctly informed, support for policies to
mitigate climate change rises, falls, and is sometimes tepid. Despite activists' persistent efforts to develop committed environ-
mentalists, the links between policy support and knowledge
are not steady; activists must keep on persuading the same
people to take the same actions that they took sometime in the
past and then stopped doing.

Analytically, the status of the inactive informed tends more
toward instability than stability. That is because its elements are
inherently contradictory; knowing an important fact implies a
(rebuttable) presumption that one should act in accord with
it. Thus, when the dissonance between one's knowledge and
one's commitment to commensurate activity is made explicit
and challenged, the internal conflict can sometimes become
uncomfortable enough to motivate change (Festinger 1957;

Cooper 2007; Mendelberg 2001). Recall the eventual success of the reports of the surgeons general on the harm of smoking, and note the rise in recycling in the United States as a partial response to climate change.[23] So we see the Lewinskyan stability as an important exception to the general rule that informed inactivity is an indeterminate and uncomfortable state of affairs.

Informed Inactivity and Good Governance

Informed inactivity is frustrating to proponents of the Jeffersonian ideal of informed activity. Nonetheless, the cases suggest three reasons for nuance of that core claim. First, there are two routes to resolving the contradictions of informed disengagement. One can indeed escape the strains of cognitive dissonance or embarrassment about laziness by engaging in more activity in accord with one's knowledge. But one can instead resolve the dissonance by moving in the other direction—accepting misinformation that appears to justify one's preferred political or policy stances, or simple inactivity. For example, if one shifts to the view that global warming is not occurring or is not caused by human activity, as many Americans did in the late 2000s, one can oppose a carbon tax with a clear conscience. Or if one shifts to the view that inhaling someone else's smoke is not physically harmful, one can light a cigarette in a crowded room with a clear conscience. Those choices are worse than remaining in a state of uncertainty. Thus the degree to which informed inactivity is problematic for good governance depends on the answer to the old question, "compared to what?"

Second, as we have noted, given its internal contradiction and instability, the stance of being informed but disengaged can be accessible to persuasion. Thus, the blurry boundary between the inactive and active informed might be grounds for relative optimism about democratic governance rather than pure frustration.

Finally, there may be occasions on which knowing the facts but refusing to act on them is actually good for democratic governance. In our view, that is the lesson of the Lewinsky case. Arguably, Clinton's supporters were relying on more important information than the affair and its legal complications; they were judging his presidency in terms of its economic, social, and foreign policy performances. As Zaller (1998: 182) put it, Clinton's consistently high job rating demonstrates "the importance of political substance, as against media hype, in American politics." If people are using one set of facts to justify their inactivity with regard to another set, that may accord, at least roughly, with the Jeffersonian ideal. It depends on whether the offsetting array of facts is better suited to the circumstances or the task at hand; the question is again, "compared to what?"

These three reasons for nuance do not eliminate the frustration inherent in the fact that many people are correctly informed about important social facts but do not act on them. They do, however, open the possibility that the inactive informed are less harmful to democratic governance than the active misinformed. In our years of working on *Do Facts Matter?* we have identified no instances in which the active use of misinformation has had a benign effect on democratic governance; it is sometimes genuinely harmful. The next three chapters explore the pernicious use of false facts in democratic decision making.

CHAPTER 4

USING INCORRECT INFORMATION IN MAKING POLITICAL JUDGMENTS

If you don't read the newspaper you are uninformed,
if you do read the newspaper you are misinformed.

Mark Twain

The power of people who vote en bloc and don't care
about the facts can be fearsome.

Michael Tomasky, "How the House
Really Works," 2012

THE INACTIVE INFORMED are frustrating to observers, as the increasing fury of Clinton's opponents throughout 1998 and the increasingly urgent messages from climate scientists at present make clear. But the active misinformed—those holding false information and using it to make or justify political choices—are not merely frustrating but "fearsome" for democratic governance. That is so for three reasons.

First, difficult though it can be to persuade people to act in accord with their correct information, it is much harder to induce people to relinquish misinformation in favor of facts (Kuklinski et al. 2000; Lewandowsky et al. 2013) and *then* to act on their new knowledge in the public arena. Moving from informed inactivity to informed activity requires only one step, which, moreover, resolves cognitive dissonance and so has its own rewards. In contrast, an engaged but misinformed individual must take two steps to become informed—and the first involves admitting a mistake, which increases the sense of dissonance and disruption. The incentives push in opposite directions in the two circumstances.

Second, as the literature on persuasion shows, people most readily accept new information when it comes from trusted elites or friends (Miller and Krosnick 2000; Huckfeldt and Sprague 1995) and when it accords with their beliefs and loyalties (Gilens 2012: chap. 1; and see chapter 3, note 14 of this volume). Hence people using false information are likely to feel increasingly close to others who hold and use similar supposed knowledge and correspondingly distant from the rest of the population, especially those who try to correct them (Sunstein 2011; Mutz 2006; Kuklinski and Quirk 2000; Kuklinski et al. 2000). Put less formally, people tend to keep going in the direction in which they have started, and they appreciate and pay attention to people who agree with them more than to those who disagree. In principle, the competition involved in running for office or seeking to "sell" one's argument in a marketplace of ideas is a countervailing force to biased persuasion. And competition can have that effect; "facts matter." But in practice one can sometimes avoid the marketplace of ideas by promoting one's argument to the already convinced, and politicians can sometimes win election by mobilizing their base rather than persuading the undecided. In short, even if compromising with those who understand the world very differently is not always better than passionate commitment for democratic governance, growing polarization associated with misinformed activity leads to trouble.

Third, "false facts" are indeed false. Developing public policies in response to pressures linked to misinformation risks making bad decisions and implementing them poorly. It matters for racial policy whether a tenth (as about 7 percent of Americans believe) or a third (as about 15 percent of Americans believe) or half (as about 8 percent of Americans believe) of the American population is black (2000 GSS). It matters for criminal justice policy whether a majority of Americans think crime is rising throughout a decade in which it is falling.[1] It matters for foreign policy whether most Americans believe that some other nation is stockpiling weapons of mass destruction. Even though implementation does not flow predictably from policy design or policies from public or expert opinion, programs are likely to be more effective and less plagued with unintended consequences if they are not created in a context of public misinformation.

As we do in chapter 3 with regard to the inactive informed, in this chapter we use two case studies to explore the active misinformed. And, as before, we focus less on the usual social science question of what *causes* people to acquire and use misinformation than on an analysis, to be completed in later chapters, of the *consequences* of using misinformation. Our cases, the 2010 Affordable Care Act and Clarence Thomas's 1991 confirmation to the Supreme Court, are disparate substantively and politically. Both, however, illuminate the dynamics of using false belief in activities, with a particular focus on the ways that group membership underlies individuals' readiness to acquire and act on misinformation.

THE AFFORDABLE CARE ACT

"Knowing" Misinformation

Most Americans knew in April 2010 that Congress had recently passed and President Obama had signed the Patient Protection and Affordable Care Act.[2] Most also knew that the law was massive and complicated, and that the politics leading to its passage had been dauntingly byzantine. Over half agreed, appropriately, that "confused" described their "feelings about the health reform law," and over half agreed that they lacked "enough information about the health reform law to understand how it would impact [them] personally." (Kaiser Health Tracking Poll [HTP], Apr. 2010).[3]

Nevertheless, many already held false information about the law. The Kaiser Foundation asked each of two half-samples whether the new law included eight specific provisions, for a total of sixteen items; anywhere from a sixth to a third of the respondents reported incorrectly that a given item was not in the law. For twelve of the sixteen items, a higher proportion (occasionally almost three times greater) gave the wrong answer than said they did not know. Almost half agreed mistakenly that "the independent Congressional Budget Office said that the health reform law will increase . . . the federal budget deficit over the next ten years" (an honest 13 percent confessed ignorance of the CBO report).

A few months later, a parallel survey showed that the share of the population fulfilling the first criterion for misinformed activity—possession of wrong factual knowledge—had grown. On fourteen of the sixteen repeated items, more Kaiser respondents agreed incorrectly that a given provision was not in the ACA. Between 21 and 38 percent reported false knowledge; that share was always greater than the share who did not know. By the end of 2010, the Kaiser surveys revealed a new type of mistake—belief that the ACA contained provisions that were *not* in the law. Two-thirds of respondents agreed incorrectly that the law required all businesses of any size to provide health insurance for employees; three-fifths discerned a public insurance option; and at least two-fifths thought it included undocumented immigrants, created Sarah Palin's death panels (see below), or cut Medicare benefits (Kaiser HTP, all Dec. 2010). Thirty-six percent of respondents correctly answered four or fewer of the ten questions about factual states of affairs, and 25 percent answered seven or more incorrectly (Kaiser "Pop Quiz," Dec. 2010).

Over the next few years, Kaiser respondents remained just as misinformed. Usually more (often twice as many) gave the wrong answer as admitted unawareness of crucial ACA components. As late as September 2013, at least two-fifths agreed incorrectly that the ACA cut Medicare benefits to current recipients, retained copays and deductibles for preventive services, provided government subsidies to undocumented immigrants for health insurance, or established government death panels. Over half wrongly perceived a public option (Kaiser HTP, Sept. 2013). In February 2011, 22 percent agreed that the ACA had been repealed; a year later 14 percent reported its overturn by the Supreme Court (Kaiser HTP, Feb. 3–6, 2011; Mar. 2012). Conversely, in June 2012 a fifth believed that the Court had *not* ruled (an additional 4 percent thought it had struck down the law; all Kaiser HTP). Even in August 2013, about 15 percent thought the ACA had been repealed or struck down, and another 30 percent admitted ignorance (Kaiser HTP, Aug. 15–18, 2013; see also Kaiser HTP, Apr. 18–21, 2013).[4]

Elites' Contribution to Misinformation

Political and media elites who probably knew better contributed to the stock of false information available to the public. Two instances stand out. Although Representative Joe Wilson (R-SC) soon offered "sincere apologies" for his "lack of civility" in shouting "You lie" during President Obama's September 9, 2009, speech to Congress about the health care bill, his substantive views remained intact. Two months after the speech, Wilson and four congressional colleagues announced a press conference to "discuss the weak verification measures in Pelosi's health care takeover bill" and to propose amendments "that will prevent American taxpayers from being forced to finance benefits for illegal immigrants" (*U.S. Congressman Joe Wilson* 2009). This press conference probably passed unnoticed by almost everyone, but it suggests the ease with which the motivated could find support from elite actors for mistaken factual claims if they tried to do so.

The strange career of death panels provides a more prominent instance in which elites deliberately purveyed false information. Former Alaska governor Sarah Palin introduced the phrase in her Facebook posting on August 7, 2009: "And who will suffer the most when they ration care? The sick, the elderly, and the disabled, of course. The America I know and love is not one in which my parents or my baby with Down Syndrome will have to stand in front of Obama's 'death panel' so his bureaucrats can decide, based on a subjective judgment of their 'level of productivity in society,' whether they are worthy of health care. Such a system is downright evil."

Senator Charles Grassley (R-Iowa) similarly told constituents that "there is some fear because in the House bill, there
is counseling for end-of-life. And from that standpoint, you
have every right to fear. . . . We should not have a government
program that determines if you're going to pull the plug on
grandma" (Aug. 13, 2009; he later agreed, less publicly, that the
health care bill "won't do that").

Palin's Facebook page received 8,500 "likes" on the day she
wrote about death panels, and the message was sent directly
to her more than 800,000 Facebook fans. The number of fans
grew exponentially over the succeeding week (Holliday 2009).
In the ten days after August 7, "death panel" appeared in 179
headlines or lead paragraphs of U.S. newspapers and wires
and in 396 transcripts of the ten television and radio shows
that LexisNexis then monitored. Over the same period, 513 of
the blogs and web-based publications tracked by LexisNexis
included the phrase "death panel."[5] By August 18, 86 percent
of Americans had heard about "the creation of so-called 'death
panels'" in the health care bill, and 30 percent of that group
believed that they were included (Pew, Aug. 14–17, 2009).

Within a few months, "death panel" had spread even further,
appearing by December 7, 2010, in 726 headlines or lead paragraphs of U.S. newspapers and wires and in 1,603 television and
radio transcripts, according to LexisNexis. By then two-fifths of
Americans thought the new law included "a government panel
to make decisions about end-of-life care for people on Medicare" (Kaiser HTP, Dec. 14, 2010). The phrase was catnip for the
media, and many Americans were as responsive as kittens.

Elites can also foster falsehood by denying the misinformed
access to the truth. A category of consultants called "navigators" or "assisters" has grown up around complex federal
laws to help individuals understand options, constraints, and
resources that vary in particular circumstances. Using state or
federal grants, churches, civic groups, nonprofits, and state
governments sponsor these helpers; they have never been controversial or even much noticed by public officials. With regard
to the ACA, however,

whether by fees, background checks, tests, extra training, certi-
fications, threats of civil penalties, or delays, Republican legis-
latures and officials in at least 17 states across the country have
thrown up all manner of bureaucratic roadblocks in front of the
program. The officials say the regulations are necessary to protect consumers and their personal information, but health care
reform advocates say the regulations, adopted only in states
controlled by Republicans, are just part of a multipronged campaign to obstruct the implementation of the Affordable Care Act
at every turn. (Seitz-Wald 2013; see also Galewitz 2013)

Not just reform advocates describe the constraints on navigators as obstructionism: "In Georgia, Insurance Commis-
sioner Ralph Hudgens boasted in a speech two months ago
about a new state law that requires navigators to be licensed by
his office. 'Let me tell you what we're doing: Everything in our
power to be an obstructionist,' Hudgens said to cheers" (Seitz-
Wald 2013). A Robert Wood Johnson Foundation Health Policy
Brief found that the job of "educating and enrolling people . . .
will be more difficult in states that are hostile to the law" (*Health
Affairs* 2013: 4), and a federal judge issued an injunction against
Missouri's new law to control navigators on the grounds that it
"obstructs the federal purpose" (Pear 2014).

In short, elites can actively disseminate misinformation and
can take steps to prevent anyone from disseminating correct
information; the two actions may reach the same goal through
slightly different paths. And the failure to provide or permit
correct information can work. Residents of states that declined
to create their own health care exchanges—all with Republican governors—were twice as likely to say, mistakenly, that
exchanges would not be available in their state compared with
residents of states that established their own system (Pew Research Center 2013a: 3).

Acting Politically in Conjunction with Falsehood

Being wrong about something relevant makes one eligible for
the category of active misinformed. But only if one takes political action or links one's misinformation to political and policy

views does a person become a full-fledged member of this set. Surveys rarely include the questions needed to reveal the links between misinformation and activity, but some Kaiser polls do. In June 2010, for example, a third of respondents with at least one piece of misinformation about the ACA reported that a member of Congress's support for the law would increase their opposition in the upcoming November election; only half as many of the correctly informed gave the same answer.

One can also identify the active misinformed by pulling on the other end of the string—that is, by examining activists' (lack of) knowledge. A careful study of Tea Party adherents found many "deeply misinformed about" the ACA, with regard to both states of affairs and causal connections. "One Virginia Tea Partier regaled us at length with (a completely factually untrue) account of the strong public options supposedly contained in the law. . . . Another Virginia Tea Party member told us that the Affordable Care law included 'death panels' and would abolish Medicare. . . . [Activists] claim that health reform will help immigrants without legal authorization to be in the United States. . . . We were also assured that ObamaCare will be financed through a tax on real estate transactions" (Skocpol and Williamson 2012: 54, 72, 199). Again, we make no claim about the causal direction of being wrong and being politically active; it is enough for our purposes to note the close and mutually reinforcing links between misinformation and public engagement.

CLARENCE THOMAS

On July 1, 1991, President George H. W. Bush nominated Clarence Thomas, then a judge on the Court of Appeals for the District of Columbia, to the Supreme Court. The Senate Judiciary Committee held confirmation hearings from September 10 through 20. After hearing mixed views from senators and other witnesses, the committee split 7 to 7, largely along party lines. It sent the nomination to the Senate floor without endorsement. The Senate's subsequent consideration of Judge Thomas's nomination was interrupted by charges that he had frequently spoken to Anita Hill inappropriately about sexual matters while she had been his employee. Thomas denied the assertions, and the Judiciary Committee held new hearings on October 11 through 13. The hearings ended inconclusively; on October 15, 1991, the Senate confirmed Clarence Thomas by a vote of 52 to 48.[6]

The American public was less conflicted about Thomas's confirmation than the Senate was. Many expressed no view, initially because they knew too little to have an opinion and later because they wanted to wait until the Hill hearings were completed before making up their mind. But in all twenty-nine relevant survey questions in iPoll from July through October 1991, more Americans endorsed than opposed Thomas's appointment. Support rose by a few percentage points after the Hill hearings.[7]

African Americans' support for confirmation got stronger over time. In three polls, September 3 and 20 and October 9, high proportions of black respondents reported no opinion. But roughly three-fifths of blacks endorsed the nominee in the other seven polls, opinions solidified during the second set of hearings, and some of the remaining two-fifths were not sure rather than opposed. Roughly a third of blacks believed that Thomas should be confirmed even if Hill's accusations proved accurate (*Los Angeles Times,* Oct. 12, 1991; *New York Times*/CBS, Oct. 13, 1991).[8] As Thomas Edsall and E. J. Dionne (1991) summarized, "Trends in polling show that backing for Thomas among men, black and white, fell from 65 percent on Sept. 15 to a low of 51 percent on Oct. 9, and then rose back into the 60s by Monday, according to ABC. Thomas made an even sharper rebound among women, going from a low of 43 percent to 57 percent on Monday. *Blacks were even more supportive of the Thomas nomination, the data suggested*" (emphasis added).

Why Is Blacks' Support for Thomas Evidence of Active Misinformation?

Like opponents of the ACA whose misinformation affects their view of congressional candidates, black supporters of Judge Thomas's confirmation are in the active misinformed group only if they satisfy two criteria: they are wrong in what they think they know, and they take policy stances or political action in accord with this error. We begin with the second point.

We have already shown that a majority of blacks supported Thomas's confirmation. That support was reinforced by a Gallup poll held just after the confirmation vote and a few weeks before election day. Gallup asked registered voters whether they were more likely to vote for their senator's reelection if he (only two senators were women in 1991) had endorsed Thomas's confirmation. A third of black voters said yes, and on a separate question a fifth made the even stronger statement that they would vote *against* their senator if he had opposed confirmation (Gallup, Oct. 17–20, 1991). Seventeen percent of blacks in another poll described the Thomas vote as "one of the biggest factors" (rather than "one of many factors") in their upcoming vote choice (ABC/*Washington Post*, Oct. 16–21, 1991).

Arguably, these views had a much greater impact than their numbers would suggest. Politicians facing (re)election are notably attentive to strong opinions held by intensely engaged constituents (Sharp 1996), so senators likely paid close attention to blacks' views on confirmation and on the role their confirmation vote would play in the upcoming election. Senators did indeed report listening closely to constituents' views; as one newspaper put it, "A number of Southern Democrats are up for election next year after narrow victories in 1986 and they noted privately that black voters in their states backed Judge Thomas" (Rowley 1991). The New Orleans *Times Picayune* agreed: "In charging racism, Thomas appeared to gain support from black viewers—an important consideration for many of the swing Democratic senators because their states have large black populations. President Bush sought to put further pressure on the wavering Democrats [the day before the vote] by publicly thanking blacks for siding with Thomas" (Hutchings 2003: 39). Edsall and Dionne (1991) put the link between views and votes baldly: "Clarence Thomas was confirmed yesterday because his nomination split core Democratic constituencies, pitting blacks against feminist groups."

Social scientists retrospectively confirmed journalists' judgments: "Black opinion carried perhaps more weight than usual.
In the final 52–48 vote, a number of his swing Southern Democratic backers in the Senate attributed much of their decision
to Thomas's strong support in the black community." The
opinions of black women were especially crucial; "had black
women turned against Thomas, feminist supporters of Anita
Hill might have had more influence in the outcome" (Tate 2002;
see also Overby et al. 1992; Frankovic and Gelb 1992).

So African Americans who supported Thomas's confirmation and then proposed to reward or punish their senators accordingly satisfy the criterion of voting in accord with their
views. But were they misinformed? The first criterion for the
category of active misinformed is complicated in this case,
since it requires something closer to a judgment than to adherence to a purely objective fact. In our view, black support
for Thomas was indeed factually mistaken because it generally rested on the belief that, despite his conservative profile
as Judge Thomas, Justice Thomas would act on behalf of the
black population in ways that most African Americans, who
are overwhelmingly liberal or Democratic, would approve.

Some African Americans were misinformed about the actual
state of affairs, not realizing Thomas's conservative beliefs; in
one early poll, 15 percent predicted he would be "too liberal"
(Gallup, July 11, 1991). But more were misinformed about what
to them was a crucial causal link: Thomas's racial identity, personal history, and statements implied that he would act in the
interests of blacks as the majority understood those interests.
Thus, in a poll soon after his nomination, almost half of blacks
perceived Thomas to be "a role model for blacks because he
overcame poverty and racism to rise to prominence" (Gordon
Black/*USA Today*, July 3, 1991). In another early poll, almost
half of black respondents agreed that Thomas's performance
would be "just about right"; only a quarter worried that he
might be "too conservative" (Gallup, July 11, 1991).

The data in figure 4.1 give more contour to African Americans' belief that Thomas would act in their interests as they

Figure 4.1. Black respondents' characterizations of Clarence Thomas, July 1991.

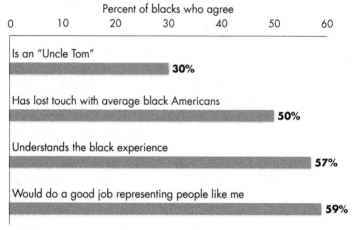

Source: Authors' analysis of *Time*/CNN Poll, July 17, 1991
Copyright © 2015 University of Oklahoma Press.

understood them. Half worried that Thomas had lost touch with ordinary blacks, but larger majorities agreed that he understood the black experience, was not an Uncle Tom, and would represent black interests on the Court (*Time*/CNN, July 17, 1991). Two September polls found similar results (CBS/*New York Times*, Sept. 3–5, 1991; ABC, Sept. 13–15, 1991).

In sum, at no point in the confirmation process did all African Americans concur in praising Thomas; at least two-fifths consistently expressed no view or rejected the proffered reasons for endorsing his confirmation. Nevertheless, a majority unfailingly agreed with favorable statements about how Thomas would behave once confirmed. Many were certain enough of these presumed facts that they supported Thomas even in the face of his own recent actions as a public official and Hill's charges of sexually inappropriate behavior.

Elites' Contribution to Misinformation, Take 2

Many elite actors fostered African Americans' false beliefs, although unlike the ACA situation the motivation was sometimes wishful thinking rather than deliberate distortion. The Southern Christian Leadership Conference endorsed Thomas on the grounds, as its president the Reverend Joseph Lowery put it, that he was the best available option for people wanting "a strong voice for justice on the Court. . . . Our choice for the Court is not between Thomas and a proven progressive, but between Thomas and an appointee like arch-conservative members of the present Court whose votes have turned back the clock on civil rights, freedom of speech and the criminal justice system" (Applebome 1991). The poet Maya Angelou (1991) warned that, "if efforts to scuttle his appointment are successful, another conservative possibly more harmful, and one who has neither our history nor culture in common with us, will be seated firmly on the bench. . . . Because Clarence Thomas has been poor, has been nearly suffocated by the acrid odor of racial discrimination, is intelligent, well trained, black, and young enough to be won over again, I support him." Virginia governor Douglas Wilder and columnist William Raspberry endorsed Thomas on the same grounds. Although the national NAACP opposed Thomas, one local branch and the former chair of its board endorsed him (Pinderhughes 1992; Burnham 1992; Marable 1992; Williams 1995).

The *Washington Post* takes its role as the premier media outlet in a majority black city seriously, so its support of Thomas's candidacy, although cautious, may have influenced African American readers:

> Clarence Thomas is qualified to sit on the court. He is surely not the most eminent jurist who could have been selected, but neither have many of his predecessors been. His views, particularly on what are called broad remedies in civil rights cases, are conservative. . . . It is not clear to us that in every respect these views are wrong or that Judge Thomas's mind is closed. . . . Nor do we think Judge Thomas comes to the court or this

point in his life with a malign or distorted agenda. Quite the
contrary. . . . He will have a clearer sense of discrimination and
its remedies than any other member of the court, [or] any other
nominee this administration is likely to send up. (*Washington
Post* 1991a)

The *Post* reaffirmed its endorsement after the Hill hearings,
albeit with even less enthusiasm (*Washington Post* 1991b).[9]

Some scholars who cared deeply about the interests of African Americans also endorsed the nomination. One sociologist
observed that "Hugo Black's Ku Klux Klan membership did
not prevent him from being a good and decent Associate Justice. A conservative black Georgian can be another Hugo Black.
. . . Thomas is more likely than a [Thurgood] Marshall clone
to move it [the current Supreme Court] toward racially equi-
table compromises on such controversial issues as affirmative
action" (Jackson 1991: 49). The president of Lincoln University
and the sociologist Orlando Patterson also espoused his cause.
Dean Guido Calabresi of Yale Law School testified to the Senate
Judiciary Committee that "many of his [Thomas's] views have
changed several times since those days [when he was a student
at Yale Law School]. . . . I would expect that at least some of
his views may change again. . . . [Thomas's] history of struggle
and his past openness to argument, together with his capacity
to make up his own mind, make him a much more likely candidate for growth than others. . . . Many a justice has changed his
mind dramatically since going on the court" (quoted in Phelps
and Winternitz 1992: 207). Calabresi even discerned a significant chance that Thomas would prove to be "a powerful figure
in defense of civil rights" on the Court (Aukofer 1991).

Politicians made the same calculation. Senator James Exon,
for example, justified his yes vote through the rather weak "belief that he will not turn out to be the doctrinaire ideologue on
the court that he is projected to be. . . . Time will tell" (quoted in
Phelps and Winternitz 1992: 406).

Whether cynically or sincerely, Thomas himself sometimes
provided grounds for believing that as a justice he would act
on behalf of the disadvantaged and in the interests of his race as

the majority understood those interests. A speech to civil rights leaders was what led to Rev. Lowery's cautious endorsement (Applebome 1991). Thomas's opening statement to the Senate Judiciary Committee lauded the civil rights movement: "But for the efforts of so many others who have gone before me, I would not be here today. It would be unimaginable." Thurgood Marshall was "one of the great architects of the legal battles to open doors that seemed so hopelessly and permanently sealed and to knock down barriers that seemed so insurmountable to those of us in the Pin Point, Georgia's of the world." Thomas even praised iconic civil rights groups, despite the opposition of many of their current leaders: "The civil rights movement— Reverend Martin Luther King and the SCLC [Southern Christian Leadership Conference], Roy Wilkins and the NAACP, Whitney Young and the Urban League, Fannie Lou Hamer, Rosa Parks and Dorothy Height. They changed society and made it reach out and affirmatively help. I have benefited greatly from their efforts. But for them, there would have been no road to travel."

Thomas returned to this theme in the first hearings: "I certainly count myself among those Americans who are for safe working environments and who are strongly for protections from abuses and exploitation from individuals who have more clout and more power. . . . And I'm certainly, as I've made clear during my tenure at EEOC, strongly in favor of laws that prevent employers from discriminating against individuals." He explained away a speech praising a natural law justification for outlawing abortion as an effort to connect with the Heritage Foundation so "that they would be more apt to accept that concept as an underlying principle for being more aggressive on civil rights." He did not repeat his earlier affirmation of "very strong libertarian leanings" or his observation that the civil rights movement is "really out of touch with reality" (Kauffman 1987). Instead, Thomas insisted that "we all have to do as much as possible to include members of my race, minorities, women, anyone who's excluded, into our society. I believe that. I've always believed that. And I've worked to achieve that."

We have no direct evidence on whether black voters were persuaded by trusted elites, Thomas's statements, or some other source.[10] And they did hear opposite evaluations and predictions, also from trusted elites. They also had available to them Thomas's record as chair of the Equal Employment Opportunity Commission, during which he halted class-action discrimination lawsuits and focused only on cases of asserted individual discrimination. Nevertheless, many believed that Justice Thomas would issue rulings approved by and of benefit to black Americans, the majority of whom were liberal.

Justice Thomas's jurisprudence is a subject for other books, but no one can argue that he turned out to be a racial, political, or economic liberal. That fact is what makes African Americans' support for him on the grounds that he would pursue their interests, as they understood those interests, mistaken. A measure known as the Martin-Quinn score rates every Supreme Court justice in every year since 1937 (currently through 2012) on their relative liberalism or conservatism. Justice Marshall had been one of the most liberal, scoring at least −4.3 in the final five years of his term ending in 1990 (an ideologically neutral justice scores 0; negative scores indicate liberalism and positive scores indicate conservatism). Justice Thomas scored 2.75 in his first term of 1991–92, and his scores have always been over 4.6 since 2005. That compares, for example, with Justice Antonin Scalia's scores in the range of 3.3 since 2005, or Chief Justice Roberts's scores, which have edged up from 1.8 to 2.8 since 2005. Only Chief Justice William Rehnquist has come anywhere close to Thomas's level of conservatism for about a decade, although he moved toward the center after the 1970s.[11] We return to Justice Thomas's conservatism, and the consequences of blacks' misinformation about him, in chapter 6.

GROUP MEMBERSHIP AND THE ENGAGED MISINFORMED

We remind the reader that *Do Facts Matter?* does not seek to explain why a given person would become more or less active and misinformed. Instead, in light of our focus on consequences rather than causes, we seek to identify the politically manipulable levers that can be used to encourage people to move into or out of the status of misinformed activity. As we found for the inactive informed, group membership dominates all other characteristics.

Partisanship and the ACA

As political scientists have shown many times, factual misinformation often has a political partisan cast. Democrats were more than twice as likely as Republicans to perceive incorrectly a rise in crime over the course of George W. Bush's presidency (Gallup, Jan. 2–4, 2009). Republicans were more likely than Democrats to report mistakenly that crime was worsening during the Obama presidency (CBS/*New York Times*, July 11–12, 2012). A majority of strong Democratic partisans agreed in the 1988 ANES that inflation had worsened during President Reagan's two terms; in fact, it had fallen from 13.5 to 4.1 percent. Conversely, strong Republicans were much more likely than Democrats to agree in the 2000 ANES that the federal budget deficit had increased under President Clinton; it had shrunk from $255 to $22 billion (Bartels 2002). More Republicans than Democrats mistakenly believed that "the percentages of Americans in prison today" is "lower" or "about the same as in other countries around the world" (National Center for State Courts, Mar. 6–Apr. 9, 2006). More Democrats than Republicans mistakenly agreed that "when TARP [the Troubled Asset Relief Program] was voted on [in 2008], Democrats did not mostly favor it" (WorldPublicOpinion.Org 2010).

The ACA fits this pattern exactly.[12] Over half of Republicans, and just over half of conservatives, held false beliefs about the ACA in June 2010 *and* planned to vote in accord with their representative's position on the law. Fewer than a quarter of independents, a tenth of Democrats, and a few moderates and liberals were in the same analytical space. Furthermore, as figure 4.2 shows, this imbalance is not a matter of general ignorance. Active misinformed Republicans—those who hold false factual beliefs and are politically engaged around this issue—are unusually well-educated. As the light gray bars show, Democrats with a college degree are much less likely

Figure 4.2. Percentage of respondents who are engaged and misinformed about the Affordable Care Act, by party identification and education, 2010.

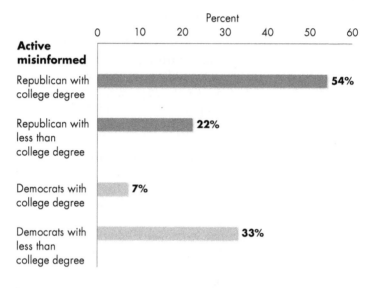

Source: Kaiser HTP, June 2010
Copyright © 2015 University of Oklahoma Press.

than less-educated Democrats to be mistaken about the ACA and to plan to use their views in their vote choice. In contrast, as the dark gray bars show, Republicans with a college degree are much more likely than those without to be mistaken about the ACA and to plan to use their views in their vote choice. (Note that proportionally fewer poorly educated Republicans than Democrats hold and plan to use mistaken factual information; partisanship is not everything.)

We cannot say whether highly educated Republicans oppose the ACA and its proponents because they are misinformed, or are misinformed because they oppose the ACA and its proponents, or are both misinformed and opposed because of some other reason such as fear or racism. But we can point to a large number of Americans whose good schooling has not inoculated them against holding and using mistaken understandings. More sophisticated statistical techniques confirm the importance of partisanship in making sense of active misinformation. In both OLS and tobit regressions that control for education, gender, income, health insurance status, and race, partisanship still has an overwhelming impact. Even with controls, Republicans are much more likely than Democrats to be misinformed about the ACA *and* to use that misinformation in forging judgments about candidates for office.[13]

Again we note that partisanship is not everything; with the same controls in place, blacks and Hispanics are less likely to be active but misinformed than are non-Hispanic whites. So the second driver of public opinion, group identity, also is associated with being active and misinformed about the ACA. Surprisingly, however, the third driver of public opinion, material interests, plays no discernible role. The best measure of interests in the survey, whether you and your family have health insurance, had no statistical or substantive relationship with active misinformation about the ACA.[14]

Race and Clarence Thomas

With few exceptions, political partisanship has dominated our explanations so far for membership in the categories of inactive informed and active misinformed. The case of Clarence Thomas, however—"one of the great set-pieces of recent American history" (Toobin 2011: 46)—is an important exception; racial identity swamped all other components of public opinion.

The importance of race in characterizing the engaged misinformed is not unique to this case. In 1985, middle-class African Americans were much more likely than all other Americans to agree incorrectly that "the percentage of blacks living in poverty has been increasing from year to year" and to overestimate the proportion of the poor who were black (*Los Angeles Times*, Apr. 20–26, 1985). A decade later, 40 percent of blacks incorrectly agreed that a majority of the poor are black; whites estimated more accurately (*Washington Post,* Sept. 29, 1995). But as we show above, blacks' views on Thomas's confirmation had much more impact on the political and policy arenas than public attitudes usually do, and they present a classic case of the role of racial group membership in understanding the use of facts in politics. So they warrant close examination.

Polling data illustrate the potent association between race and attitudes in this case when one compares white Democrats' and all blacks' views of Thomas during the confirmation process. African Americans support the Democratic Party in most votes and on most policy issues (Tate 1993; Dawson 1994; Kinder and Winter 2001), and since the 1960s nine-tenths have regularly identified as Democrats (Abramowitz 2010: 72). We might therefore expect blacks and white Democrats to hold similar views of a Supreme Court nominee. But, eventually, they did not.

In the weeks soon after his nomination, when few Americans had any view of Thomas, blacks' and white Democrats' views fluctuated dramatically, and in tandem. As the Senate hearings unfolded and opinions developed, however, the gap between white Democrats and all blacks grew. In five of the six polls between September 20 and confirmation, African Americans were on average twenty percentage points more likely than white Democrats to endorse confirmation.

Michael Dawson's (1994) analysis of racial linked fate and the black utility heuristic provides a plausible explanation for this unusual gap. Despite growing economic and social diversity within the black community, a majority of African Americans consistently perceive race to have a potent effect on their life chances. They consequently use group interests as a proxy for their own individual interests. Since a majority of blacks believed during this period that Thomas would represent the interests of their group on the Supreme Court, they supported him; white Democrats had no racial link, were more inclined to project his future opinions from his past actions, and therefore tended to oppose him.

STABILITY OF THE ACTIVE MISINFORMED

With occasional and important exceptions, group membership is deeply stable. People seldom change their ethnic identity even if they can, and changing one's racial identity is vanishingly rare. People can and do change partisan loyalties, but reinforcement is much more likely than abandonment. Gender is analogous to race in this context. Americans sometimes do change their religious identity (Putnam and Campbell 2012), but a safe generalization is that people are more likely to burrow into their group than to leave it.

In chapter 3 we portray the tensions inherent in being correctly informed but politically inactive, which make that category unstable. In contrast, group membership interacts with misinformation in a way that makes the active misinformed difficult to dislodge from their stance. Factors like race and partisanship are not just associated with the likelihood of believing false information; they also spur individuals to retain that misinformation and use it when making political or policy choices. If people like me are acquiring what they understand to be facts and using them in their judgments, I am supported in my own acquisition and use of these supposed facts. Even stronger, if people unlike me or hostile to me are insisting that what I take to be facts are wrong—and that I am foolish, misguided, or venal in using them—I am likely to be even more convinced that my (mis)information is correct and appropriately used (Haidt 2013).

This strong connection between group membership and use of misinformation implies that moving the active misinformed into possession of correct information is not simply a matter of correcting individual mistakes; would-be persuaders arguably need to alter perceptions of broad community interests. An advocacy organization hoping to move black opinion on Clarence Thomas from the active misinformed to the active informed would need not only to convince blacks that Thomas does *not* "do a good job representing people like me" but also to change the widely shared view that almost any descriptive representation in prominent offices furthers African Americans' aims. Democrats hoping to increase Americans' enthusiasm for the ACA would need not only to insist that death panels are a chimera but also to change Republicans' view that any federal activism or new expenditure threatens the United States' economy and moral fiber. Such changes do occur—as James Stimson (2004: 108) says, "Opinion is not infinitely malleable. . . . Facts matter." But they are likely to occur only under pressure, for many people at a time, and in particular circumstances; we return to this issue in chapter 7.

Thus, although our typology in figure 1.1 portrays the inactive informed and active misinformed as equidistant from the Jeffersonian ideal of the active informed, they are not. The inactive informed are generally in a dissonant and therefore unstable position, but the active misinformed are in a consonant and thus stable position. This logic underscores our claim that, although the inactive informed are at times frustrating to proponents of democratic governance, the active misinformed actually threaten it. People who use falsehoods in their political activity are in an emotionally and cognitively stable position; disagreement with their stance is arguably more likely to make them dig in than to feel embarrassed, as with the inactive informed. They are relatively inaccessible to teachers, advocates, candidates, book authors, or others who are outside their group. Sometimes this stance simply generates high-voltage political conflict, but at other times it has severe consequences. The next chapter explores some of these.

CHAPTER 5

ENDANGERING
A DEMOCRATIC POLITY

It was a great presentation, but unfortunately the
substance didn't hold up.

> CIA director George Tenet (2007), on Colin Powell's
> UN speech about weapons of
> mass destruction in Iraq

The argument is "Oh no, I'm putting off vaccines. I'm
part of a group that's smart enough to understand that
government is a pawn of big pharma."

> Doctor describing his patients (2011)

TO OBSERVERS WHO KNOW the facts, others' use of misinformation in the public arena can be amusing in a rather patronizing
way. One can only shake one's head at the North Carolina and
Ohio polls two months before the 2012 presidential election in
which 6 percent of respondents gave Governor Mitt Romney
credit for the assassination of Osama bin Laden and an additional three-tenths were not sure whether President Obama or
Romney "deserves more credit for the killing" (Public Policy
Polling 2012a, 2012b). (Obama ordered Bin Laden's assassination on May 2, 2011, two and a half years into his first term of
office.) Or what about the Jewish foreboding complex? A series of 1985 polls of contributors to the San Francisco Jewish
Community Federation revealed that one-third of respondents
agreed that a Jew could not be elected to Congress from San
Francisco. In fact, in 1985 all three members of Congress from
the city or adjacent districts were Jewish, along with a large

portion of the city council, the mayor, and two state senators (Lipset 1997: 172, citing Raab 1988).

But even slightly cruel amusement fades in contemplation of the harm to American politics and policy that can result from misinformed activity. Chapter 4 shows African Americans' cautious support for Clarence Thomas's confirmation to the Supreme Court to have been based on mistaken or misleading assertions that Thomas would support blacks' interests as they understood them; we see in chapter 6 how, during the subsequent decade, their hopes turned to disillusionment. Chapter 4 also shows the breadth and depth of false knowledge about the ACA, including among those who stand to gain a great deal of health care provision from its implementation. Moreover, chapter 4 underscores that, unlike the inactive informed, the active misinformed are remarkably difficult to edge toward the Jeffersonian ideal of informed activity. The disparity between knowledge and behavior creates dissonance for the inactive informed, which makes their stance inherently unstable; thus, they can sometimes be persuaded into political or policy support that is factually appropriate. But for the active misinformed, political views and knowledge of incorrect facts become mutually reinforcing through the mechanism of group membership. This concordance renders their attitudes far more stable.

Stability among the engaged misinformed is dangerous to democratic politics, as the cases in this chapter demonstrate. "Danger" is not an overstatement; people have died as a result of the actions described below.

We do not want to exaggerate the distinction between the active misinformed and the inactive informed, since failure to act on correct information may also yield tragic results. Global warming illustrates the point. Inaction on climate change is already having real, identifiable, and devastating effects on weather events—including droughts, wildfires, and flooding—that in turn threaten not only people's livelihoods but also their lives (Melillo et al. 2014; Nordhaus 2013). Nonetheless, the active misinformed are uniquely threatening to democratic polities because, unlike the inactive informed, they are in a relatively stable, consonant position and therefore much less likely to shift positions on issues like climate change even when confronted with new realities.[1] Thus, nudging them toward the Jeffersonian ideal is very difficult; what may be required is conversion.

We return to this point in the next two chapters; for now, we focus on showing just how harmful the active use of misinformation can be. We do so for two reasons: to highlight the importance of moving Americans toward informed engagement, and to remind readers that the stability of the stance of misinformed engagement makes it plausible that other, equally devastating cases will occur in the future.

IRAQ AND WEAPONS OF MASS DESTRUCTION

On February 5, 2003, almost a year and a half after the terrorist attacks of September 11, 2001, Secretary of State Colin Powell spoke to the United Nations, reporting the American government's evidence that the Iraqi government was developing weapons of mass destruction (WMDs). Powell had a reputation as deliberate and cautious, and he was known to be skeptical about the virtues of invasion, so his speech was a defining moment both internationally and domestically. At least three-fifths of American adults reported reading about or hearing Powell's speech, and a majority found his argument and evidence convincing. A tenth even reported that they had opposed intervention before the speech but changed their minds as a consequence of it (*Los Angeles Times,* Feb. 7–8, 2003). More generally, several survey organizations repeatedly asked a question about support for invasion during the months preceding the sending of troops; three of those series showed an upward spike in support just after Powell's speech. The higher level of support persisted through the day of the invasion several weeks later, at which point the focus of survey questions shifted.[2] By mid-March 2003, at least two-thirds of Americans, and more in many polls, enthusiastically endorsed or unambiguously accepted the U.S.-led invasion of Iraq.

Powell's UN assertions about Iraq's weapons were in crowded and bipartisan company. The main spokesperson, of course, was President George W. Bush. In his 2002 State of the Union speech, Bush described Iraq as one third of an "axis of evil" and reported that "the Iraqi regime has plotted to develop anthrax and nerve gas and nuclear weapons for over a decade. . . . By seeking weapons of mass destruction, these regimes pose a grave and growing danger" (Jan. 29, 2002). A year later, President Bush again pressed the case for war against Iraq and its frightful weapons:

> Saddam Hussein . . . agreed to disarm of all weapons of mass destruction. For the next twelve years, he systematically violated that agreement. He pursued chemical, biological and nuclear weapons even while inspectors were in his country. Nothing to date has restrained him from his pursuit of these weapons: not economic sanctions, not isolation from the civilized world, not even cruise missile strikes on his military facilities. . . . The dictator of Iraq is not disarming. . . .
>
> Imagine those 19 hijackers with other weapons and other plans, this time armed by Saddam Hussein. It would take one vial, one canister, one crate slipped into this country to bring a day of horror like none we have ever known. We will do everything in our power to make sure that that day never comes. (Jan. 28, 2003)

And so on for an additional 1,300 words—an eternity in a State of the Union address. Three quarters of Americans claimed to have heard or watched all of the speech and the rest had gotten "some" of it (Gallup/CNN/*USA Today*, Jan. 28, 2003). Like Powell's, Bush's speech had an impact: a tenth of respondents to one poll said they "did not [previously] favor U.S. military action against Iraq, but the speech changed my mind and I favor it now" (*Los Angeles Times*, Jan. 30–Feb. 2, 2003).

President Bush and his secretary of state were preceded and followed by many others of varied political persuasions, as the following sample of public officials' comments suggests:

- "Simply stated, there is no doubt that Saddam Hussein now has weapons of mass destruction." (Vice President Dick Cheney, Aug. 26, 2002)

- "Every day Saddam remains in power with chemical weapons, biological weapons, and the development of nuclear weapons is a day of danger for the United States." (Senator Joseph Lieberman, D-CT, Sept. 4, 2002)
- "Iraq . . . [is] continuing to possess and develop a significant chemical and biological weapons capability, actively seeking a nuclear weapons capability, and supporting and harboring terrorist organizations." (Senator Hillary Clinton, D-NY, Feb. 5, 2003)
- "We are asked to accept Saddam decided to destroy those weapons. I say that such a claim is palpably absurd." (British prime minister Tony Blair, Mar. 18, 2003)
- "Well, there is no question that we have evidence and information that Iraq has weapons of mass destruction, biological and chemical particularly." (White House Press Secretary Ari Fleisher, Mar. 21, 2003)
- "We know where they are. They are in the area around Tikrit and Baghdad." (Secretary of Defense Donald Rumsfeld, Mar. 30, 2003; for other such statements, see CounterPunch Wire 2003; Eichenwald 2012)

Mainstream media also reported the views and words of Bush administration officials much more than those of either Democrats or Republicans outside the administration (Hayes and Guardino 2013: 71–79; these authors also show, in any case, how little most prominent Democratic actors dissented).

Ordinary Americans, of course, had no direct evidence about the existence of WMDs. But they appear to have been listening carefully to their leaders in 2002 and 2003—and well beyond—as figure 5.1 shows with crystal clarity.[3] Surveys seldom show agreement to any query in the 80–95 percent range over a long period of time and with different sampling procedures, question wording, or response categories. Yet that is the proportion of respondents who mistakenly "knew" or thought it highly likely that Iraq possessed weapons of mass destruction before and during the invasion.

It is no surprise in this context that half or more of Americans endorsed the invasion and that many supported the war over the next few years. What is more surprising is how many

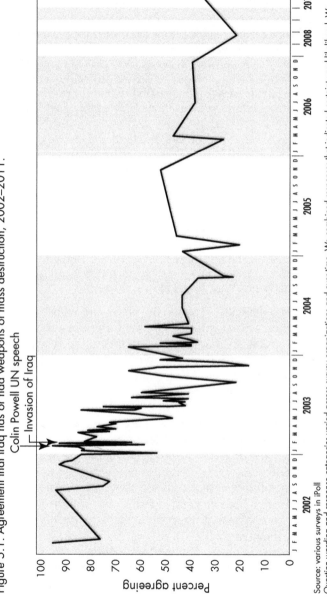

Figure 5.1. Agreement that Iraq has or had weapons of mass destruction, 2002–2011.

Source: various surveys in iPoll

Question wording and response categories varied across survey organizations and over time. We combined responses that indicated certainty and likelihood. We included questions that asked if Iraq currently had weapons of mass destruction or facilities to make them, as well as questions that asked if Iraq has had such weapons or facilities before the Coalition invasion. A few samples included only registered voters; their views resembled those of the full adult public.

Copyright © 2015 University of Oklahoma Press.

continued to believe that the United States was saving the world from biological, chemical, or nuclear attack months and even years after no weapons were found. Some Americans were so persuaded that Iraq possessed WMDs that, in April 2003, 36 percent agreed that the United States had "been successful in . . . finding evidence of" them (NBC/*Wall Street Journal*, Apr. 12–13, 2003; see also Holsti 2011, esp. chap. 3). A quarter believed that the weapons had been found through August 2003 and a fifth through the fall of 2003; since 2004, the proportion of believers has remained between 15 and 40 percent.[4]

Not only did large segments of the American population hold mistaken views about Iraq's possession of WMDs, but also—as is necessary for them to be in the category of the active misinformed—these beliefs were strongly associated with their political and policy views. Figure 5.2 shows the link between supporting the Iraq war and believing that Iraq contained WMDs. We randomly selected four surveys from the large set shown in figure 5.1: one before Colin Powell's speech, one after Powell's speech but before the invasion, and two after Coalition forces invaded Iraq. For each survey, we compared support for the war among those who incorrectly believed that Iraq possessed WMDs with those who were not misinformed in this way. Our awkwardly worded "not misinformed" category includes both respondents who thought that Iraq did not have WMDs and respondents who said "don't know" to queries on the topic.

As figure 5.2 shows, both long before, shortly before, and after the invasion, those who mistakenly thought that Iraq possessed WMDs were at least twice as likely as their correctly informed counterparts to endorse the Iraq war.

Agreement that Iraq possessed such weapons was associated with political partisanship even long after the invasion; Republicans were more likely to believe it initially and more likely to maintain the belief. One study found that, after the Bush administration stated in the fall of 2004 that it was unlikely ever to find WMDs, "Democrats concluded that the WMDs had not existed" and Republicans argued that "Iraq moved the WMDs;

Figure 5.2. Support for the Iraq War, misinformed versus not misinformed, 2002–2003.

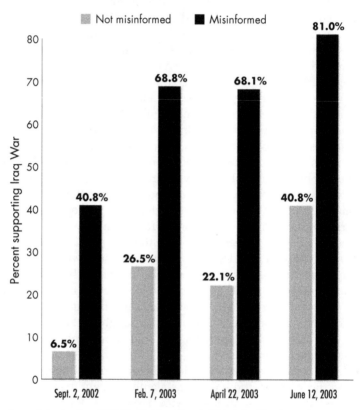

Source: Authors' analysis of CBS/*New York Times*, Sept. 2, 2002; Gallup/CNN/*USA Today*, Feb. 7, April 22, 2003; CBS News, June 12, 2003.

Copyright © 2015 University of Oklahoma Press.

it destroyed them; or, they had not yet been found" (Gaines et al. 2007: 965). In March 2006, 18 percent of a national adult sample agreed that the United States had found WMDs in Iraq. There were no substantively or statistically significant differences by age, education, gender, income, or region between those who agreed and those who did not—but Republicans were almost five times more likely than Democrats (27 percent to 6 percent) to report that the weapons had been found (22 percent of independents concurred; PIPA, Mar. 1–6, 2006).

Crucial for our analysis, the connection between beliefs and policy preferences was not simply a matter of partisan identification. Running the same cross-tabulations as in figure 5.2 for only Democrats showed that misinformed Democrats—though ten percentage points less likely to endorse the war than the misinformed public as a whole—were still far more likely to support the war than were Democrats with a more accurate view of the situation. Misinformed Democrats held views more like those of correctly or incorrectly informed Republicans than like those of correctly informed Democrats.

Perhaps the United States would have gone to war in Iraq even if Americans had not strongly supported the invasion. Or perhaps Americans would have supported the invasion even if they had not believed (because they were consistently told) that Saddam Hussein possessed and planned to use WMDs. After all, leaders hinted at at least one other apparently good reason to invade Iraq—that "Saddam Hussein was personally involved in the September 11th terrorist attacks," to quote one widely used survey item.[5]

Perhaps even Operation Iraqi Freedom and Operation New Dawn were the right policy choices, for the United States or for Iraq. We cannot replay history. But we do note two deeply destructive outcomes. For one, many Americans became (even more) alienated from their elected officials. As early as May 2003, half of the respondents to an NPR poll agreed either that "the war in Iraq was a success but was not worth the cost in U.S. lives and dollars" or that "the war in Iraq was not a success" (NPR, May 27–29, 2003; by 2011, two-thirds agreed that it was not worth it [CBS, Nov. 6–10, 2011]). By July 2003, two-fifths of respondents in a Gallup poll agreed that "the Bush administration deliberately misled the American public about whether Iraq has weapons of mass destruction" (Gallup, July 18–20, 2003; within a few years, a majority agreed). In November of the same year, over half thought that President Bush was either lying or "hiding important elements of what he knew" (CBS, Nov. 10–12, 2003; the proportion agreeing also rose over time). By 2011, half or more Americans agreed that the outcome was a "stalemate" or "defeat," that the war was not "morally justified," that the war's cost was harming the U.S. economy, that the war had a "negative effect on life in the United States," or that the invasion and occupation would not prevent civil war and violence in Iraq or terrorism at home (CNN/ORC, Dec. 16–18, 2011). ABC asked respondents to weigh "the costs to the United States versus the benefits" six times between January 2009 and November 2011; in five of the six cases, three-fifths or more said "not worth it," and a majority concurred in the sixth case (ABC/*Washington Post*, Jan. 13–16, Feb. 19–22, July 15–18, 2009, July 7–11, Aug. 30–Sept. 2, 2010, Oct. 31–Nov. 3, 2011).

Even more important, 4,500 Americans died in the Iraqi war between March 2003 and January 2012, and an additional 32,000 were wounded.[6] Estimates of non-American deaths range from 170,000 (Iraq Body Count 2013) to over a million (Opinion Business Research 2008). The latter figure is almost certainly too high, but regardless of the actual number, there were a lot of casualties.

Opposition, disillusionment, and deaths do not themselves mean that the war was a disastrous mistake. But if, as our analyses suggest, the invasion was made more likely by the American public's support, which was itself partly due to misinformation intentionally or inadvertently purveyed by leaders, one must think hard about the role of facts in politics. Even if the causal arrow goes in both directions or is reversed— that is, even if Americans engaged in "inferred justification" (Prasad et al. 2009)—the entanglements among wrong beliefs, public support for war, politicians' manipulation of the facts, disillusionment with and anger at elected officials, and hundreds of thousands of deaths raise deep concerns about policy making in a democratic polity.

CHILDHOOD VACCINATION

Few Americans had independent information about whether Iraq possessed WMDs in the early 2000s; they took their cues from an almost uniform set of elite messages. We have just argued that such an acceptance and use of misinformation is dangerous to a democratic polity and to individuals in (and outside of) it. Another case, however, shows that the use of misinformation that derives from the *failure* to accept an almost uniform set of elite messages also endangers the people in a democratic polity (see Hochschild 2012 for more on this inconsistency). These two cases differ on whether mainstream elites are responsible for the public's acquisition and use of misinformation; they are united in showing that acting in accord with false knowledge can get people killed.

Despite scientists' consensus that there is no connection between autism and vaccination against measles, mumps, and rubella (DeStefano 2007; Miller and Reynolds 2009), "there's been a dramatic rise in the number of communities where vaccination rates have fallen below the 90 to 95 percent threshold needed to maintain herd immunities. An overwhelming percentage of those are left-leaning, well-educated enclaves. . . . The consequences of these trends are as tragic as they are predictable" (Mnookin 2011: 304–305). In 2009, California saw a resurgence of pertussis greater than any since 1947, before a vaccine came into wide use. Ten children died from the infection, all but one infants. France had almost eliminated measles in 2007, but more than 20,000 people had the disease between 2008 and 2011. The head of the World Health Organization's office on vaccine-preventable diseases and immunization commented, "This is a lot of cases. . . . There's been a buildup of children who have not been immunized over the years" (Heilprin 2011). "U.S. Measles Cases in 2013 Spike to *Three Times*

Normal," blared one headline, with the article continuing, "and they are all due to people not getting vaccinated" (Plait 2013).

More soberly, the *New England Journal of Medicine* has inveighed against the "damage to individual and community well-being from outbreaks of previously controlled diseases, withdrawal of vaccine manufacturers from the market, compromising of national security (in the case of anthrax and smallpox vaccines), and lost productivity" (Poland and Jacobson 2011). The editor-in-chief of the *Canadian Medical Association Journal* similarly pointed to "a huge impact from the Wakefield fiasco. This spawned a whole anti-vaccine movement. Great Britain has seen measles outbreaks. It probably resulted in a lot of deaths" (Ross 2011). Referring to the same 1998 article, which first drew public attention to the purported harmful effects of vaccines, one pediatrician said, "That paper killed four children" (Gupta 2011).[7] Epidemiologists predict that more people will become seriously ill or die from infectious diseases in the foreseeable future, since it takes some time for such diseases to take hold and spread.[8]

Active resistance to vaccination in the United States is low overall but growing in some states and high in some localities. Despite the 90–95 percent threshold for herd immunity, among the fifteen vaccines that the CDC tracks no more than 53 percent (for hepatitis A) or 69 percent (for rotavirus) of young American children had received the recommended doses as of 2012 (CDC 2013a). Across the nation, the rate of exemption from school immunizations rose from just over 1 percent in 2006 to over 2 percent in 2011 (Omer et al. 2012). Either religious or philosophical exemptions enabled 5 percent of Oregon's public school kindergartners and 10.3 percent of its private school kindergartners to avoid vaccinations; comparable figures for Vermont are 5.1 percent and 10.8 percent. These rates do not include medical exemptions, which add a few more percentage points to the set of unvaccinated children (CDC 2013b). Nor do they account for homeschooled children, who are not subject to school regulations. In California, some private schools have vaccination compliance rates of less than 20 percent. Even among public schools in the state, vaccination rates can be distressingly low; fewer than three-fifths of the kindergartners in one of Malibu's three elementary schools were up to date on their vaccinations in 2013 (Shapiro 2013). In New York City, "vaccination rates at some . . . private schools are worse than those of developing countries" (Friedman 2014).

Americans are relatively tolerant of others' refusal to vaccinate their children, and acceptance may be growing. In 2001 and again in 2009, 6 percent of a national sample agreed that vaccines are "dangerous" or "not safe" and another few percent did not know. Since then, between one-fifth and two-fifths have responded to other poll questions in ways that imply sympathy for or agreement with nonvaccinators, or at least caution about vaccination—and many other respondents do not venture an opinion.[9] In the most recent survey of 2012, three in ten flatly agreed that autism is "linked to vaccines" (Berinsky 2012a).

As is no surprise, parents with doubts about vaccine safety are responsible for a disproportionate share of unvaccinated children. In 2010, 13 percent of parents of young children reported following an "alternative vaccination schedule" from that recommended by pediatricians. Most alternative-schedule parents refused only certain vaccines, but more than three quarters rejected H1N1 or seasonal influenza vaccines altogether and more than four in ten rejected rotavirus or varicella vaccines. Others delayed the vaccination until the child was older than recommended or prolonged intervals between doses. Two percent of the sample refused all vaccines, including polio and hepatitis. "The vast majority of parents identified as alternative vaccinators had anti-vaccination attitudes (80%–95%, depending on the attitude statement)" (Dempsey et al. 2011: 850). Only a small share of alternative-schedule parents were concerned that unvaccinated children would spread infections to other people.

Case studies of school districts and some (though not all) systematic evidence suggest that, in contrast to the usual characteristics of people who hold and use false information, parents who resist vaccination are disproportionately well off

and often politically liberal. In the 2009 Pew survey on parental choice, respondents with at least some college education and relatively high incomes were more likely to endorse
choice than were those with high school education or less, or
the poor.[10] Whites endorsed choice more than did blacks or
Hispanics. A study of all 39,000 newborns in Colorado in 2008
found that mothers with "higher education, private insurance,
and white race" were less likely to have their newborns vaccinated against hepatitis B than were Hispanic mothers, those
with little education, and those without private insurance (i.e.,
poorer mothers; O'Leary et al. 2010: abstract). Similarly, in the
2010 survey published in *Pediatrics*, nonblack parents were
significantly more likely to follow an alternative schedule (no
other parental characteristics attained statistical significance in
the multivariate model), and parents with higher incomes were
more likely to hold anti-vaccination beliefs (Dempsey et al.
2011). CDC data show that private schools have a much higher
rate of exemption than public schools in almost all states that
permit philosophical or religious exemptions from childhood
vaccines.

The link between political partisanship or ideology and opposition to childhood vaccination is complex. As an epigraph
to this chapter suggests, opposition stems largely from mistrust
of the federal government and large corporations—a position
occupied by both libertarians and some liberals. The school
districts with the highest levels of nonvaccination—Malibu,
California; Boulder, Colorado; Ashland, Oregon—tend to be
communities with many residents who see themselves as pro-
gressives. But in the two 2009 surveys with large enough samples to permit cross-tabulations, one shows Republicans (but
not conservatives) and the other shows conservatives (but not
Republicans) to be slightly more opposed to vaccination than
their opposites. Members of Congress who have raised public
doubts about vaccination have been Republicans. In short, people who hold and act on misinformation about childhood vaccination may be liberal, conservative, or libertarian, but they
are united in their rejection of medical expertise on this topic

and in their apparent indifference to the links between acting on misinformation and children's deaths.

The social status of the active misinformed with regard to vaccination is not our central concern; the fact that many people occupy that category with dangerous consequences is what matters here. But the vaccination case reminds us that education, affluence, social status, and liberal politics are not necessarily associated with holding and using correct rather than incorrect information. Some of the most sophisticated people in the most progressive communities in the wealthiest Western societies are using what scientists have shown to be misinformation to make decisions that endanger the health and lives of their own and others' children.

This case also reminds us that the meaning of a group can be very flexible. In most of our cases, explaining which category a person is in involves a group that is large, stable, and visible—a political party, a race or ethnicity, an economic stratum. In the case of anti-vaccinators, the group is either amorphous and not mutually recognized (people who have no political affinity except for their mistrust of the government and large corporations) or small and almost serendipitous (a school district in which a critical mass of like-minded people happen to reside). Scholars are increasingly aware of how important social networks can be; even friends of friends are statistically associated with whether one is obese, a smoker, or fearful of one's neighbors (Kadushin 2011; Christakis and Fowler 2007; Putnam 2007). Apparently a few influential parents with the right connections can also constitute a publicly consequential group.

Given that the active misinformed can be impervious to persuasion—and, at a minimum, have no strong incentive to change their views—and that their behavior can be destructive to a democratic polity and its residents, we might expect public officials vigorously to combat the use of misinformation. Some do. But many do not, which raises a further obstacle to the attainment of the Jeffersonian ideal of informed activity. The next chapter examines why.

CHAPTER 6

POLITICAL ASYMMETRY

Virtuous motives, trammeled by inertia and timidity,
are no match for armed and resolute wickedness.

Winston Churchill, 1936, demanding
British rearmament

CHURCHILL'S PROSE IS melodramatic, but his underlying point
is central to our argument. Absent strenuous effort, inertia or
timidity trammels virtuous motives in the political as in other
arenas. It is easier not to act than to take action; it is easier to
maintain one's beliefs than to question and then change them;
it is safer to encourage or tolerate use of misinformation than to
challenge falsehoods. There is an imbalance, in short, between
the likelihood of people's staying informed but inactive or misinformed and active and the likelihood of their moving out of
either of those positions toward engaged use of information.
From the politician's vantage point, people with the virtuous
motives of promoting Jefferson's ideal are usually no match for
those promoting the active use of misinformation, even assuming the absence of resolute wickedness (or arms).

In less fanciful terms, this chapter analyzes the deep asymmetries embedded in the typology we have been developing.
The cases already discussed reveal some of them; others are
best illustrated through new cases. In this chapter we focus on
three crucial asymmetries that emerge as one looks at the role
of facts in politics from the perspective of political actors. First,
inertia is more likely than change for people in any category.
Second, conditional on the general inclination toward inertia,
actors who focus on the inactive informed have the goal of
moving people out of that category (into the active informed),

102

whereas actors who focus on the active misinformed have the easier task of encouraging people to remain as they are. Thus, inertia works against the first set of actors and on behalf of the second set. Third and related, politicians' incentives to keep people misinformed but active tend to be much more powerful than (other) politicians' incentives to try to move people out of using falsehoods into using facts. Cumulatively, these asymmetries underline the importance of, and help to explain, the core claim of *Do Facts Matter?*—that, from the perspective of Jefferson's ideal democracy in which knowledgeable citizens take appropriate action, those who know but do not act can be exasperating, but those who act on wrong knowledge are dangerous.

Thus, although this chapter presents what we hope are broadly useful analytical arguments, it focuses especially on why the active misinformed can be uniquely harmful to democratic governance. We show in chapter 4 that the cognitive and emotional consonance of misinformation and group membership makes these individuals difficult to persuade away from their status. Chapter 5 adds the point that the active use of misinformation can have deadly consequences. This chapter builds on those arguments by contending that some politicians have an incentive to keep citizens misinformed, thus exacerbating both the challenges of persuasion and the risks of misinformed activity.

INERTIA IS MORE LIKELY THAN CHANGE

By this point in the book, we need not say much more about the first asymmetry; our central cases have already demonstrated how much more likely people are to remain in the status in which they started than they are to move. We offer, therefore, only a brief summary.

With regard to the inactive informed: once Americans got past the initial shock of the discovery of Clinton's affair with Lewinsky, the president's approval ratings rebounded to their prediscovery levels. Ratings changed little from that point on even in the face of increasingly lurid and detailed revelations. Americans knew altogether too much about the affair and its legal complications, but the majority did not choose the action (impeachment, conviction, or resignation) that would have been, in the eyes of the minority, commensurate with the president's moral or legal failings. Similarly, many Americans accept scientists' growing concurrence on the certainty and momentum of human-induced global warming; nonetheless, knowledgeable citizens' support for government action beyond encouraging companies to change lightbulbs and individuals to recycle newspapers remains stably low to moderate.

With regard to the active misinformed: despite the fact that no death panels have surfaced in the years since the ACA became law, as many Americans still agree that the law creates government committees to rule on end-of-life care for Medicare recipients as agree that the law does not.[1] The polls have shown little change since July 2010 in the proportion of respondents who are mistaken on this issue. Similarly, few African Americans who supported Clarence Thomas's Supreme Court confirmation were swayed by Anita Hill's charges or the NAACP's opposition. Most supported confirmation in the belief that Thomas would act on behalf of black interests as commonly understood. Up to two-fifths of Americans, albeit with "extreme partisan differences" (Shapiro and Bloch-Elkon 2008: 128, and citations therein), continued to believe for years after the 2003 invasion that Iraq had weapons of mass destruction, despite the total lack of evidence.

POLITICIANS' INCENTIVES TO REDUCE INFORMED INACTIVITY AND SUSTAIN MISINFORMED ACTIVITY

We lack the data that would permit a direct comparison of the likelihood of moving out of one or the other category into the Jeffersonian ideal. A fully persuasive comparison would require defining a population of cases featuring the inactive informed and another of the active misinformed, and then tracing the movements of individuals in a representative sample of each population or in the full sets of cases. Such evidence does not exist, and it is difficult to envision how one would define the relevant populations.

Instead we offer indirect support for our claim about the second asymmetry by showing, in conjunction with evidence from other scholars, important instances of efforts to move people out of inactive information and other efforts to keep people in the realm of active misinformation. We also offer theories to explain these differences in politicians' use of scarce resources. Our cases remain, nevertheless, selective and illustrative rather than probative. Remember also that our point here is *relative* ease of movement, within the context of the fact that inertia is always easier than change.

Efforts to Move People into Activity to Match Their Knowledge

"The industrial East is lost anyway, sure to support Kennedy. So is the northern Negro vote, overwhelmingly Democratic. Therefore, in Goldwater's words, the Republicans should . . . 'go hunting where the ducks are.' The ducks are in the electoral votes of the West, the Middle West and the South" (Alsop 1963). Goldwater was quoting an old adage, used with equal aptness by contemporary scholars seeking once again to explain candidates' micro-targeting: "Turn on the local news during campaign season, and you're likely to see a political ad. Watch MTV for an hour, and you probably won't see any ads at all. Parties and candidates hunt where the ducks are, airing messages that will be seen by potential voters. . . . The new media environment presents parties with new opportunities to communicate with their core, committed supporters. This has facilitated fundraising, the recruitment of volunteers, and mobilization" (Hayes 2010: 48, 44).

In other words, parties in campaign mode (are there any other modes?) not only seek to induce supporters who are already informed and active to vote and contribute time or money but also try strenuously to mobilize copartisans who are informed but disengaged. By definition, inactive informed supporters are the ducks (who already endorse the party's candidate), but they need to be hunted so that they will add an action such as voting to their knowledge.[2] That is the job of campaign activists, from precinct captains carrying turkeys and buckets of coal to media whiz-kids with Facebook pages and Twitter feeds.

As all of that activity suggests, adding action to partisanship is not easy, since inertia is more likely than change. Despite strenuous efforts, a political party is never able to persuade all of its disengaged informed supporters to move to the Jeffersonian ideal of participation. Seldom do more than three-fifths of the voting-age population turn out even in presidential campaigns, and many fewer contribute time or money. Nevertheless, parties commit large and perhaps increasing amounts of resources and effort to identifying and mobilizing passive supporters, even at the expense of general broad-gauged advertising of candidates or positions. Donald Green and Alan Gerber have conducted the most systematic and influential studies of "how to increase voter turnout" (their book's subtitle). Their message is clear: "A personal approach to mobilizing voters is usually more successful than an impersonal approach. That is, the more personal the interaction between campaign and potential voter, the more it raises a person's chances of voting" (Green and Gerber 2008: 10). Targeted media efforts in communities full of likely supporters are one strategy, to which are added door-to-door canvassing, phone calls from neighbors or coworkers, direct mail, or e-mail with a personal touch. Some get-out-the-vote organizations such as Rock the Vote or the League of Women Voters are nonpartisan, seeking to raise the proportion of eligible voters who actually submit a ballot regardless of what party they endorse. In contrast, party organizations seek to galvanize only party loyalists or those leaning toward their candidate: "Canvassing begins with a target population, that is, a set of potential voters whom you think it worthwhile to mobilize. . . . Many nonvoters need just a nudge to motivate them to vote. A personal invitation sometimes makes all the difference" (Green and Gerber 2008: 28, 45; see also Garcia Bedolla and Michelson 2012).

Some analysts attribute Obama's 2012 win partly to his campaign's extensive and sophisticated operation to hunt where the ducks are. Discussing the campaign's 125 million voter contacts, Obama's national field director Jeremy Bird assured reporters that "many [field campaigns] have historically favored quantity over quality. We do not. . . . They are personal outreach conversations. . . . In each conversation we have with the voter, our goal is to make a difference" (Dwyer 2012). Critical for our (and their) purposes, "Persuasion wasn't part of the [volunteer's] assignment; the people on the list have already been identified as potential Obama voters. The point was to make sure they turned out" (Drew 2012: 28)—that is, that they moved from inactive to active use of factual information. Obama's opponents agree on this point, if on no other: "In retrospect, the Romney team is in awe and full of praise of the Obama operation. 'They spent four years working block by block, person by person to build their coalition,' says a top aide. . . . 'We did everything we set out to do,' says a top strategist about the Ohio effort [for Romney]. 'We just didn't expect the African-American vote to be so high'" (Dickerson 2012; see also Issenberg 2012).

Some systematic research has found the targeted ground game to be highly effective—by one calculation, enough to turn three uncertain states into Democratic victories in 2008 (Masket 2009; see Darr and Levendusky 2014 on 2012). But other researchers are more skeptical. Many factors contributed to Obama's election, and even Green and Gerber (2008: 37) calculate that, "as a rule of thumb, one additional vote is produced for every fourteen people who are successfully contacted by canvassers"—confirmation of the first asymmetry, that inertia is more likely than change. The most extensive analysis of the 2012 presidential campaign found that Obama's "field operation . . . likely did not decide the election" (Sides and Vavreck 2013: 222). It is simply too difficult to mobilize enough of the inactive informed to win a national election on that basis alone.

Nevertheless, evidence is accumulating that persuasion directed at people whose views are in tension with their actions can motivate some to reduce that dissonance by moving from inactivity to the active use of valid information, at least for a while. The reports of the surgeons general (understood, broadly, as a sustained anti-smoking campaign) have, after all, been associated with a reduction in Americans' cigarette consumption; we offer other examples in the next chapter.

Working to Keep People Misinformed and Active

Green and Gerber pay little attention to the possibility of persuading active adherents of one party to vote for the candidate of another, and usually neither do party operatives. Large-scale party switching is rare enough that its exemplars are given labels—Reagan Democrats, Labour Thatcherites,[3] recipients of a wedge strategy (Hillygus and Shields 2009)—and searching for them is hunting where the ducks seldom roost. To the contrary: the active misinformed unite their purported knowledge and their political actions, so they have little incentive to abandon old beliefs, accept new ones, abandon old allegiances, find a new group, and change their behavior. So party activists largely ignore the active misinformed who support their opponents and instead concentrate on keeping their own supporters, regardless of whether they are misinformed, politically engaged.

A dramatic case of politicians yielding to the temptation of encouraging the active misinformed to remain in that condition is that of (what their opponents call) birthers—people who believe that Barack Obama was born outside U.S. borders and is therefore not constitutionally permitted to be its president.[4] A lot is at stake here; as one columnist put it, "If (and it is a very big if) it could be proved that Obama was born outside the United States, then the legitimacy of any legislation he has signed into law would be instantly questionable. So long, Obamacare?" (Patterson 2011). It is also a clean case; the state of affairs of where Obama was born is not genuinely in dispute or subject to alternative interpretations.

Although Hillary Clinton's chief strategist inadvertently started the birther snowball rolling,[5] Republican elites have boosted, or at least permitted, its growth into an avalanche. Thirteen Republican members of Congress cosponsored a bill in 2009 requiring presidential candidates to "include within the [campaign] committee's statement of organization a copy of the candidate's birth certificate" along with appropriate documentation. In 2011, to choose only one year, legislators in seventeen states filed bills requiring presidential candidates to prove their constitutional citizenship before being allowed onto a state ballot. Most prominent Republicans on the national scene have been a bit more coy. House of Representatives Speaker John Boehner (R-OH) observed that "the state of Hawaii has said that President Obama was born there. That's good enough for me." But when asked his response to members of Congress sponsoring the birth certificate bill, he demurred, "It's not up to me to tell them what to think" (Jan. 6, 2011). Representative Michele Bachmann (R-MN) declared that "it's not for me to state [whether the president is a native-born citizen or a Christian]. That's for the president to state. . . . I think we should take the president at his word" (Mar. 17, 2011). Asked about Obama's birth certificate, former Arkansas governor and hopeful presidential candidate Michael Huckabee responded, "I would love to know more. What I know is troubling enough" (Mar. 1, 2011); would-be presidential candidate Herman Cain made a similar comment (Mar. 31, 2011). Sarah Palin observed, when asked about aspiring presidential candidate Donald Trump's focus on the issue of Obama's birth, "You know, more power to him. He's not just throwing stones from the sidelines. . . . He's digging in there. He's paying for researchers to know why President Obama would have spent $2 million to *not* show his birth certificate." She agreed that Obama was in fact born in Hawaii but, "obviously, if there's something there that the president doesn't want people to see on that birth certificate. Then he seems to go to great lengths to make sure it isn't shown, and that's kind of perplexing for a lot of people" (Apr. 10, 2011). A spokesperson for Louisiana governor Bobby Jindal reported that a bill requiring confirmation of a candidate's birthplace "is not part of our package, but if the legislature passes it we'll sign it" (Apr. 19, 2011).[6]

As John Zaller's (1992) model of followership would predict, many though not all Americans followed this lead, agreeing mistakenly that Obama was born somewhere in Africa, or perhaps Asia, but at least not in the United States. How many actually believed it, any more than elites did, remains an open question, but figure 6.1 shows the proportions willing to declare themselves birthers or to state that the question remains unresolved. The totals and partisan proportions vary greatly over time, depending on methodological differences among survey houses in sampling rules, question wording and response categories, our classification choices for disparate response categories, and public discourse just before the poll was taken. These views, in other words, are not firmly fixed for many Americans. Nonetheless, although our methodological choices were cautious,[7] the crucial point comes through clearly: from 2010 through the spring of 2014, a substantial proportion of Republicans (and conservatives) agreed that Obama was born outside the United States or were uncertain or unwilling to venture an opinion (see Berinsky 2005 and Shoemaker et al. 2002 on the substantive importance of survey nonresponses).

Not merely partisanship, but also its intensity, is associated with birtherism. In 2012, 52 percent of self-defined strong Republicans, but only(!) 32 percent of weak Republicans, agreed that Obama probably or certainly was born outside the United States; in comparison, 8 percent of strong Democrats and 13 percent of weak Democrats concurred (2012 ANES). Self-defined supporters of the Tea Party were often even more willing than Republicans or conservatives to agree that Obama is not a constitutionally legitimate president. In the January 2010 Field Poll of California's registered voters, for example, 22 percent of Tea Party supporters, compared with 18 percent of conservatives, agreed that Obama was born outside the United States. In the ABC/*Washington Post* poll a few months later, a quarter of Tea Party supporters, compared with just under a fifth of Republicans, concurred. In a 2010 national survey, 46 percent of Tea Party supporters, compared with 37 percent of other Republicans, agreed that Obama was not native born (Abramowitz 2011; see also Jacobson 2011). Identification with the Tea Party is especially important for our purposes because it signals the second of the two criteria for the active misinformed: holding political or policy views, or voting, in accord with one's misinformation.

Figure 6.1. Agreement that Barack Obama definitely or perhaps was not born in the United States, by party identification, 2010–2014.

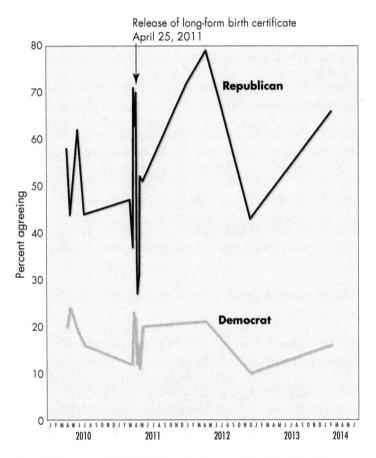

Source: ANES, surveys in iPoll, and 2010 Cooperative Congressional Election Study (thanks to Alan Abramowitz for data in last poll).

Note: We include "Don't know" and "No answer" in these results, since up to a quarter of respondents chose one of those answer categories in some surveys. See Berinsky (2005) on the substantive importance of "DK/NA" in some polls. However, we treat those who agree that Obama was "probably born in the U.S." as nonbirthers. For some polls, agreement levels were available only for respondents identifying with one or the other political party.

Copyright © 2015 University of Oklahoma Press.

As we and others have noted, the direction of causality among belief, emotion, and action is unclear here, as is the degree to which birtherism is a genuine expression of false belief rather than exploitation of any chance to express hostility to the president. On the one hand, according to the former head of polling at ABC News, "People in fact may voice an attitude not as an affirmed belief—a statement of perceived factual reality —but rather as . . . 'expressed belief'— . . . to throw verbal stones at that which they so thoroughly dislike" (Langer 2010). On the other hand, Adam Berinsky's (2012b) careful analysis of the "verbal stones" hypothesis shows that agreement with partisan-inflected misinformation is usually a genuine belief. We have little at stake with regard to the causal question; what matters politically is that many Americans are wrong about this state of affairs, link it to their partisan identity, are emotionally invested in their position, and have been encouraged to maintain this stance by partisan elites.

President Obama initially found birtherism amusing; at the 2011 Gridiron Club Dinner, he asked Bruce Springsteen to play "Born in the U.S.A." But in the face of apparently growing skepticism about his American birth, in April 2011 the president requested the state of Hawaii to release his "long form" birth certificate.

Facts do matter. As figure 6.1 shows, birtherism plunged in the days after the document was made public. Even among conservative Republicans, the proportion agreeing that Obama was born outside the United States was cut in half from a year earlier. Donald Trump, who had been running for the Republican presidential nomination largely on the birther issue— "Barack Hussein Obama has made mincemeat out of our great and cherished Constitution!" (Apr. 7, 2011)—withdrew from the race shortly thereafter. Asked about the future of this story, Representative Bachmann, no ally of Obama, told CNN, "I guess it's over" (Apr. 20, 2011). Speaker Boehner's spokesperson declared it "a settled issue" (Apr. 27, 2011). Most Republicans seemed ready to follow Karl Rove's advice from a few months earlier: "Stop falling into the trap of the White House and focus on the real issues" (Feb. 17, 2011).[8]

But facts may not matter for everyone, or matter for long, especially when politicians cannot resist the temptation to give misinformation a friendly boost. Although 14 percent of respondents in one post-release survey admitted, "I had my doubts, but now I am satisfied that the President was born in America," 18 percent "still [had] doubts" and another 10 percent remained "sure that the birth certificate . . . is a forgery" (*SurveyUSA* 2011). The latter groups were presumably gratified by comments of some of Obama's opponents, even long after the April 2011 release of the birth certificate:

- Asked in 2011 if he believed that the president was born in the United States, Texas governor Rick Perry responded, "I have no reason to think otherwise." Has he seen the birth certificate? "I don't know. . . . I don't have any idea." Two days later, he explained his caginess: "It's fun to poke at him a little bit and say, 'hey, how about—let's see your grades and your birth certificate.' . . . It's a good issue to keep alive." (Oct. 23 and 25, 2011)

- Early in 2012, Sheriff Joe Arpaio of Maricopa County, Arizona, called a news conference to announce that his cold-case posse had found probable cause to believe that the birth certificate was forged. "I cannot in good faith report to you that these documents are authentic" (he made the same claim about Obama's 1980 selective service card). Four months later, Arpaio's investigators declared the birth certificate to be "definitely fraudulent." (Mar. 9 and July 17, 2012)

- Campaigning on behalf of his son, senatorial candidate Ted Cruz, Rafael Cruz told a group of supporters that "we need to send Barack Obama back to Chicago. I would like to send him back to Kenya." (Mar. 2012)

- Arizona's secretary of state, Ken Bennett, announced that he was seeking verification of the birth certificate's authenticity from Hawaii state officials in order to determine if Obama could be on the ballot in November 2012. "I'm not a birther. I believe the president was born in Hawaii—or at least I hope he was." He eventually declared that he had received the needed verification, so the president could run for reelection in Arizona. "If I embarrassed the state, I apologize"; nevertheless, "What is so sacred or untouchable about this question that you can't even ask the question?" (May 17 and 22, 2012)

- Campaigning for the presidency in Michigan, Mitt Romney declared, "Now, I love being home in this place where Ann and I were raised, where both of us were born. . . . No one's ever asked to see my birth certificate. They know that this is the place that we were born and raised." (Aug. 24, 2012)

- Campaigning for his father, the senatorial candidate and former Wisconsin governor Tommy Thompson, Jason Thompson asserted, "The election here in November will chart our course as a country not only for our generation, but our kids' generation. We have the opportunity to send President Obama back to Chicago. Or Kenya." Upon his father's request, he apologized the next day. (Oct. 13 and 14, 2012)

- At the low point of this dismal sequence, in December 2013 Donald Trump hinted at something suspicious in the death during a plane crash of the health director of Hawaii who had authorized release of Obama's long-form birth certificate in 2011. He tweeted, "How amazing, the State Health Director who verified copies of Obama's 'birth certificate' died in plane crash today. All others lived." (Lavender 2013)

Except for Trump's sinister hint, at one level these comments are simply teasing, examples of politicians breaking the tedium of campaigning with a joke at one another's expense, like Obama's reference to Romney's dog Seamus.[9] Furthermore, birtherism's persistence may be in part merely an instance of citizens' more general ignorance; a tenth of Americans are not sure whether Hawaii is a state in the United States (Associated Press, Aug. 30–Sept. 11, 2012). But sophisticated, ambitious politicians would not keep on raising the issue of Obama's citizenship if there were not a more serious edge to it, and the many comments would not matter if repetition had no independent impact. But it does; demagogues have known for centuries, and systematic research has shown, that the more people hear an assertion of fact, the more inclined they are to accept it as true (Schwarz et al. 2007; citations in Gilbert et al. 1993). Garry

Trudeau's *Doonesbury* (figure 6.2) captures the thin line between deniability and demagoguery.

Republican politicians may not be actually trying to persuade Americans that Obama is an unconstitutional president. They may instead be keeping the issue of his American-ness salient, as Obama himself does in the opposite direction with the ubiquitous U.S. flag lapel pin. If, by framing him as a literal outsider in supposed jokes, Republican leaders can add anxiety about whether Obama is a metaphorical outsider to their other disagreements with him, their followers have that much more motivation to go to the polls to vote against the president and his party. Salience, or what one reader of an earlier version of this book called available information as distinguished from true information, matters a great deal in politics.

But birtherism goes a step beyond usual get-out-the-vote tactics. It does not rise to the level of war casualties and infants dying of pertussis or measles. Nevertheless, we see politicians' continual return to the issue as harmful for democratic governance rather than merely a subject for amusement or bemusement. There are three reasons for the slightly melodramatic language of danger in this case.

Obama and Rove both pointed out the first reason: birtherism wastes scarce resources of energy for and attention to politics. The president noted that top network anchors attended the press conference at which he announced release of his birth certificate only because of rumors about developments on the issue; they would not interrupt scheduled programming for a speech on national security, the proposed federal budget, or his social welfare goals. "During that entire week the dominant news story wasn't about these huge, monumental choices that we're going to have to make as a nation. It was about my birth certificate."[10] Obama then moved beyond presidential pique into genuine disquietude: "I just want to make a larger point here. We've got some enormous challenges out there. . . . We're not going to be able to do it ['solve these problems'] if we spend time vilifying each other . . . , if we just make stuff up and pretend that facts are not facts . . . , if we get distracted

by sideshows and carnival barkers. . . . We do not have time for this kind of silliness. We've got better stuff to do. . . . We have got big problems to solve" (Apr. 27, 2011).

Some in the media agreed. In a classic case of postmodern self-referentialism, the *New York Times* capped its report on Obama's comments about the media's excessive attention to the issue of his birth with yet another report headlined "In Trying to Debunk a Theory, the News Media Extended Its Life." The *Times* reporter noted with some exasperation that "in waves of media coverage . . . reporters tried to debunk those theories. . . . There was distaste evident in the voices of television anchors," and many talk show hosts found the issue "ludicrous." Nevertheless, they kept talking about it—the liberal MSNBC more than the neutral CNN or the conservative Fox News[11]—and "the very fact of the debate caused the issue to fester in more minds" (Stelter 2011). Given most individuals' limited taste for politics, attention to birtherism arguably detracted from attention to more consequential concerns.

Birtherism is also harmful, as well as irresistible to some politicians, because it stokes citizens' ineffective frustration with contemporary American politics. Conservative commentator Christopher Caldwell (2011) quoted a Tea Party member: "The birther issue definitely isn't part of our core values, but what Donald Trump is doing is questioning things and saying, 'Why do we have to just accept everything?'" He then observed, "To hold the birther view is to affiliate oneself with an attitude, not a truth claim. . . . Your average Trump supporter may think that the proper attitude to have toward America's politicians is contempt." Caldwell himself opposes this stance: if people use birther claims to express "a laudable cynicism toward those in power, . . . then a terrible trap has been laid: the more absurd the untruth, the more politically trustworthy the one who peddles it."

Setting aside any causal claim based on cross-sectional data, the evidence is clear that people who doubt Obama's birth in the United States are also especially mistrustful of the federal government. In the 2012 ANES, many, 58 percent, of those who

accepted Obama's native-born status were highly mistrustful
of the federal government—but a full 73 percent of those who
rejected his native-born status also rejected the government.
The pattern persists, somewhat more weakly, with controls
for party identification. Even more dramatic, three quarters
of birthers and three-fifths of those who thought Obama was
"probably" born in the United States agreed that the federal
government's power posed a threat to the rights and freedoms
of American citizens, compared with only(!) 37 percent of those
who were certain of Obama's native-born status. Even with
controls for party identification, Republican birthers are significantly more likely than Republican nonbirthers to say that
the federal government threatens its own citizens.[12]

Finally, as an extension of the earlier point about get-out-
the-vote mobilization, birtherism may tempt politicians as a
respectable vehicle for reinforcing some individuals' view that
Obama's race or foreign ancestry pushes him out of the legitimate American mainstream. This too is dangerous for a democratic polity. As Michael Tomasky (2011) limns this view:

> The president is . . . an Other with a capital O, who, to their way
> of thinking, could not possibly have been legitimately elected
> the president of any United States they know. . . . A conspiracy
> of immense proportions, concocted all the way back in 1961,
> had to be the only explanation for how this black man got to the
> White House. And if you think race isn't what this is about at
> its core, ask yourself if there would even be a birther conspiracy
> if Barack Obama were white and named Bart Oberstar. If you
> think there would be, you are delusional.

Survey data support Tomasky's argument. In the 2010 Evaluations of Government and Society Survey (part of the ANES),
even with controls for party identification and ideology, racial resentment was positively related to whites' doubts about
Obama's American birth (Abramowitz 2011).[13] Another survey
found not only an association between resentment of blacks and
birtherism but also that, even with controls for partisanship,
ideology, and birtherism, "individuals with the most favorable
impression of Muslims were 45 percentage points more likely

to say Obama was American-born than were those with very unfavorable feelings about Muslims" (Tesler and Sears 2010: 15; see also Hehman et al. 2011). In the 2012 ANES, birthers were much more likely than nonbirthers to agree that blacks and Hispanics—but not whites—have too much influence in American politics. The pattern remains highly significant when one controls for partisan identification, as figure 6.3 shows.

As Tesler and Sears' analysis suggests, birtherism and the related assertion that Obama is a Muslim may reflect, and provide a legitimate way to express, hostility to some foreigners as well as to African Americans. Representative Bachmann assured her listeners that "most Americans are wild about America and they are very concerned to have a president who doesn't share those values" (or, more simply, Obama may have "anti-American views" [Oct. 17, 2008], which she later called a misstatement). Governor Huckabee not only found the purported ambiguity about the birth certificate "troubling" but also observed, "One thing I do know is his having grown up in Kenya, his view of the Brits for example, [is] very different than the average American. . . . His perspective as growing up in Kenya with a Kenyan father and grandfather, their view of the Mau Mau Revolution in Kenya is very different than ours because he probably grew up hearing that the British are a bunch of imperialists who persecuted his grandfather" (Mar. 1, 2011).

In short, politicians flirt with birtherism and thereby encourage people to maintain belief in and act on false statements of fact for several reasons—to be witty, to distract voters from more difficult issues, to reinforce hatred of government, and to promote hostility to Obama and all that he personifies. Albeit similar on the surface, Romney's joke about Obama's birthplace is not really comparable to Obama's joke about Romney's dog.[14]

Generalizing beyond Birtherism

Even given strong ideological commitments, over the long term most successful politicians are pragmatists. To win an election, persuade fellow legislators to vote for a cherished bill, or induce busy colleagues to invest scarce resources in their agenda

Figure 6.3. Percentage of birthers and nonbirthers agreeing that blacks, Latinos, and whites have too much influence on American politics, 2012.

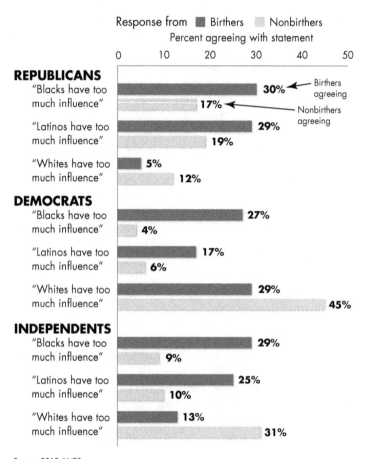

Source: 2012 ANES

Questions: (1) How much influence do Hispanics [blacks, whites] have in U.S. politics? Too much influence, just about the right amount of influence, or too little influence? (2) Was the President born in the U.S.? Definitely born in the U.S., Probably born in the U.S., Probably born in another country, or Definitely born in another country? The comparisons in figure 6.3 are understated, since we treat those who agree that Obama was "probably born in the U.S." as nonbirthers.

Copyright © 2015 University of Oklahoma Press.

rather than some other, they can seldom afford a lot of illusions or chase after many unwinnable goals. Candidates cannot instruct voters how to act; they must meet them where they are and then exhort or nudge them toward somewhere else.

Looking at democratic decision making from the opposite vantage point, ordinary people live in social networks, and their attitudes typically align with those of people with whom they identify or regularly associate. Most individuals devote only slight attention to politics and policy choices, and most prefer to hear opinions or pronouncements with which they agree rather than those that seem wrong or challenging (Oliver 2001; Mutz 2006). Most people want to view themselves as rational and consistent, as well as honorable and sensible; as Christopher Achen and Larry Bartels (2006) once titled an essay, "It Feels Like We're Thinking."

In combination, both fairly obvious points have distinct implications for the acquisition and use of facts in politics. As we have noted, the status of being inactive informed is unstable, which makes one susceptible to a concern about being irrational or having weakness of will. Others in one's social network are likely to feel a similar unease or to be acting already on their knowledge, so connections with others can reinforce a concern about inaction. A pragmatic politician can expect some success in efforts to induce people to resolve this dissonance, so it is worth investing resources in trying.

The status of being active misinformed, in contrast, can be highly stable, which makes it hard to persuade a person that he or she is not being rational or sensible. Others in one's social network are likely to be wrong about the same things and to be taking the same actions, so connections with fellow group members can reinforce a sense of rationality and coherence. A pragmatic political actor realizes that the investment of resources goes much further in efforts to work around, accommodate, or even encourage the active misinformed than in efforts to move people out of that category.

There is, in short, a deep asymmetry between political actors who seek support from the inactive informed and those who seek support from the active misinformed. The former promote the Jeffersonian ideal of informed activity; the latter undermine it.

ACTIVE MISINFORMATION: ENCOURAGING PEOPLE TO STAY IN, SHRUGGING ONE'S SHOULDERS, AND MOVING PEOPLE OUT

Politicians do try occasionally to move the active misinformed. Obama held a (rare) press conference to announce release of his birth certificate; a few members of Congress insisted that the ACA does not include death panels; the national NAACP opposed Clarence Thomas's confirmation to the Supreme Court. Public officials make considerable efforts to correct harmful misinformation about themselves or their policy positions. To understand more fully when and why political actors resist or accommodate individuals who are active but misinformed, we turn to the third asymmetry—the fact that politicians' incentives to keep people acting on misinformation are almost always greater than (other) politicians' incentives to move those individuals into the Jeffersonian ideal or even into inactivity.

Assume for the sake of argument that political elites know that the active misinformed are indeed mistaken and are acting on their misapprehensions politically—thus probably working against their own true interests or against the interests of the polity as a whole. These elites have three basic choices: to encourage people to remain misinformed, to ignore the dangers of actively using misinformation and work with people wherever they are, and to try to move people into the ranks of the active informed. The first is easiest and potentially advantageous, the second is a reasonable choice for a pragmatist, and the third is hard but best for democratic governance.

Encouraging People to Stay Active and Misinformed

What might appear to an observer as a challenge to democratic governance may be an opportunity for some actors to use public opinion in pursuit of a cherished goal. Consider again the issue of Iraqi WMDs in 2003. Neither President Bush nor many other leaders sought to correct misperceptions about the presence of such weapons even months after the Coalition forces found none. After all, the belief reinforced support for the Iraqi invasion, which was, in this view, what mattered most. This need not have been (only) a cynical calculation; Saddam Hussein was a terrible person and ruler, and arguably Iraqis as well as Americans were better off with his defeat and the subsequent Coalition control of Iraq.

Taking political or policy advantage of the active misinformed can be more or less assertive. President George W. Bush and his administration probably condoned public misinformation well past the point of themselves believing that there were Iraqi WMDs. A decade earlier, President George H. W. Bush had taken a step further into encouraging the use of misinformation by deliberately reinforcing misperceptions about what the American Bar Association meant in declaring then-judge Clarence Thomas "qualified" to be a Supreme Court justice. The ABA's rating was intended to be, and was understood by the knowledgeable as, "arguably the worst rating ever given to a Supreme Court nominee. . . . It was—or should have been—a stunning blow to Thomas" (Phelps and Winternitz 1992: 140–41). But to the vast majority of Americans who know nothing about the ABA, "qualified" seemed, sensibly enough, to mean what it said—that Thomas was qualified to be on the Court. Despite the White House staff's deeper knowledge, the president's spokesperson simply stated that "we are very pleased that the ABA's Standing Committee on the Federal Judiciary has found Judge Thomas qualified to be an associate justice of the United States Supreme Court" (Reuters 1991). Senator John Danforth concurred that, "as the ABA will testify, he is certainly qualified for the job" (United States Senate 1991: 100). It was a brilliant move: "How could it be explained . . . that when the ABA said qualified, it really meant barely acceptable. To most people, qualified sounds like an endorsement" (Phelps and Winternitz 1992: 141).

Sarah Palin moved even deeper into boosting the use of misinformation by inventing and continuing to foster belief in nonexistent ACA death panels. She is not alone in creating rather than merely encouraging or tolerating misinformation. In 2011, Senator Jon Kyl (R-AZ) falsely stated on the Senate floor, "If you want an abortion, you go to Planned Parenthood, and that's well over 90 percent of what Planned Parenthood does." Not so: fewer than 3 percent of Planned Parenthood's services are abortions.[15] In these cases and others, one set of political actors or one policy position benefited from the stability of the category of active misinformation and sought to raise the salience of particular bits of misinformation. They took to heart the aphorism attributed to Lee Atwater: "Politics and facts don't belong in the same room."

Shrugging One's Shoulders

Not all political actors condone, encourage, or create citizens' active use of misinformation. Recall the member of Congress who declared that "I have the best platform from which to educate of anyone in the country. To me, there's no difference between leadership and education. . . . What is politics if it's not teaching?" His hearer, however, observed soon thereafter that "the only generalization supportable by the evidence is the apparent paucity of educational effort" (Fenno 1978: 162, 163).

To test the disparate claims of Fenno and his informant— more broadly, to examine how energetically elected officials work to spur the active use of facts—we conducted two parallel studies (elaborated in the appendix to this chapter). One analyzed district-wide constituent newsletters from two different sessions of Congress. We focused on representatives who have been elected at least twice, on the grounds that winners of at least two elections have presumably worked out the right answer to the question of how much information to convey to voters, at least better than their opponents did. (Table 6.1, in the appendix to this chapter, gives information about the sample of members of Congress.) We examined newsletters because, given the rules and norms of congressional communication, they present the most direct, unmediated communication from politicians to all constituents.[16] Furthermore, the newsletter format encourages communication of facts more than, say, meeting notices or campaign ads do—so if Fenno's informant is right, we should see evidence of educational efforts in successful legislators' newsletters.

In particular, we explored politicians' provision of what we term "social facts"—pieces of information that might contextualize legislation through factual statements about society at large. Such statements could be precise states of affairs, explicit or implicit comparisons of one state of affairs to another, or even causal claims. Examples include "Oil prices have risen by 33 percent," "Oil prices are rapidly rising," "Oil prices are higher than they've ever been," and "Conflict in the Middle East is causing oil prices to rise."

We found that members of Congress are mostly uninterested in purveying social facts. The appendix provides details of the analysis, but the central conclusion is simple: roughly 14 percent of all coded paragraphs in the 2004/5 and 2006/7 sessions (combination of rows 1 and 2, table 6.2) contained a social fact. And even when politicians do seek to educate their constituents, in both years over half of the social facts appeared in the same paragraph as partisan appeals or David Mayhew's categories of position taking, advertising, and credit claiming (Mayhew 1974). In contrast, newsletter writers provide many legislative facts, that is, bits of information about bills, new laws, and speeches or other procedural activities; examples include "The House voted 403–30 to pass the housing bill" and "This new law offers tax breaks to families making below $10,500." In both 2004/5 and 2006/7, well over half of the coded newsletter paragraphs contained legislative facts either alone or combined with partisan or personal appeals.[17]

Thus, elected officials tell their constituents a great deal about the good things that Congress is doing and vigorously urge them to ensure that their representative can continue doing those things—but they give constituents little information that provides context, explains and justifies, or simply makes sense of the plethora of legislative facts and personal or partisan appeals. Almost by definition, since we sampled newsletters from electorally successful candidates, this strategy is electorally successful. But it does not support a claim that "Educating your constituency . . . [is] the most important job we have" (Fenno 1978: 162).

Our second study of political actors' commitment to educating their constituency paralleled the first but focused on State of the Union addresses. For reasons explained in the appendix, we analyzed the first State of the Union addresses given by George H. W. Bush, Bill Clinton, George W. Bush, and Barack Obama after their initial elections and, if relevant, their reelections. The results are uncannily similar to those of members of Congress (see table 6.3); recent presidents have devoted an average of 16 percent of the paragraphs in these speeches to educating their listeners about social facts. The proportion of paragraphs devoted to social facts was also surprisingly similar given the presidents' very different styles, ranging from 10 percent in George H. W. Bush's analyzed speeches to 25 percent in Barack Obama's.

This consistency in levels of social fact provision suggests that successful elites have evolved a norm of occasionally, but infrequently, trying to nudge citizens into the active use of knowledge. More often, they seek partisan or policy gains by starting where citizens are substantively and trying to galvanize them politically from that starting point. They seek to make some facts more salient than others, and the information they promote may be more accurate than the information they deemphasize. But the level of accuracy may be accidental, and providing explanation or context is not a priority; politicians seeking (re)election have more pressing goals than pursuit of the Jeffersonian democratic ideal.

Moving People from the Active Misinformed to the Active Informed

The previous claim, however, has exceptions, even beyond the occasional assiduous efforts of politicians to correct misinformation about themselves. A political actor who perceives that people's misinformation is linked to a harmful partisan or policy view may devote resources to try to explain to them the real situation, and then persuade them to use their new knowledge.

The issue of vaccination provides a good example of both the motivation for and the difficulties of moving people from active misinformation toward the Jeffersonian ideal. The CDC has a website partly devoted to convincing people to vaccinate their children (motto: "Love. Protect. Immunize."). It tracks the number of very young children who have gotten measles from travel abroad since 2001 (the year after "measles was declared eliminated in the United States") and points out that almost all sickened babies had not been immunized and that some were hospitalized and developed complications. Carefully avoiding blame, the CDC notes that "all of these infections and the associated sequelae were potentially preventable through adherence to recommendations for vaccination of children traveling outside the United States" (CDC 2011). The CDC also sponsors National Infant Immunization Week, "an annual observance to highlight the importance of protecting infants from vaccine-preventable diseases and celebrate the achievements of immunization programs and their partners in promoting healthy communities." Promotions range from fact sheets and growth charts for parents in English and Spanish to coloring sheets for children. Community outreach programs range from informational sessions for parents and childcare providers to "Safe Summer Slam, a youth empowerment event and neighborhood festival." Researchers urge public health officials also to "engage in more proactive social marketing campaigns . . . [including] newer media such as social-networking sites and Twitter" (Freed et al. 2011: S111).

Other public actors join the CDC, with varying degrees of urgency and efficacy. The American Medical Association's website offers a rather bland page on "Pediatric Vaccination" with a stern message: "Unfortunately, the immense success of vaccination in America has lulled many parents into complacency with regard to vaccine preventable diseases. . . . In order for previous successes to be maintained, the public and their appointed legislators must realize these diseases still exist and can still debilitate and kill." It assures readers that there is "no relationship between thimerosal vaccines and autism" and that "infant immunizations [are] not shown to be harmful to infants' systems," but it expends little energy on a persuasive message (American Medical Association c. 2013).

The American Academy of Pediatrics tries harder, with web pages featuring colorful pictures of cute children, stories about presumably real patients,[18] an FAQ page, an information-filled page dedicated to families, and an invitation to "Pediatric Best Practices: Submit Yours!" (American Academy of Pediatrics 2013). But it is unlikely that any of these efforts reached more than a small fraction of the people who heard Representative Bachmann state that "a mother . . . told me that her little daughter took that vaccine, that injection, and she suffered from mental retardation thereafter" (Fox News interview, Sept. 12, 2011), or who saw Jenny McCarthy's 45-minute heart-rending interview on the *Oprah Winfrey Show* (2007: 5):

> "What number [of autism diagnoses] will it take for people just to start listening to what the mothers of children who have seen autism have been saying for years, which is, 'We vaccinated our baby and *something* happened.'"

> "Right before his [her son's] MMR shot, I said to the doctor, 'I have a very bad feeling about this shot. This is the autism shot, isn't it?' And he said, 'No, that is ridiculous. It is a mother's desperate attempt to blame something,' and he swore at me, and then the nurse gave [Evan] the shot. And soon thereafter—boom—the soul's gone from his eyes."

> Despite her belief, Jenny says she is not against vaccines. "I am all for them, but there needs to be a safer vaccine schedule. There needs to be something done. The fact that the CDC acts as if these vaccines are one size fits all is just crazy to me. People need to start listening to what the moms have been saying."

Few elected officials challenge these "mother warriors," as Winfrey describes the courageous mothers of autistic sons, despite the concern that declining vaccination rates are linked to deaths from infectious diseases. Upon Winfrey's invitation, the CDC responded to McCarthy's comments with a long, carefully worded, and sympathetic statement that might be compelling to medical professionals but had none of McCarthy's

flair (*Oprah Winfrey Show* 2007: 6). Even worse, CDC-type responses may be not only ineffective against mother warriors
but also counterproductive. In one study, subjects were shown
a CDC flyer countering "myths" against flu vaccination. Those
asked to recall the information immediately after reading it did
so accurately, but those asked to recall the information a half-
hour later were significantly more likely to perceive myths as
facts than the reverse and less likely to say that they would get
a flu shot than those who had responded immediately. In short,
the effort to correct misinformation about vaccines backfired
(Berinsky 2012b: 32).[19]

Even if providing information does not backfire, note once
more the asymmetry between action and inaction. A public
actor can expect little success from efforts to induce people to
abandon their false beliefs, reject the views and behaviors of
their group, acquire new knowledge, and change their activity
accordingly. That may be especially true for parents of young
children, but it holds more generally. Such an effort requires a
large investment of resources, probably over a long period of
time and for many group members simultaneously. There are
always battles to be fought and important policies to be promulgated; except for those with a professional responsibility to
do so, trying to move frightened parents from the active use of
falsehoods to the active application of correct information may
seem, and be, a poor use of scarce resources.

WHAT DOES IT TAKE TO MOVE PEOPLE FROM ACTIVE USE OF MISINFORMATION TO ACTIVE USE OF INFORMATION?

Up to this point, we have emphasized three forms of asymmetry that cumulate in the great stability of the active misinformed: (1) inertia is easier than change; (2) movement from
inactive information to active information takes one step that
resolves tension, whereas movement from active misinformation to active information takes two steps that create tension;
and (3) political actors' incentives to encourage active use of
misinformation are much stronger than other political actors'

incentives to prevent people from actively using misinformation. Indeed, the association between active misinformation and group membership may be increasing in some important cases. Recall figure 3.3: Republicans (and, to a lesser degree, independents) were much more likely in 2013 than in 1997 to agree that the media exaggerate global warming.

Nevertheless, it is at times possible to persuade individuals to stop acting on falsehoods in their political or policy choices. Facts matter. Or, as Newt Gingrich put it when contemplating his failed presidential campaign, "I think you have to at some point be honest with what's happening in the real world, as opposed to what you'd like to have happened" (Apr. 25, 2012). On occasion, large numbers of people eschew incorrect information in favor of knowledge. A proof of principle on this point is essential for our discussion in the next chapter of how best to promote a Jeffersonian democracy, so we return to the case of Clarence Thomas.

Asymmetry operated powerfully with regard to views on his confirmation to the Supreme Court. During the crucial few months of his nomination, Thomas's supporters had only to reinforce, or merely not contest, many blacks' mistaken expectations about Thomas's likely liberalism once confirmed. Supporters were highly strategic; Thomas's confirmation process inaugurated "a new style of 'judicial campaigning' for membership on the Court" (Caldeira and Smith 1996: 656). Although some wanted to promote his conservatism, those who managed his nomination mostly sought to "duck volatile issues and go with crafting the image of a man who had pulled himself up by his bootstraps from Pin Point, Georgia." As one White House source put it, "Their main strategy was . . . to split the black community, get public pressure, particularly on the Southern Democrats" (Phelps and Winternitz 1992: 72).

President Bush initiated that strategy, mentioning Pin Point, Georgia, in the second paragraph of his nomination speech. Although race purportedly played no role in his choice of a justice ("I . . . pick[ed] the best man for the job on the merits"), Bush noted "the fact that he's a minority—you heard his testimony to the kind of life he's had, and I think that speaks eloquently for itself" (Bush 1991). Senators Strom Thurmond, John Danforth, and others made similar statements, often using similar words. Thomas was no less forthcoming in his own opening statement to the Senate Judiciary Committee: "My earliest memories . . . are those of Pin Point, Georgia, a life far removed in space and time from this room, this day and this moment. . . . We lived in one room in a tenement. We shared a kitchen with other tenants and we had a common bathroom in the backyard which was unworkable and unusable. It was hard, but it was all we had and all there was." His trajectory since then has proved that "hard work and strong values can make for a better life" (United States Senate 1991: 108).

The quotations could easily be multiplied but are unnecessary; careful framing enabled Thomas and his supporters to take advantage of the beliefs held by a majority of blacks that Thomas "understands the black experience" and "would do a good job representing people like me" (see figure 4.1).

Thomas's opponents had a much more difficult task, which they failed to accomplish. They needed to make the delicate argument that a very dark skinned black man who had worked his way up from deep poverty and racism in a tiny southern town did not deserve to sit on the Supreme Court. In particular, opponents had to convince African Americans that they were mistaken in believing that their race would benefit from having the only available black man elevated to the Court, that they were misinformed about his racial solidarity, or that their predictions of how his racial solidarity would be manifested in judicial decisions would prove wrong. Given their own political and racial liberalism, the actors most concerned about Thomas's ideology and plausible future rulings were precisely those who found it most difficult to tell black voters that their views were naïve and wrong.

Thus, opponents tended to tie themselves into knots trying to prevent the active use of misinformation while maintaining their own and Thomas's dignity. The national NAACP's statement provides an unfortunately good example:

The story of Judge Thomas's rise from the poverty of his youth to his present eminence is captivating and inspiring. . . . We have no basic quarrel with Judge Thomas's devotion to self-reliance and self-help. Indeed, we share it. What is overlooked in the emphasis on self-reliance is any concern for what government and other sectors of society ought to do to alleviate many problems in the minority community. . . . We earnestly desire the appointment of an African-American to the supreme bench. But if there is reason to believe the African-American nominee would join in the further and continued erosion of threatened civil rights gains, we don't need that appointee. (Hooks et al. 1991–92)

This message may have been subtle, profound, and correct—but it was hard to convey. Opponents never found a way to counter Thomas's declaration that "as a child, I could not dare dream that I would ever see the Supreme Court—not to mention be nominated to it. . . . Only in America could this have been possible" (July 1, 1991). Had more than a third of blacks used accurate information, a few senators' votes would probably have been different and Thomas would have been denied the confirmation he craved. But the incentives captured by the phrase "political asymmetry" meant that Americans were much more likely to act on their misinformation than to use a painful set of facts appropriately.

The logic of asymmetry between active misinformation and active information did not change after confirmation. What did change was the dissemination of new information about Thomas's positions on the Court—positions that made him by far the most conservative justice since 1937 (when the Martin-Quinn scoring system described in chapter 4 began). The number of people of any race who ponder Martin-Quinn scores is miniscule. But the media quickly and consistently made the scores' message clear to the public. From June 1 to October 1, 1992, that is, in the four months immediately after his first Supreme Court term, the words "Clarence Thomas" and "conservative" appeared in seventy-nine television or radio transcripts tracked by LexisNexis. A *CBS News* show observed that "Justice Scalia is holding the far right. He is frequently joined . . .

more and more by the newest justice, Clarence Thomas, who certainly is every bit as conservative as his supporters hoped he would be and as his critics feared he would be. He has headed with Justice Scalia often to that distant right that would do a lot of changing of the country, I think" (Kuralt 1992a). Another Charles Kuralt Sunday news show described "an extraordinary diversity of leadership . . . [among blacks, including] Supreme Court Justice Clarence Thomas. His is one of a growing number of conservative black voices" (Kuralt 1992b).

Mainstream print media echoed television. The *Houston Chronicle* editorialized: "If you are ever tempted to think that being black, Hispanic, or any other minority automatically means being tolerant, sensitive, and compassionate, from now until the end of your life you should remember Supreme Court Justice Clarence Thomas. . . . Give Thomas a chance, said minorities and pragmatists alike. President Bush was going to nominate a conservative to succeed retiring Justice Thurgood Marshall, no matter what. And better a conservative of color than one who was not. Live and learn" (Rodriguez 1992). Conservative James Kilpatrick praised him in the *Atlanta Journal and Constitution* in an article headlined, "Justice Thomas Is Off to a Good Start after a Solidly Conservative First Term" (Kilpatrick 1992). The *St. Louis Post Dispatch* (1992) noted that "Rookie Justice Thomas Pleased Conservatives."

Media oriented toward nonwhite audiences conveyed the same message, almost always without Kilpatrick-type approbation. As of April 2014, ProQuest's Ethnic NewsWatch identified 1,525 items in minority-oriented newspapers and magazines since Thomas's confirmation that contained the search terms "Clarence Thomas" and "conservative." Headlines include "African American Conservatives Surface" (*Big Red News*, Dec. 7, 1991), "Clarence Thomas: Cruel and Unusual" (*Call and Post*, Mar. 12, 1992), "Clarence Thomas Isn't the Victim We Thought He Was" (*Philadelphia Tribune*, Apr. 3, 1992), "All We Get from Thomas Are the Sounds of Silence" (*Tennessee Tribune*, Jan. 3, 2001), and "Clarence Thomas Should Be the Last Person to Whine about Race" (*Chicago Defender*, Feb. 26, 2014).

In a 2007 appearance on the *Tavis Smiley Show*, the president of the National Urban League described Thomas as "hostile towards [black] advancement."[20] In short, African Americans had plenty of opportunity in the years after confirmation to learn that their predictions of Thomas's likely behavior on the Supreme Court were wrong.

And they did learn it. In the year after confirmation, blacks on average continued to feel relatively cold toward Anita Hill (on a feeling thermometer) and warm toward Thomas (Gimpel and Ringel 1995; Sapiro and Soss 1999). But support for Thomas eventually eroded. Figure 6.4 shows the decline in African Americans' favorable view of Clarence Thomas from confirmation through the most recent relevant poll question we could find, in 2012. The proportion of supporters dropped from roughly three-fifths in the first year to less than a third about five years later. By 2012, black support for Thomas remained low at 40 percent.

In more analytical terms, by the late 1990s most African Americans had given up the liberal optimism, racial nationalism, or commitment to the Horatio Alger story that had spurred them to rely on mistaken causal claims about the relationship between Thomas's race or background and his judicial actions. They moved into the Jeffersonian ideal (ironically named in this case) by realizing that Justice Thomas is a conservative whose views differ from those of most black Americans.[21] As one person put it in 1998, "Ultimately, this is how people have to be judged: how their actions, activities, decisions, power, influence etc. impede the growth and advancement of African Americans. So far, Thomas has been a major—and concrete—impediment" (Akwasi Osei, e-mail on H-NET Discussion List for African American Studies, July 22, 1998). From a more scholarly perspective, "the thesis that *any* Black could be counted on to defend the interests of *all* Blacks was substantially valid as long as Jim Crow segregation lasted. . . . [But with the] development of a more class-divided Black America, . . . descriptive representation no longer worked with bureaucrats and politicians such as Thomas, who feel no sense of allegiance

Figure 6.4. Percentage of black respondents viewing Justice Clarence Thomas favorably, 1991–2012.

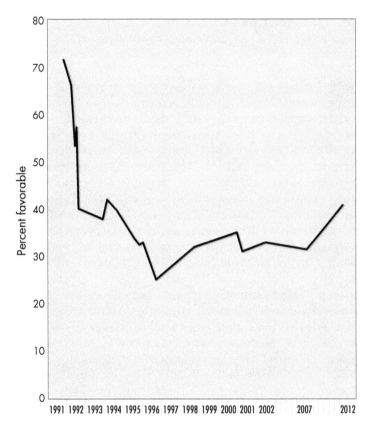

Source: In addition to surveys in iPoll, see Joint Center for Political and Economic Studies, July 1992, Jan. 3, 1996, Sept. 5, 1998; National Black Politics Study, Dec. 4, 1993; National Black Election Study, Sept. 9, 1996; 2012 Outlook Survey.

Copyright © 2015 University of Oklahoma Press.

to the historic Black freedom struggle" (Williams 1995: 249–50). Justice Thomas was forty-three years old when appointed and could easily serve on the Supreme Court for four decades. The active use of misinformation was a costly mistake from the perspective of most African Americans.

CONCLUSION

People can unlearn long-held views and learn new ones; if facts are "presented in a way that 'hits them between the eyes' . . . such information can have a substantial effect" (Kuklinski et al. 2000: 805). A majority of Americans eventually stopped believing that Iraq harbored WMDs; a majority of African Americans eventually stopped believing that Justice Thomas would rule in ways that matched their understanding of their race's interests; some parents whose children got infectious diseases rue their failure to vaccinate. But substantial changes of this sort are rare. It is hard for a political actor to move people to action even when they hold correct information, and it is yet harder for an overstretched political actor (is there any other kind?) to change what people think they know and then to move them to action based on newly acquired facts. From the perspective of the individual, moving from inactive to active use of knowledge requires some effort but has the reward of reducing dissonance—whereas moving from the active use of misinformation to actively applying new understandings of facts not only requires great effort but also increases dissonance and discomfort since it entails abandoning communities of belief. A conversion experience is profound, but rare.

Nevertheless, change can occur. Our motivation for writing *Do Facts Matter?* is to enhance democratic governance, so we turn in the final chapter to the question of how to promote membership in the category of active informed.

APPENDIX:
ANALYSIS OF CONGRESSIONAL NEWSLETTERS
AND PRESIDENTIAL SPEECHES

We examined newsletters for a random sample of 186 members of Congress before and after the 2004 election and 186 members before and after the 2006 election. The sample includes only members who had held at least one term in office *and* won the 2004 or 2006 election. Those two years provide variation in electoral context; Republicans dominated the 2004 election cycle, and Democrats dominated in 2006. The sample is divided into four groups designed to vary by several independent variables, as shown in table 6.1.

For each sampled representative, we collected the two newsletters sent most recently before the 2004 or 2006 election and the first two newsletters sent after February 2005 or 2007; we selected February rather than the first two newsletters after the election to avoid celebratory mailings not likely to have substantive content. We excluded electronic newsletters in favor of their print counterparts to ensure that the documents were targeted toward the widest possible audience.

We examined the first two pages containing substantive content (i.e., not a title page) of each newsletter. We treated a paragraph as a single unit (following Yiannakis 1982; Lipinski 2001, 2004). Our coding scheme had fourteen categories, but its chief purpose was to distinguish "social facts" from other types of statements. We coded a paragraph as a social fact if it included factual statements about society at large, whether they were precise states of affairs, comparisons of one state of affairs to another, or causal statements.

"Legislative facts" are also relevant to this book. A paragraph with a legislative fact offers details about votes or broader statements about a piece of legislation.

To ensure validity, we compared our coding decisions on ten newsletters with those of two research assistants unfamiliar with the project. After a concordance rate of 78 percent with

Table 6.1. Categories of sampled members of Congress

		Political Party	
		Democrats in competitive seats 2004: $N = 36$ 2006: $N = 36^*$	Republicans in competitive seats 2004: $N = 50$ 2006: $N = 50$
Competitiveness of Election		Democrats in safe seats[†] 2004: $N = 50$ 2006: $N = 50$	Republicans in safe seats[†] 2004: $N = 50$ 2006: $N = 50$

Source: Congressional Quarterly.
[*]In both years, there were only 36 competitive Democratic seats in which the sitting member had won in 2002 and 2004 (for the 2004 sample) or in 2004 and 2006 (for the 2006 sample).
[†]A safe seat is one in which a member of Congress won at least 60 percent of the vote in the 2002 and 2004 primary and general elections (for a 2004–2005 member of Congress) or the 2004 and 2006 primary and general elections (for a 2006–2007 member of Congress).

the first research assistant, we revised the codebook slightly to clarify vague categories. Using the revised codebook, the second research assistant agreed with 84 percent of our coding decisions.

Our main dependent variable is the proportion of paragraphs in each newsletter containing social facts, either alone or in combination with other types of statements. Our secondary dependent variable is the proportion of paragraphs with legislative facts, either alone or in combination.[22] Table 6.2 provides the proportions of paragraphs in various categories, overall for each year and separately by party, electoral competitiveness, and newsletter timing in relation to the 2004 and 2006 elections.

The analysis of presidential speeches used the same logic, code sheet, and procedures. To parallel the congressional study, we focused on the most recent successful Democratic and Republican candidates for an open office and the most recent Democratic and Republican reelected presidents; those are, respectively, Barack Obama in 2008, George H. W. Bush in 1988, Bill Clinton in 1996, and George W. Bush in 2004.[23] In each case, we coded the first State of the Union speech given after each election and reelection. Table 6.3 provides the evidence on the presidents from which the discussion in the text is drawn.

Table 6.2. Percentage of newsletter paragraphs in various categories

A. 2004

Category	Total	Democrat	Republican	Before 2004 election	After 2004 election	Competitive district	Safe district
1. Social fact	5.7	3.6	7.4	5.6	5.8	6.2	5.1
2. Social fact + other categories*	7.6	9.3	6.3	8.7	6.5	6.6	8.8
3. Legislative fact	28.4	21.0	34.3	28.8	28.0	30.0	26.8
4. Legislative fact + other categories*†	29.0	33.3	25.5	28.2	29.8	30.0	28.0
5. Other categories*	29.2	32.7	26.5	28.7	29.9	27.1	31.6
	100%	100%	100%	100%	100%	100%	100%

B. 2006

Category	Total	Democrat	Republican	Before 2006 election	After 2006 election	Competitive district	Safe district
1. Social fact	6.8	6.2	7.3	7.6	5.9	5.0	8.6
2. Social fact + other categories*	7.4	8.6	6.4	8.0	6.6	7.9	6.9
3. Legislative fact	25.6	26.5	24.9	28.5	22.3	26.5	24.8
4. Legislative fact + other categories*†	32.8	33.8	32.0	31.8	34.0	37.2	28.4
5. Other categories*	26.7	25.0	29.4	24.0	31.3	23.6	31.3
	100%	100%	100%	100%	100%	100%	100%

Source: Authors' coding of congressional newsletters.
*"Other categories" include logistics, partisan appeal, self-appeal, and other. Almost all of the coded paragraphs address logistics or self-appeal.
†To avoid double-counting, this row does not include paragraphs containing both legislative and social facts. Both types of facts appear in about 5 percent of all coded paragraphs and are included in row 2, "Social fact + other categories."

Table 6.3. Percentage of State of the Union paragraphs
containing social facts

George H. W. Bush	10.0
Bill Clinton	15.4
George W. Bush	11.3
Barack Obama	25.4
Average	15.6

Source: Authors' coding of presidents' speeches.

We did not check the veracity or relevance of social facts contained in newsletters or presidential speeches. Politicians may
use these forms of communication to lie and manipulate rather
than to educate—and, of course, one person's "fact" is often another's manipulative distortion. Nevertheless, having roughly
equal samples from both major political parties means that partisan bias is likely to be neutralized in our analysis, assuming
that bias is roughly equally distributed across the parties.

CHAPTER 7

PROMOTING JEFFERSON'S IDEAL

[I feel] a need to present a point of view, educate,
conscious raise, on issues that are important, . . . and that
may or may not be the things that people, either in your
constituency or your fellow legislators, are aware of.

State legislator on why he holds office (c. 2003)

Do we see sometimes us going overboard in our
campaign, are there mistakes that are made, areas where
there's no doubt somebody could dispute how we are
presenting things? You know, that happens in politics.

President Barack Obama, *60 Minutes*
unaired excerpts, 2012

Guys like me were "in what we call the reality-based
community," which he defined as people who "believe
that solutions emerge from your judicious study of
discernible reality. . . . That's not the way the world really
works anymore."

Top-level aide to President George W. Bush,
speaking to a journalist

POLITICIANS HAVE VARIED relationships with facts and their
use. As in the first epigraph, some see themselves as educators,
showing their constituents and colleagues the unrecognized
realities underlying important issues. As in the second, others
admit with some embarrassment and unusual candor that in
the heat of debate "mistakes are made." Still others boast that
their administration has moved beyond the mundane triviali-
ties of the reality-based community into the realm of creating

new truths. Regardless of the ratio of embarrassment to boast in the purveyance of misinformation, the previous chapters show clearly that Richard Fenno (1978: 163) is right to point to the apparent paucity of genuine educational effort by political actors.

Politicians who misinform their hearers may be making the right strategic choice given their goals; like other researchers, we see reasons for pessimism about Americans' use of facts when forging political judgments. Beyond the core imbalance that inertia is easier than change, we especially note worrisome asymmetries. First, some elites have strong incentives to encourage individuals to stay misinformed and to act on their false beliefs, and others have only weak incentives to rebut misinformation. Furthermore, holding factual knowledge but not acting on it can generate discomfort that partly offsets basic inertia, whereas holding misinformation and acting on it can generate gratification that reinforces basic inertia. Politicians know and act on that imbalance. Together, these asymmetries make democratic governance and good policy difficult to attain and may even contribute to situations in which people die.

In this final chapter, we address possible solutions available to scholars, public officials, advocates, and ordinary Americans who seek to reduce the risks of informed inactivity and (especially) misinformed activity. Three strategies might improve democratic governance. One is the perennial favorite of book writers: research and education to teach the facts and the importance of acting on them. It is a direct, frontal rejoinder to the difficulty of mobilizing people out of informed inactivity and the even greater difficulty of persuading people to leave the category of the active misinformed.

Education by itself is often a weak reed, but two other strategies can reinforce or perhaps substitute for it. Given the dangers of misinformed activity, perhaps public officials should seek ways to work around, ignore, or reject public opinion. That strategy is not very democratic on its face, but it may be essential for good democratic governance understood more broadly. Alternatively, reformers might try to change elites' incentive structure, to overcome political actors' motives to keep people in the category of the active misinformed. Political entrepreneurs—whether allies or competitors—can try to create moments in which politicians themselves benefit from challenging the public use of misinformation.

A final proposal is less a strategy than a hope, backed by some evidence that it can actually come to pass. On rare but electrifying occasions, members of the public themselves have taken steps to mobilize the disengaged informed or correct the false ideas of the engaged misinformed. A social movement can, once in a while, change the terms of the debate, as a favorite student once put it in explaining a sit-in, and thereby change politics and policy. There is no clear recipe for creating a successful social movement, as countless activists and scholars have discovered, but we want at least to point to a possibility that goes beyond educational campaigns or policy design.

None of our proposals or suggestions are new, but to our knowledge they have not before been systematically linked to the diverse routes through which facts enter politics. Making those connections provides an analytical structure for classifying and interrelating the many proposals to improve the quantity and quality of public participation in decision making. In short, having examined individuals' behavior, group membership, and political actors' vantage points, we turn to the question "What now?"

RESEARCH AND EDUCATION

The Reports of the Surgeons General

We begin seeking solutions to the defects of facts in politics by returning to the vignette of the surgeon general's reports. Government actors' persistent efforts to acquire, disseminate, and promulgate policies appropriate to new knowledge about states of affairs (smoke in lungs) and causal relationships (smoke in lungs causes cancer) largely succeeded. The proportion of smokers declined, heavy smoking decreased, fewer young adults started to smoke, and cigarette consumption reversed its upward trend soon after the surgeons general spoke out, and especially after taxes and regulations were promulgated.

We emphasize two features of this vignette. First, the surgeon general's reports, understood broadly, are an existence proof; they show that a large number of Americans can learn new facts, retain them over time and across generations, and use their new knowledge to change individual behaviors and social norms even when doing so entails nontrivial sacrifices of pleasure. That is no small thing. Second, the new information was associated with policy changes that have explicitly or implicitly retained majority support; political partisanship seems to have played little to no role in the issuance of reports, policy development, and changes in individuals' behavior. Thus, Jefferson's ideal has been reasonably well met; the "people at large" have been given "knowledge of . . . facts" and have "exert[ed] their natural powers" to contest, not quite tyranny, but nonetheless a pleasure as addictive as it is destructive.

Creating Jeffersonian democrats is not easy; even in this exemplary case, not everyone got the message. Perhaps the most illuminating survey item ever written appeared in a 1978 poll of adult American smokers: "Why do you smoke in light of the evidence that smoking causes cancer?" Only 10 percent denied or questioned the premise, and a few others tried to twist away from it (1 percent: "Worse things than smoking cause cancer"). They are the active misinformed. Another 7 percent did not know why, but at least four-fifths of the respondents agreed with the premise and simply offered a more or less dignified excuse (ranging from "enjoy it" to "stupidity") (Public and Worker Attitudes toward Carcinogens and Cancer Risk Survey, Apr. 1978). They are the inactive informed, and they have not disappeared. The CDC reported roughly 480,000 preventable tobacco-related deaths in the United States in 2014, in addition to lower life expectancy and productivity losses compared with the counterfactual of no smoking. Nevertheless, it is indisputable that education combined with policies and changes in social norms have moved millions from inactive information and even active misinformation into the active use of knowledge.

*Other Uses of Education to Promote
the Jeffersonian Ideal*

The designers of the ACA appear to have drawn a lesson from the surgeon general's reports. Among the ACA's 420,000 words are some that explicitly authorize programs to promote knowledge and appropriate action. To choose only one example, one section of the law authorizes the Department of Health and Human Services' new Personal Responsibility Education Program, which provides grants to states and other organizations to "educate adolescents and young adults on both abstinence and contraception for the prevention of pregnancy and sexually transmitted infections, including HIV/AIDS." The provision is not mere verbiage; the ACA allocated roughly $100 million per year through 2014 for grants under this program (Catalogue of Federal Domestic Assistance c. 2010). Other sections promote additional forms of "health literacy, including public education, consumer assistance programs and new ways to compare coverage options" (*CoverMissouri.org* 2011: 2).

Historical hindsight illuminates a very different case. Historians debate furiously over when various U.S. officials shifted during the early 1940s from being misinformed about Nazi "work camps" to awareness that Jews were being slaughtered in extermination camps. They debate with equal strenuousness about whether the choice not to intervene directly—that is, officials' failure to use their new knowledge—was militarily and morally defensible. But they generally concur that knowledge eventually overcame falsehood and provided at least some impetus even to those reluctant to act.

Until late 1942, key State Department officials believed, or perhaps wanted to believe, that the Nazis had created work camps but not death camps for Jews. For example, the Bern legation passed an August 1942 report from the secretary of the World Jewish Congress about a plan to exterminate up to four million Jews to the State Department. But in doing so it noted, "Legation has no information which would tend to confirm this report which is however forwarded in accordance with

Riegner's wishes. . . . The report has earmarks of war rumor
inspired by fear and what is commonly understood to be the
actually miserable condition of these refugees."[1] Undersecre-
tary of State Sumner Welles, generally understood to sympa-
thize with the Jews' plight, is similarly reported to have told
the leader of American Jewry and recipient of Riegner's report
that "the real purpose of the Nazi government is to use Jews in
connection with war work" (Wallance 2012: 102).

It is the State Department's responsibility to be cautious
about dramatic rumors, and the systematic killing of millions
of Europeans across the continent was, in fact, almost impossible to imagine. Intelligence during wartime was confused and
fragmentary; the CIA did not yet exist. So the fact that the administration's policy rested on the assumption that Jews were
being held in work camps, not killed in death camps, may be
one of the rare cases in which the active use of misinformation is understandable.[2] But eventually education of federal
officials (along with the end of the war) led them to abandon
the use of misinformation, cease ignoring the facts, and instead actively apply their new knowledge. We cannot recount
here the history of postwar international relations, so as a brief
stand-in we offer the summary of the U.S. Holocaust Memorial
Museum (n.d.):

> In the aftermath of World War II, the world . . . confronted its
> legacy. . . . In light of the moral failures that allowed the holo-
> caust to happen—
>   • Nations pledged to prevent and punish the crime of
>   "genocide."
>   • Criminal trials established that government officials who
>   commit crimes against humanity could be held account-
>   able by international tribunals.
>   • International protection of human rights expanded
>   dramatically.
>   • The idea of "informed consent" influenced ethical ap-
>   proaches to medical experimentation on human beings.
>   • Protections for refugees were broadened.
>   • The movement toward reconciliation between Christians
>   and Jews advanced.
>   • The idea of a Jewish homeland gained urgency.

Even though they came too late, American and other countries' postwar policies demonstrate that, when confronted with undeniable facts, people can learn to set aside their anti-Semitism, professional caution, political calculations, or whatever else is keeping them from taking serious action.[3]

Apart from these unusual cases, what have scholars taught us about the circumstances under which, and the mechanisms through which, education can move people toward the Jeffersonian ideal? Some answers are surprisingly positive. For all their noise and misinformation, campaigns can be effective teachers. Andrew Gelman and Gary King find that "voters decide, based on their enlightened preferences, as formed by the information they have learned during the campaign, as well as basic political cues such as ideology and party identification, which candidate to support eventually. . . . The news media have an important effect on the outcome of presidential elections—not through misleading advertisements, sound bites, or spin doctors, but rather by conveying candidates' positions on important issues" (Gelman and King 1993: 409).

And, as we note earlier, even people with strong partisan affiliations—that is, those who disproportionately use incorrect information and are hard to dislodge—may respond to new information. The point is worth reiteration, since it is as important as it is underestimated:

> People are psychologically motivated to maintain and support existing evaluations. Yet it seems unlikely that voters do this ad infinitum. To do so would suggest continued motivated reasoning even in the face of extensive disconfirming information. . . . Motivated reasoning processes can be overcome simply by continuing to encounter information incongruent with expectations. . . . Voters . . . reach a tipping point after which they begin more accurately updating their evaluations. (Redlawsk et al. 2010: 563; see also Holbrook 1999; Bennett 1994)

Beyond campaigns themselves, the electoral structure can enhance information and its use: "Voters from states that heavily use [substantive policy] initiatives show an increased capacity over the long term to correctly answer factual questions about politics" (Partin 2001: 892). And governance after elections can similarly move people out of active misinformation into active use of information. Zoltan Hajnal (2006: 8) observes that "politics—even local politics—can be extremely informative and consequential. . . . Whites . . . become measurably more willing to support black incumbents when they have experienced black leadership and know more about its effects on their well-being. . . . [This] confirm[s] the critical role that information plays in the arena of racial politics."

Finally, policies can be an instrument for education. We describe in chapter 1 the extensive and probably growing set of mandates for transparency and the release of data about everything from students' test scores to the costs of caesarian sections in hospitals around the United States. Some systematic research confirms that information can make a difference: "Recipients of personal Social Security Statements [from the federal government] gained more knowledge of, and confidence in, Social Security than nonrecipients after controlling for individual differences. These results suggest that citizens' evaluations of government institutions echo, in part, the quality and quantity of information distributed to them" (Cook et al. 2010: 397).[4]

Nevertheless, *pace* Jefferson, relying mainly on education to produce informed and active citizens is unwarranted; too many efforts yield only disappointment. We can offer only a few examples here (although perhaps no others are needed in light of the resurgence of birtherism even after release of Obama's birth certificate). One study gave a random group of high school students a civics curriculum that emphasized constitutional rights and civil liberties in addition to more usual topics. Students in the treatment group did show more overall knowledge of civil liberties than those in the control group, but not greater support, which was the main target of the experimental curriculum. Students moved, in other words, from ignorance into disengaged information but not into informed activity (Green et al. 2011). And as we note in chapter 3, despite scientists' and educators' fond hopes, increasing knowledge about climate change is not always allied with support for policy actions to combat it. Instead, in one recent study subjects with the highest levels of scientific literacy exhibited the greatest "cultural polarization"; the best educated were the most severely cross-pressured between personal interests in allying with others like them and collective interests in the mitigation of global warming (Gilens et al. 2007). Despite, or perhaps because of, their cognitive sophistication, the knowledgeable were stuck in the realm of inactive information.[5]

Efforts at education can even have perverse consequences, as we note in chapter 6; this point too is worth repeating because of its importance and counterintuitive quality. An experimental study randomly assigned people to read articles that did or did not correct the claim that the ACA included death panels. Compared with controls, people who viewed Sarah Palin unfavorably and those who supported her but had little prior political knowledge did indeed become less likely to believe in death panels. But the educational effort "backfired among politically knowledgeable Palin supporters, who were more likely to believe in death panels and to strongly oppose reform if they received the correction" (Nyhan et al. 2013: 127; for another instance of backfiring, see Nyhan et al. 2014). In some (we hope unusual) contexts, efforts at education can be worse than a waste of time.

What is most puzzling is that, although cross-sectional data show that compared with the poorly schooled the well-educated participate more in democratic governance, show more ideological and policy coherence, know more relevant facts, and are more tolerant of disagreement, longitudinal data show little salutary impact of schooling. Even though Americans as a whole are much better educated in the 2000s than their counterparts were in the 1950s, scholars do not find a more informed and engaged electorate now than in earlier decades (Nie et al. 1996; Gilens et al. 2007).

Given our profession as educators, as well as proofs of concept such as the surgeon general's reports and blacks' eventual loss of faith in Clarence Thomas, we remain cautiously optimistic that education and the repetition of brute facts can spur the active use of knowledge. But education alone is insufficient given inertia and incentives to remain with one's group in actively using misinformation. We turn next to tougher-minded strategies.

MANEUVERING AROUND THE PUBLIC

Mobilization is hard; reeducation and then mobilization are harder; politicians have many urgent tasks and few incentives to take on what might be a thankless and hopeless effort. So policy makers who both believe in democratic governance and perceive public inactivity or misinformation may seek strategies that limit the damage citizens can do or that compensate for their failure to act.

Nudge

A classic case is what Richard Thaler and Cass Sunstein (2009; Sunstein 2013) call a nudge, or the design of "choice architecture" so that people are encouraged to take the path that they would choose if they had perfect (or at least more) information and were motivated to use it. For example, Americans without health insurance can face a bewildering array of options in state exchanges, each with a different structure of benefits, deductibles, monthly costs, and constraints. In such a situation it is difficult not to acquire distorted or otherwise mistaken information, so people might make choices that are undesirable compared to what they would choose if fully informed. A policy maker could combat this problem by designing a website so that after providing several pieces of pertinent information a purchaser is offered only a few options, all appropriate though varying in details.

Offering people a few appropriate choices would address the problem of misinformation. Requiring them to make a choice through a fine for inaction, or enrolling them in one plan if they failed to make a choice, would address the problem of inactivity. In short, it is possible to design and implement a policy that minimizes the risks of acting on misinformation, minimizes the frustrations of not acting even if correctly informed, and maximizes the likelihood of acting on correct information.[6] Some argue that this sort of nudge gives too much power to the choice architects. And nudges can surely be mistaken or ineffective themselves. Nonetheless, a correctly designed structure of choices with incentives to act or penalties for not acting may be the best feasible way to move a large number of individuals into the realm of active information, so long as their inactivity or misinformed activity is unintentional or not fiercely partisan.

Ignore the Active Misinformed

How should policy makers deal with the fiercely partisan misinformed activist? In the 1950s, American localities, states, and the federal government debated the merits of fluoridated water. Scientists found that public water supplies treated with appropriate amounts of fluoride substantially reduced cavities especially but not only in children. They found no harmful side effects unless the amounts of fluoride were too high. Three surveys on the topic in the early 1950s asked about knowledge of, support for, and residence in a community that fluoridated its water (see table 7.1). Solid majorities of the informed public, itself a solid majority, endorsed fluoridation, putting them into the category of the engaged informed based on the best research evidence at the time. A majority of informed Americans have continued to support fluoridation for the succeeding six decades.[7]

Confirmatory research started to accumulate, and the U.S. Public Health Service officially endorsed fluoridation of local water supplies in the mid-1950s. Researchers refined measures of the appropriate levels of fluoridation and further demonstrated its benefits. Conditions seemed to be set for widespread adoption, and that did occur over the next few decades. By 2010, two-thirds of all U.S. residents, and three-quarters of those using community water systems, drank fluoridated water. The mean number of cavities among children in communities with treated water declined from four to one in the

Table 7.1. Knowledge of and views on fluoridation, 1952–1956

	1952	1953	1956
Have you ever heard or read anything about the use of fluoride in city water to help prevent tooth decay? Percentage answering YES	56	68	75
Does your community use fluoride in its water supply? (asked of those who had heard or read about it) Percentage answering YES	13	10	12
Would you favor or oppose a plan for putting fluoride in the water supplied to your community? Percentage answering FAVOR	66*	59**	60**

Sources: Gallup polls in iPoll.
*Asked only of respondents who have heard or read about the use of fluoride in city water.
**Asked only of respondents living in communities without fluoridated water.

two decades after 1967 (CDC 1999a). The CDC identified fluoridation of drinking water as one of the "ten great public health achievements" of the twentieth century (CDC 1999b).

Nonetheless, fluoridation has always been and remains controversial.[8] Three objections arose in early debates, and with some variation they persist. Two of the three involve misinformation: some people challenged the efficacy of fluoride in preventing cavities, and others went further to claim that even approved doses can be harmful.[9] Whether as a result of these or other arguments, fluoridation has often lost in referenda or votes for candidates. More than a thousand Florida communities defeated referenda on introducing fluoride during the 1950s and 1960s, and 80 percent of fluoridation referenda were defeated in the same state between 1977 and 1980. Indeed, across the nation, efforts to attain fluoridation through a popular vote have frequently failed over the past half-century (Musto 1987; see also Crain et al. 1969).[10]

What was to be done? The answer lay in administrative orders and, in some states, compulsory fluoridation laws. In 2002,

California took a rebellious town to court in order to require it to fluoridate its water supply; California won the case, and the courts have unanimously held that mandatory fluoridation is legal. A study of more than seven hundred cities found that "when local political power structures allowed little citizen input into decision-making, . . . the decision was most likely to favor fluoridation. . . . Because most referenda oppose fluoridation, the more participative polities have had fewer adoptions of fluoridation" (Martin 1989, summarizing Crain et al. 1969; note also that "the most educated communities have most trouble with fluoridation" [Crain et al. 1969: 215]).

In short, public officials have ignored the views of the active misinformed where they could and occasionally challenged them in court when they could not ignore them. As a result of community fluoridation (among other changes), cavities and tooth loss have declined for all age groups in the United States. Under what conditions one should draw the lesson from this case that ignoring the views of the active misinformed is a legitimate political choice and the right policy strategy remains a question worth pondering.

Superimpose Expertise

Another strategy for maneuvering around the dangers attendant on misinformed activity mandates, or at least strongly encourages, access to correct information held by experts. A good illustration is the marketing of genomic information. In 2007, companies began offering direct-to-consumer (DTC) testing of part of an individual's genome through the simple process of mailing in saliva or a buccal (cheek) swab. There are no systematic data on how many Americans have availed themselves of this opportunity, but it is in the hundreds of thousands and is likely to grow as the cost plummets and information spreads (Wright 2010; Booz Allen Hamilton n.d.).[11] DTC companies claim that sequencing enables accurate information on physical or medical conditions ranging from the likelihood of excessive ear wax to the chances for developing Huntington's or Alzheimer's disease or breast cancer. They also provide information about an individual's likely response to some drugs.

This enterprise remained under the regulatory radar screen until one firm proposed in 2010 to sell its DTC tests in more than six thousand Walgreens stores, at which point the Food and Drug Administration (FDA) sent letters to twenty-three companies warning of possible violations of the Food, Drug, and Cosmetic Act. Regulators, along with experts and observers, have offered an array of concerns. Some concerns focus on the absence of information; scientists simply do not know the function of many genes and have even less knowledge of how genes interact with each other, the environment, other parts of the genome, and other bodily processes. So consumers may be buying a bill of goods when they pay for genomic sequencing and its purported interpretation.

Other concerns are more relevant to our analyses. Bioethicists and empirical researchers have been pointing to risks since the first days of individual genomic sequencing, and their rhetoric has become more urgent as tests and users proliferate.[12] Regulators fear that DTC companies may unintentionally purvey false or misleading information, that consumers may misconstrue the facts they receive, and that doctors may make diagnostic or prescriptive mistakes in seeking to use these novel data. Errors in this arena can be dangerous, says the FDA; people might choose prophylactic mastectomies to prevent breast cancer or make decisions about marriage or child bearing based on predictions about the future presentation of a genetic disease.

Although to this date there are no federal laws or judicial decisions directly on DTC testing, the regulatory arena is complex, with variation across states, levels of government, and agencies. Luckily, we need to focus on only a small part of this rapidly evolving enterprise—the move toward urging or requiring a connection between the consumer and trained medical personnel in order to obtain results from genomic testing.

In response to the FDA's 2010 letter of inquiry, Pathway Genomics, the would-be seller through Walgreens, withdrew from the DTC market and now sells genomic sequencing and interpretation to individuals only through physicians. This point is emphasized many times in Pathway's website promoting its services:

A physician will need to register with Pathway and order the report for you. . . . When your kit is sent in, we will return your genetics report to your doctor and they can review the results with you. With the doctor's authorization, your report will also be available directly to you through your secure online account. . . . Knowing your genetic information can lead you and your physician to make choices about your behavior and environment that could result in a better and healthier life for you. . . . An analysis of your genetic makeup can reveal to your physician your risk for developing these and other diseases and potentially how you would respond to treatment.

By far the largest company in the DTC market, 23andMe, has been in negotiations with the FDA about which genetic medical tests are to be regulated and how stringently. Since receiving the 2010 warning letter, its website has included safeguards, warnings, and suggestions for contacting medical experts—even while enticing potential users with promises of information that is important ("Understand your genetic health risks") or fascinating (What is your Neanderthal percentage?).[13] The Health Overview page notes that "the information on this page is intended for research and educational purposes only, and is not for diagnostic use." Sensitive genetic results are "locked"; once opened after the user explicitly agrees, the unlocked screen offers to connect the user with a genetic counselor. The section on drug responses states, "Do not discontinue or change an existing drug regimen based on this information; you should consult your physician if your genetics indicates a non-standard drug sensitivity or an increased risk of side effects." And so on. None of these notices mandate a specific connection with a medical expert, but cumulatively they imply that the consumer should beware of being misinformed and should not act before consulting an expert and checking for misinterpretations of the evidence.

The warnings were not enough. In November 2013, the FDA ordered 23andMe to "immediately discontinue marketing the PGS [Personal Genome Service] until such time as it receives FDA marketing authorization." The FDA focused squarely on the dangers of misinformed activity: "Some of the uses for

which PGS is intended are particularly concerning . . . because
of the potential health consequences that could result from
false positive or false negative assessments for high-risk indi-
cations. . . . Serious concerns are raised if test results are not
adequately understood by patients or if incorrect test results
are reported." Although only implied, the preferred solution in
the FDA letter, as in the case of Pathway Genomics, is that individuals' health care be managed by experts: "Risks are typically mitigated by INR management under a physician's care"
(Gara 2013).

It is not hard to find other instances in which political actors, even from different parties, have joined to pass legislation
or promulgate regulations that they believed the public would
have supported had they possessed the right information. Examples range from establishing commissions to recommend
closure of redundant military bases or underused schools
to creating the Federal Reserve Board to passing—and then
quickly rescinding—the Medicare Catastrophic Coverage Act
of 1989. The latter introduces a cautionary note. The law "was
supposed to protect older Americans from bankruptcy due to
medical bills. Instead it became a catastrophe for Democratic
and Republican lawmakers, who learned the hard way that
many older Americans did not want to be helped in that particular way" (Hulse 2013). The history of that legislation suggests,
in fact, two cautionary notes: policy makers can get it wrong,
to their cost and perhaps the cost of others, and the strategy
of "giving the public what it would want if it knew what we
know" can readily violate the ideals of democratic governance
that it purportedly supports. So this strategy is worth developing, but cautiously.

CHANGING POLITICAL ACTORS' INCENTIVES

To this point, we have offered two pathways toward good
democratic governance even in the face of inertia: directly
educating or mobilizing people, perhaps by structuring individuals' choices, and working around those obstructing good
policy, perhaps by mandating protection from the dangers of

misinformed activity. A third set of strategies engages with the third asymmetry, the fact that political actors who benefit from active misinformation have stronger incentives than do political actors who do not so benefit. These strategies seek to change political actors' incentives.

Inducing politicians, the media, and advocacy groups to address flaws in their use of facts in politics is arguably the most difficult but also the most important of the three sets of responses to the problems identified in *Do Facts Matter?* It is also the least developed, so our illustrative cases lack the systematic evidence of effectiveness that a strong policy recommendation ought to have.

Shaming and Punishment

Efforts to change incentives can be negative—making public actors' lives more difficult if they purvey or acquiesce in the use of false information. Fact checking is one way to do that. Journalists sometimes take on the mission of reporting elites' inaccurate or dishonest claims:

> *Facts Take a Beating in Acceptance Speeches* [headline]. Representative Paul D. Ryan used his convention speech on Wednesday to fault President Obama for failing to act on a deficit-reduction plan that he himself had helped kill. He chided Democrats for seeking $716 billion in Medicare cuts that he too had sought. . . . And Mitt Romney, in his acceptance speech on Thursday night, asserted that President Obama's policies had "not helped create jobs" and . . . warned that the president's Medicare cuts would "hurt today's seniors," claims that have already been labeled false or misleading.
>
> The two speeches—peppered with statements that were incorrect or incomplete—seemed to signal the arrival of a new kind of presidential campaign, one in which concerns about fact-checking have been largely set aside. (Cooper 2012)

Comedians use a different tactic with the same goal of shaming public actors into disavowing misinformation. Stephen Colbert challenged Representative Bill Posey (R-FL), who introduced the bill into the House of Representatives requiring birth certificates for presidential candidates, to provide a DNA test to "quell the persistent rumors" that "Florida congressmen are part alligator. I have had enough with the reckless whispering!" After describing rumors about Posey's grandmother and an alligator in a swamp one night, Colbert concluded piously, "I hope that's the end of this, because it probably didn't happen."

Fact-checking organizations also try to shame political actors publicly into conveying correct rather than incorrect information, again with a range of approaches. FactCheck.org describes itself as "a nonpartisan, nonprofit 'consumer advocate' for voters that aims to reduce the level of deception and confusion in U.S. politics. We monitor the factual accuracy of what is said by major U.S. political players. . . . Our goal is to . . . increase public knowledge and understanding" (*Fact-Check.org* c. 2012). Its website is sober and informative, focused on correctly depicting states of affairs and occasionally causal claims. Politifact.com is much more assertive about its shaming mission, and more fun. It ranks public actors' statements on a "truth-o-meter" whose categories run from "true" and "mostly true" to "false" and "pants on fire"—with vivid graphics of a meter engulfed with flames and cartoon pigs with wings flying across the computer screen.

A serious purpose lies behind the clever graphics; perhaps one can change political actors' incentives to promulgate or tolerate misinformation by embarrassing them into honesty. Satire is an old and honorable profession. Efforts to discipline elites' public statements are valuable because they attack misinformation at its source. They have at least two serious problems, however. First, like education, they are weak reeds; little evidence shows that candidates for office, pundits, or advocacy group spokespeople have dropped or changed an argument because journalists or fact checkers showed its falsity. The *New York Times* article quoted above made this point with unusual explicitness: "The growing number of misrepresentations [by presidential and vice-presidential candidates] appear to reflect a calculation in both parties that shame is overrated, and that no independent arbiters command the stature or the platform to hold the campaigns to account in the increasingly polarized and balkanized media firmament. Any unmasking of the lies or distortions, the thinking goes, rarely seeps into the public consciousness" (Cooper 2012).[14]

The old Latin proverb "Who will guard the guardians?" points to another problem with relying on experts to hold elites accountable: who will fact-check the fact checkers? Few members of the public have sufficient knowledge to determine whether the National Academy of Sciences' many reports on evolutionary theory or the Discovery Institute's Center for Science and Culture, which promotes the theory of intelligent design, more accurately conveys the science of human development. There is nothing to prevent a purported fact-checking organization of the partisan left or right from promulgating its own shaming revelations of purported misinformation, and it is easy to see how even a citizen who is seeking knowledge could get caught in a reverberating hall of mirrors.

There are other ways to raise the cost of purveying or tolerating untruths. In recent decades, public actors ranging from President Clinton to former president Richard Nixon, Michael Nifong (the district attorney of Durham County, North Carolina), and Andrew Thomas (former county attorney of Maricopa County, Arizona) were partly or fully disbarred as punishment for perjury, obstruction of justice, prosecutorial misconduct, and bringing unfounded and malicious charges against political opponents, respectively. The cases of presidents Clinton and Nixon are well known and, one hopes, salutary for other presidents tempted to lie to the public. Michael Nifong was responsible for the 2006 prosecution of Duke University students accused of raping a woman hired to dance at a party. He gave many highly charged interviews with the press, withheld exculpatory evidence, and otherwise took actions involving "dishonesty, fraud, deceit, and misrepresentation," according to the chair of the North Carolina State Bar Disciplinary Committee. Andrew Thomas charged two county supervisors with hundreds of counts of financial disclosure irregularities, filed a racketeering lawsuit against the board of supervisors, and otherwise "outrageously exploited power, flagrantly fostered fear, and disgracefully misused the law," according to the Arizona Supreme Court.

These are unusual, even extraordinary, cases, but they are not unique. (There is a thriving cottage industry of research on prosecutorial misconduct, and a smaller one on abuse of power.) Their purpose here is to underline the point that laws or the court system can, in some circumstances, raise the costs of purveying misinformation beyond the level that even a dedicated liar can withstand. Although there would be offsetting social and political costs, the court system could expand its role in punishing public actors' falsehoods or penalizing members of the public whose misinformed activity endangers others. For example, legal scholars have proposed tort liability for parents who refuse to vaccinate their children if the children can be shown to have infected another person (Baxter forthcoming; Caplan et al. 2012; see also *First Impressions* 2009). One could extend this argument to propose tort liability for misinforming the public in ways that demonstrably inhibit attainment of urgently needed health care.

Disbarment can be like the proverbial two-by-four, finally getting the mule's attention. Nonetheless, psychologists (and kindergarten teachers) know that positive incentives are generally more effective than shaming or punishing, especially for people who are under no compulsion to change their behavior. Appealing to professional norms is one such positive strategy. Atul Gawande (2013) describes a program to teach birth attendants in India appropriate procedures for caring for newborns. Most attendants are highly skilled, deeply experienced, and committed to their role and their patients. They have received instructions about avoiding hypothermia and infection. Yet they continue to act on misinformation about, for example, swaddling infants rather than placing them against the mother's skin for warmth. "You have to understand . . . barriers to change. . . . What would happen if we hired a cadre of childbirth-improvement workers to visit birth attendants and hospital leaders, show them why and how to follow a checklist of essential practices, understand their difficulties and objections, and help them practice doing things differently?" (41, 44). The project is new, so there are no systematic results yet, but case studies are promising; people who care about the results of their work can sometimes be persuaded to abandon misinformed activity in favor of informed activity that has better outcomes.

Other organizations similarly appeal to professional norms to induce leaders to overcome misinformed activity. An article in *Teaching Tolerance,* the Southern Poverty Law Center's online magazine for teachers, provides rebuttals to "10 Myths about Immigration." It urges teachers to "guide students to find a reliable source and help them figure out how to check the facts" and identifies "a few of the most frequently heard misconceptions along with information to help you and your students separate fact from fear." A recent article in the *New England Journal of Medicine* similarly identified "Myths, Presumptions, and Facts about Obesity" for its medical professional readers:

> Many beliefs about obesity persist in the absence of supporting scientific evidence (presumptions); some persist despite contradicting evidence (myths). . . . When the public, mass media, government agencies, and even academic scientists espouse unsupported beliefs, the result may be ineffective policy, unhelpful or unsafe clinical and public health recommendations, and an unproductive allocation of resources. (Casazza 2013: 446)

After refuting a series of presumptions and myths by reference to confirmatory randomized studies, the authors move from urging medical professionals not to act on misinformation to urging them to take action based on correct information:

> There are things we do know with reasonable confidence. Table 3 lists nine such facts and their practical implications for public health, policy, or clinical recommendations. The first two facts help establish a framework in which intervention and preventive techniques may work. The next four facts are more prescriptive, offering tools that can be conveyed to the public as well established. The last three facts are suited to clinical settings. (451–52)

They conclude that, "as a scientific community, we must always be open and honest with the public about the state of our knowledge and should rigorously evaluate unproved strategies" (452–53).[15]

This final appeal implies a third variant among the strategies aiming to change the asymmetry between political actors' strong incentives to keep people active but misinformed and other actors' weaker incentives to move people into informed activity. This variant moves beyond shaming, punishment, and even a call to professional norms into out-and-out exhortation. Thomas Patterson's book *Informing the News* offers "The Need for Knowledge-Based Journalism" as its subtitle. Patterson (2013: 5) cites Walter Lippmann's observation that democracy falters "if there is no steady supply of trustworthy and relevant news" and then states flatly that "journalists are failing to deliver it." Americans are "mired in misinformation" because they "have been ill-served by their intermediaries—journalists, politicians, talk show hosts, pundits, and bloggers—that claim to be their trusted guides." After developing and supporting this claim, Patterson pleads for knowledge-based journalism on the grounds that "the traditional news media . . . alone have the necessary infrastructure, personnel, and organizational routines, as well as norms that charge them with being 'custodians of the facts.' . . . Knowledge offers journalists their best chance of delivering an authoritative version of the news" and thereby sustaining a Jeffersonian democracy (141, 143).

As we note in chapter 2, two scholars of equal distinction and a long history of nonpartisan analyses exhort an even more difficult target—Congress. Ornstein and Mann (2013: 66, 123, 23) castigate the "viral e-mails and word-of-mouth campaigns [that] are expanding sharply, mostly aimed at false facts about political adversaries," and analyze political moments characterized by "misleading and factually incorrect rhetoric" or statements "with no basis in fact." These authors seek ways to resolve the current impasse but conclude with only a forlorn call to "balance individualism with community, freedom with equality, markets with regulation, state with national power,

. . . [and] policy commitments with respect for facts, evidence, science, and a willingness to compromise" (216).

Exhortation, perhaps combined with appeals to professional norms and the threat of shaming, can be effective. The media sometimes apologize for purveying misinformation: the news show *60 Minutes* apologized and offered a correction "for its botched and mishandled report on the Benghazi attacks. . . . 'We realized we had been misled, and it was a mistake to include him [a key witness] in our report. For that, we are very sorry'" (Mirkinson 2013). A few days later, the errant reporter was put on an indeterminate leave of absence. PopularScience.com put more weight behind its commitment to avoid misinformation by deciding to no longer accept comments on new articles. It explained to readers that a "politically motivated, decades-long war on expertise has eroded the popular consensus on a wide variety of scientifically validated topics. Everything, from evolution to the origins of climate change, is just another thing up for grabs again. . . . The cynical work of undermining bedrock scientific doctrine is now being done beneath our own stories, within a website devoted to championing science" (LaBarre 2013). One need not agree that there is anything like bedrock science, or that there was ever a golden age in which the populace accepted experts' judgment without demurral, in order to applaud *Popular Science* for combatting the promulgation of misinformation.

Even public officials sometimes seek to ensure that policy choices accord with the best available information. The Agency for Healthcare Research and Quality, for example,

> promote[s] evidence-based practice in everyday care through establishment of the Evidence-based Practice Center (EPC) Program. The EPCs develop evidence reports and technology assessments on topics relevant to clinical and other health care organization and delivery issues. . . . With this program, AHRQ became a "science partner" with private and public organizations in their efforts to improve the quality, effectiveness, and appropriateness of health care by synthesizing the evidence and facilitating the translation of evidence-based research findings. (Agency for Healthcare Research and Quality c. 2012)[16]

Elected officials may do the same. Franklin Roosevelt's thirty fireside chats were sometimes political appeals, sometimes exhortations—and occasionally an insistence that facts matter: "The pressing problems that confront us are military and naval problems. We cannot afford to approach them from the point of view of wishful thinkers or sentimentalists. What we face is cold, hard fact" (May 27, 1941). Examples could be added; many public actors care about purveying and acting on the basis of knowledge, and they make serious efforts to get it right. Nevertheless, we know of no systematic evidence on how much, how well, and under what conditions public actors change in response to efforts to reshape their incentives about facts in politics. So the third set of strategies for overcoming political asymmetries remains like the first and second—plausible, hopeful, but indeterminate.

CHANGING SOCIAL FACTS AND THEIR USE

In this work we have concentrated on social facts that are uncontroversial states of affairs (the proportion of Americans who are black is more than 5 percent and less than 20 percent; setting aside military engagements, fewer people were murdered in the United States in the 2000s than in the 1970s) or are causal statements with strong scientific consensus (vaccinating 95 percent of the population provides herd immunity; human activity contributes substantially to global warming). We claim in chapter 2 that the distinction between the active informed and the active misinformed is a genuine boundary. In our final pages, we relax that constraint slightly. After all, scientific consensus about causation and even states of affairs has been spectacularly wrong (the earth is flat; the balance among four humors determines a person's health; Africans have smaller brains and therefore less intelligence than Europeans). So a final set of strategies for moving people out of the category of misinformed activity into informed activity is to challenge scientific consensus, move the boundary between the categories—that is, reinterpret false information as true, or vice versa.

How knowledge is constructed, deconstructed, and de-
bunked—that is, "what is truth?"—is much too big a topic for
the final pages of a book about something else. So we limit
ourselves to placing a well-known instance of challenging purported facts into our conceptual framework in order to open a
subject for future engagement.

Before the iconic American civil rights movement of the
1950s and 1960s began, many Americans were acting on bad
information. A survey in 1944 demonstrates the level of mistaken "knowledge."[17] Close to half of a white sample agreed
that Negroes were not as intelligent as whites, and another
tenth did not know. A fifth of the respondents agreed that "Negroes in the United States have just as good a chance as white
people to get any kind of job." Those who knew that Negroes
did not have the same job opportunities as whites were asked
why; a quarter stated that they were incompetent, and a quarter (perhaps the same people) said they were lazy, repulsive,
not trustworthy, or had an offensive odor. Still in the same survey, a quarter of white respondents agreed that "most Negroes
in the United States think they are being treated fairly" (and an
honest fifth said that they did not know). Perhaps that delusion
explains the fact that 84 percent thought "Negroes in this town
have the same chance as white people to get a good education,"
and that half thought Negroes had an equal chance to "make a
good living" in the United States. A third agreed that "Negro
blood" is "different in some way" from white blood, and another third confessed ignorance on the point.[18]

The second element of active misinformation is acting politically in accord with one's mistaken beliefs. We need not detail
here the ways that many if not most white Americans treated
blacks in the 1940s—suffice it to say that their actions fully ac-
corded with the supposed knowledge that blacks had less intelligence, different blood, a repulsive odor, an equal chance for
education and a good income, and a sense of satisfaction with
their treatment.

A different survey during the early years of the civil rights
movement illustrates the other category of failure to reach the

Jeffersonian ideal, that is, the status of informed inactivity.
Asked their views of the Supreme Court's 1954 *Brown v. Board of
Education* decision on public school desegregation, two-fifths of
respondents in one survey endorsed segregation, one-fifth endorsed immediate desegregation, and a third concurred with a
proposal to "carry out the Court's order but do it gradually and
over a period of years, starting only with the youngest children
at this time" (Gallup, Oct. 15–20, 1954). In our terminology, this
third knew the facts about segregation in schools but chose not
to act politically on that knowledge, thus exemplifying the inactive informed. Other polls through the 1950s similarly found
between a third and three-fifths of respondents agreeing that
school desegregation was appropriate, or at least that it was
the law, but that it should be delayed—for up to two decades in
some surveys (Gallup, Sept. 10–15, 1958; Roper, Sept. 4–8, 1956,
June, Oct. 1958; more generally, see Hochschild 1984).

Faced with those views, civil rights activists devoted a great
deal of energy to moving people out of both inactive information and active misinformation and into informed activity. The
Reverend Martin Luther King Jr.'s famous "Letter from Birmingham Jail," to cite only one example, was aimed squarely
at the inactive informed. King wrote to "men of genuine good
will" in order to put the "ugly record" and "hard, brutal facts
of the case" before them, and he called on them to respond
suitably. He "confess[ed]" to becoming "gravely disappointed
with the white moderate" who does not act on his knowledge
of racial oppression:

> The Negro's great stumbling block in his stride toward freedom
> is not the White Citizen's Councilor or the Ku Klux Klanner,
> but the white moderate, who is more devoted to "order" than
> to justice; who prefers a negative peace which is the absence
> of tension to a positive peace which is the presence of justice;
> who constantly says: "I agree with you in the goal you seek, but
> I cannot agree with your methods of direct action." . . . Shal-
> low understanding from people of good will is more frustrating
> than absolute misunderstanding from people of ill will. Luke-
> warm acceptance is much more bewildering than outright rejec-
> tion. (*Atlantic* 2013 [1963])

In short, King shares our characterization of inactive information as usually standing in the way of good democratic governance—but he invests his frustration with an almost unique passion and urgency.

Other civil rights activities were directed at the active misinformed to show the falsity of beliefs that blacks had equal access to education and a good living and were content with their treatment. Over and over, marchers and protesters testified to the unfairness that permeated their lives, took actions to show how thoroughly they rejected their treatment, and provoked outrageous responses in order to expose the depths of racism. Until the mid-1960s, most abjured the use of force to overcome the harms caused by the active misinformed; at least in their more idealistic moments, civil rights activists sought to educate misinformed individuals about American racial hierarchy and to inspire the newly aware to act on the basis of their knowledge.

Given the immensity of its task, the civil rights movement attained these twin goals to an amazing degree. Some of the inactive informed were inspired or shamed into marching and protesting; some kept their children in newly desegregated schools, voted for liberal and eventually for black candidates, and otherwise acted on their knowledge of American racial inequality, as Gunnar Myrdal hoped they would. And as Myrdal also predicted or at least hoped, even some of the active misinformed learned that their beliefs in a contented Negro underclass, equal opportunities in the 1950s, or African Americans' lesser intelligence were wrong.[19] Well before the end of the twentieth century, a majority of white Americans recognized the existence of racial discrimination; abjured, at least overtly, empirical claims about racial inferiority; and endorsed some policies to overcome and compensate for racial injustice.

How much the civil rights movement succeeded, what Americans know and how they choose to act with regard to racial oppression, and what the most important facts are about racial oppression—these are large and controversial issues that *Do Facts Matter?* cannot broach.[20] We evoke the movement for a more particular purpose: to show that some combination of fact finding, education, leadership, mass action, moral passion, and institutional reform can change public discourse so that what were once incorrectly seen as facts that could be justly acted on are moved into the realm of falsehoods to be rejected. The same combination of actions and reforms can also inspire the disengaged informed to match their behavior to their knowledge.

Acting on established truths is not all that matters for good governance; governance also requires values, morals, aspirations, and imagining untried possibilities. Established truths can be shown to be wrong, even pernicious. But facts do matter. Other things being equal, as they are not always, the number of instances in which people should appropriately take political and policy actions in accord with misapprehensions is vanishingly small; a democratic polity functions better when people take political and policy actions in accord with their knowledge. Informed inactivity is frustrating; misinformed activity is dangerous to life and polity. It is perhaps ironic to give Thomas Malthus the penultimate word, given his spectacularly wrong prediction about the impact of a rising population on nineteenth-century societies. But at the turn of a portentous century he put our anxieties about the asymmetries attendant on the use of facts in politics more elegantly than we can:

> The most baleful mischiefs may be expected from the unmanly conduct of not daring to face truth because it is unpleasing. . . . If we proceed without a thorough knowledge and accurate comprehension of the nature, extent, and magnitude of the difficulties we have to encounter, or if we unwisely direct our efforts towards an object in which we cannot hope for success, we shall not only exhaust our strength in fruitless exertions and remain at as great a distance as ever from the summit of our wishes, but we shall be perpetually crushed by the recoil of this rock of Sisyphus. (Malthus 2008 [1798]: 140)

We can only hope that Calvin and Hobbes—"You're ignorant, but at least you act on it"—do not get the last word in life as they do in this book.

NOTES

CHAPTER 1

1. *Do Facts Matter?* does not provide full citations for comments by contemporary public figures since they are easily found online, often from many sources. Instead, we provide the date of the comment to help readers identify the right item.

2. Delli Carpini and Keeter (1993); Galston (2001); Nie et al. (1996). Several scholars have challenged this standard finding, either on methodological grounds (Mondak 1999) or by showing that civically relevant knowledge has not increased even though years of schooling have risen over the past few decades (chap. 7).

3. As an initial indication of the dangers associated with this point, note that "those who are both highly inaccurate and highly confident tend to be the strongest partisans and thus the very people who most frequently convey their sentiments to politicians" (Kuklinski et al. 2000: 799).

4. All questions were from Gallup Poll or Louis Harris Associates and were found in the iPoll database (see next paragraph), using the keywords "cigarette smoking." A parallel series about smoking and heart disease yielded the same pattern, as did other repeated questions with different wording but a similar import.

More generally, to minimize verbiage associated with citations in this book, we use the following conventions: (1) Where we report analyses of survey data with no citation beyond identification of the survey itself, we conducted the analysis. (2) Where we report survey results or analyses of survey data with the sponsor and date (e.g., CBS, Jan. 1, 2000), the data come from iPoll, an online database maintained by the Roper Center for Public Opinion Research at the University of Connecticut (www.roper center.uconn.edu). iPoll enables one to find relevant surveys from the 1940s through the present with keywords, and sometimes includes cross-tabulations by demographic characteristics such as party identification, ideology, gender, or race. It also provides downloadable data from many surveys. (3) We include a complete citation and reference for survey results from sources not in iPoll.

5. The GSS is a national face-to-face survey of several thousand Americans who constitute a representative sample of the American population. It has been fielded every year or every other year since 1972; it includes hundreds of questions each time, many of which have been repeated over many years and thus provide a portrait of changing views or behaviors. Its focus is sociological, broadly defined. The GSS is largely funded by the National Science Foundation and is one of three academic surveys that set the standard for all other surveys and polls. For more information, see General Social Survey (c. 2013). For a recent compendium of results, see Marsden (2012).

6. A higher proportion of whites in 2013 than in 1995 (53 percent compared to 41 percent) agreed that the average black person is as well off or better off than the average white "in terms of income and overall financial situation." Only 36 percent of blacks concurred in 2013 (14 percent in 1995), but fully 56 percent of Latinos did so (26 percent in 1995) (Pew Research Center 2013b: 18).

7. Interestingly, these differences do not extend to political participation; the misinformed in this survey were just as likely to have voted in the two most recent presidential elections and the most recent congressional election.

8. Gaines et al. (2007) offer a somewhat similar typology, using the concepts "fact avoidance" and "opinion disconnect," among others. However, most of their categories fit within our category of the inactive informed, and they do not address our category of the active misinformed.

CHAPTER 2

1. Nor are Americans unique in their political ignorance. To choose only one of myriad examples, in 2004, 45 percent of a national representative sample of Britons, and more than three-fifths of respondents under age 35, reported that they had never heard of Auschwitz (Rees et al. 2004); for countervailing evidence, see Smith (1995, table 8).

2. Furthermore, some research suggests that misinformation or lack of knowledge can be overestimated. A small financial incentive sometimes increases accuracy or decreases partisan bias (Krupnikov et al. 2006; Prior and Lupia 2008; Bullock et al. 2013). Asking questions in ways that accord with "accepted practices in educational testing" increased the mean level of political knowledge in three surveys by 15 percent (Mondak and Davis 2001: 199;

see also Miller and Orr 2008). Sturgis et al. (2007) offer a counter-counterargument. Changing answer options may, or may not (Luskin and Bullock 2011), increase measured knowledge.

See Hirsch (1988) and his many critics and defenders for a parallel debate in the arena of what school children know and should be taught through explicit curricula.

3. For some of the many systematic studies of Americans' knowledge of public affairs, see Erskine (1963), Bennett (1989), repeated Pew Center surveys on public knowledge in the series "What the Public Knows," and Delli Carpini and Keeter (1993, 1996). Delli Carpini et al. (2004) review evidence on the links between Americans' (lack of) knowledge and deliberative democracy.

4. Exceptions to this statement include, but are probably not limited to, Delli Carpini and Keeter (1996), Somin (1998), and Althaus (2003).

5. The careful reader will note that John Sides and his colleagues' research sometimes demonstrates the ineffectiveness of new information in changing views and sometimes its effectiveness. Asked how to reconcile these conflicting results, he responded, "To my mind, there is no clear bottom line as yet. It's a muddle. Too few studies, too many things that are varying: policy domain, type of fact, etc." (personal communication with authors, Dec. 22, 2011).

6. By another measure, voters' "actual choices fell about halfway between what they would have been if voters had been fully informed and what they would have been if everyone had cast their ballots on the basis of a coin flip." The analysis covered six presidential elections. The respondent's level of information is defined as the interviewer's evaluation of the person's political knowledge in a given round of the American National Election Studies (ANES; see note 9, this chapter). That simple measure is the "single most effective information item" in the ANES (Zaller 1985). (Research is in Bartels 1996; quotation from Bartels 2008: 47).

7. The author notes that some perceived discrimination may not be illegal (e.g., refusing to rent to someone with poor housekeeping habits).

8. The Pew Research Center finds that "Republicans have often outperformed Democrats and Independents" in its annual examination of Americans' political knowledge (Pew Research Center 2013c: 5). In multivariate analyses with controls for age, gender, and education level (in 2010), and income as well (in 2009), partisan differences largely disappeared in 2009 but persisted in 2010.

9. The ANES is a national survey of several thousand Americans who constitute a representative sample of the American

population. It is a predominantly face-to-face survey, although in recent years telephone and online components have been added. It includes surveys before and after each presidential election, with hundreds of questions each time. Many have been repeated over many years and thus provide a portrait of changing views or behaviors. Its focus is political, broadly defined. It has been fielded in every presidential election year, and recently in years with congressional elections, since 1952. The ANES is largely funded by the National Science Foundation and is one of three academic surveys that set the standard for all other surveys and polls. For more information, see American National Election Studies (c. 2013).

10. James Fishkin (2009) and his colleagues' international study of deliberative polls provides the most extensive research program investigating the claim that information changes policy views. As he puts it, "In at least some cases, deliberation makes a considerable difference and the uninformed do not simply reach the same result" as those who have participated in deliberative polling (8). It is not clear, however, whether the mechanism that produces opinion change in these polls is deliberation, new information, persuasion by other participants, or something else. Farrar et al. (2010) make an effort to sort out the issue of mechanism.

11. One such circumstance might be protecting the privacy of a candidate for office and of his or her family; another is keeping information secret that could jeopardize national security or the safety of particular individuals.

12. Perhaps they overheard the Bush administration official quoted in the epigraph to chapter 7, denigrating "what we call the reality-based community."

CHAPTER 3

1. For useful timelines, see CNN (1998), Cosgrove (2009).

2. A curious set of poll responses appears to challenge the claim that most Americans knew the facts. Starting as early as two days after the initial news report of a rumor about an affair and extending through July 1998, in six surveys roughly twice as many Republicans as Democrats—and sometimes more—reported that they believed there had been an affair. Younger respondents, men, those with higher incomes, and the better educated were also more likely than their counterparts to perceive an affair (*Time*/CNN/Yankelovich, Jan. 22, Jan. 28–29, Feb. 4–5, Apr. 8–9, May 18–19, July 30, 1998). These variations started long before there was anything like definitive evidence and did not change over the course of hundreds of news articles in the ensuing months. In our view,

therefore, these results represent a symbolic statement of support of or opposition to the president rather than a genuine statement of what people understood to be the truth. For a parallel case, see our discussion of "birthers" in chapter 6. Thanks to John Sides for bringing these odd results to our attention.

3. Cross-tabulations of these eighty-five respondents who explicitly became informed and engaged yielded no clear patterns by gender, age, race, education, or even partisanship.

4. Powell (2012) provides a meta-analysis of 14,000 peer-reviewed articles.

5. Working Group I (2013) develops the science; Working Group II (2014) gives information on vulnerability, exposure, and possible adaptation; Working Group III (2014) develops options for mitigating the effects of climate change.

6. Half concurred in 2011 (CNN/ORC International Poll, Sept. 2011). Survey responses on this topic fluctuate, being highly responsive to the effects of question wording, question context, immediate political circumstances, sampling design, and other nonsubstantive influences. We rely mainly, therefore, on series conducted by a single organization over time.

7. We focus on the 2007 Gallup survey because it also includes useful policy items, discussed below.

8. These figures are our calculations; the Pew Research Center (2012) reports 47 percent agreement in 2006 (instead of our 40 percent).

9. The individual steps were using only fluorescent light bulbs at home, installing a solar panel to produce energy for your home, unplugging electronic equipment when not in use, buying a hybrid car, supporting construction of a nuclear energy plant nearby, spending several thousand dollars to make your home energy efficient, and riding mass transit when possible.

10. The government steps included stringent restrictions on U.S. industries and utilities, ban on vehicles averaging less than 30 miles per gallon of gas, surcharge on the utility bills of home and business owners that exceed monthly energy limits, strict land use policies to discourage suburban sprawl and encourage population density, requirements for government buildings to use renewable sources of energy even if it resulted in higher taxes, and a research effort of up to $30 billion per year to develop new sources of energy.

11. Ansolabehere and Konisky (2012) and Center for Climate Change Communication (2008) find the same pattern from different surveys.

12. As discussed in note 6, the proportion of respondents identified as inactive informed depends on nonsubstantive factors as well as the actual issues at stake. For example, the Pew Research Center's global warming items, asked annually from 2006 through 2011, had fine measures of factual information but only a very broad policy question, on how serious a problem global warming is. Over six iterations, barely 5 percent of respondents were disengaged informed using this policy measure; a plurality were engaged as well as informed.

The main conclusion here is that inadequate (for our purposes) survey questions produce unrevealing results. But a more substantive conclusion may also be warranted: perhaps respondents can link correct information to appropriate policy valences when focusing on broad attitudinal questions, even if they cannot or will not link information to preferences for robust individual or government action. That is at least a starting point for promoting Jefferson's vision of an informed and active polity.

13. For partial challenges to Zaller's formulation, see Miller (1999), Sonner and Wilcox (1999), and Shah et al. (2002). They disagree on the exact reasons, but none undermine our basic claims that the public ignored elites' expectations of Clinton's political demise or that material interests were crucial for sustaining his public support. Brian Newman (2002) argues that the Lewinsky scandal did indeed depress Clinton's approval ratings, but that support based on peace and prosperity nonetheless overrode disapproval based on the failure of probity.

14. Druckman and Leeper (2012: n34) provide an excellent bibliography of current research on motivated reasoning in the political arena. Other recent politically oriented publications include Lodge and Taber (2013), Lebo and Cassino (2007), Slothuus and de Vreese (2010), and Taber et al. (2009). Fischle (2000) applies the concept of motivated reasoning directly to attitudes about the Clinton/Lewinsky scandal. Kahan (2013: 407) shows that liberals are as prone to motivated reasoning as conservatives, and that "subjects who scored highest in cognitive reflection were the *most* likely to display ideologically motivated cognition." On the latter point, see also Friedman (2006a), and chapter 4, note 13. Kahan et al. (2013) make a parallel argument about "motivated numeracy" with regard to quantitative data.

15. The variation over time in the lines suggests not only survey noise but also the fact that people were paying attention to the news and, to some degree, changing their responses accordingly—that is, moving into the category of the active informed at

least temporarily. For example, the sharp rise in support among all three groups for Clinton leaving office in mid-August 1998 followed immediately upon his statement to the nation on August 17 that he had had an "inappropriate relationship" with Lewinsky. (We have no good explanation for the sharp drop immediately prior to that rise.)

16. "Sometimes" because other polls, notably the 2007 and 2012 Gallup surveys, show no clear link between income and policy preferences among the correctly informed.

17. We compared those with annual incomes greater and less than $30,000, and (in a separate analysis) those with annual incomes greater and less than $75,000—all among the correctly informed. The pattern held in both comparisons (ABC/Washington Post, Dec. 10–13, 2009). We made the same two sets of comparisons for the 2012 Gallup poll.

18. Similarly, in 2010 twice as many Democrats as Republicans (79 to 38 percent) agreed that climate change is occurring (Pew Research Center 2010).

19. This may not be the case; see Patterson (2013) and Boykoff and Boykoff (2004).

20. Although it is not as strong, we see the same pattern of Republican movement from inactive informed to active misinformed in the two-question Pew series. The proportion of Democrats with incorrect factual information stayed stable over five years, whereas the comparable proportion of Republicans—who denied either the occurrence of global warming or its human causes—started almost twice as high and rose an additional ten percentage points.

21. Averages are, as is often the case, misleading, since three of five informed Democrats opposed nuclear power and oil exploration on federal lands but only a tenth opposed the other policies, whereas almost half of informed Republicans opposed nuclear power but close to a quarter opposed the other seven policies. In short, informed inactivity rests on an interaction between partisanship and policy proposal.

22. This extends political scientists' earlier findings on motivated reasoning (discussed earlier), sociotropic voting (Kinder and Kiewiet 1981), and failure to use self-interest in evaluating school bussing proposals, tax policy, and other matters (Bobo and Kluegel 1993; Sears and Funk 1990; Sears et al. 1979; Gelman 2009; Fong 2001). For evidence that self-interest can matter to policy views in some circumstances, see Henderson and Hillygus (2011).

We assume here as elsewhere in Do Facts Matter? that interests and group membership can be treated as meaningfully distinct.

A future analysis might usefully relax that assumption since perceived interests and group membership may well be related and
mutually caused, just as perceived facts and group membership
are linked if the claim of motivated reasoning is correct.

23. Paper recycling rose threefold in the United States from 1960
to 2000 (from about 30 million to 90 million tons). It fell back to
about 75 million tons in 2010, but that decline "might reflect on the
habits of the wireless and paperless generation, who simply used
less paper than their predecessors" (*Green Nature* 2011).

CHAPTER 4

1. In eighteen of twenty surveys from 1989 through 2013, more
than half of Americans (over two-thirds on twelve occasions) perceived "more crime in the U.S. than there was a year ago." Between 3 and 43 percent perceived "less" crime, with an average
of 19 percent (Gallup Poll, Oct. of each year). Perceptions of crime
became much worse after 2001 than in the decade before that, although rates of violent crime continued to decline through 2010
(Sides 2009).

This finding points to the underlying puzzle: the proportion of
American households experiencing any crime other than murder,
as reported in the National Crime Victimization Survey, remained
constant at about 24 percent from 1989 through 1994, after which
it declined steadily to 13.9 percent in 2005 (Bureau of Justice Statistics 1992; *Sourcebook of Criminal Justice Statistics*, various years).
Since 2005, data have not been aggregated into "any NCVS crime"
in published documents; however, crime rates continued to decline through 2012 (the last year with reported data) in every category of crime reported (Bureau of Justice Statistics 2013).

2. In keeping with the theme of this chapter, however, 10 percent said that a health care reform bill had not been passed, and
an additional 9 percent did not know (Kaiser Health Tracking Poll
[HTP], Apr. 2010).

3. All of the following results from the Kaiser HTPs are at http://
kff.org/tag/tracking-poll/ (accessed Dec. 17, 2013).

4. For ease of exposition, we focus only on the extensive and
high-quality Kaiser Foundation series. But other survey organizations have also found misinformation about the ACA. For example, 15 percent of respondents to a 2012 Pew Research Center poll
(June 28–July 1, 2012) thought that the Supreme Court had rejected
"most provisions" of the law. Fifty-seven percent of Republicans
(and 29 percent of Democrats) agreed in the 2012 ANES that the

NOTES TO PAGES 69–81

ACA definitely or probably authorizes end-of-life decisions for Medicare patients. Given its disastrous rollout, the 22 percent of Democrats who said in November 2013 that the signup for health exchanges was going "very well" or "somewhat well" were also seriously misinformed (CBS, Nov. 15–18, 2013).

5. The search of newspapers and shows was on July 21, 2012. At that point, LexisNexis Academic included transcripts from ten major television and radio shows. We conducted a LexisNexis search of blog and web publications on February 22, 2013.

6. Wikipedia's entry for "Clarence Thomas Supreme Court nomination" offers a good description of the confirmation process.

7. See Rucinski (1993) for most of these poll results, as well as concern about the "trade-offs involved in fast reaction polls" (586).

8. Slightly fewer than a quarter of whites agreed; see Caldeira and Smith (1996).

9. In contrast, the *New York Times* opposed his confirmation on October 15, and the *Los Angeles Times* "hedged its bets": President Bush "would serve the country well by withdrawing the nomination," but senators who had supported Thomas before the Hill hearings were not now justified in changing their vote (*Los Angeles Times* 1991). More generally, see Monroe (1991).

10. A September 1991 ABC poll asked respondents if the NAACP's opposition affected their support for Thomas; 72 percent of blacks said it made little difference.

11. Martin-Quinn Scores, "Measures," at www.mqscores.wustl.edu/measures.php.

12. We generated the measure of active misinformation in two steps, corresponding to its two criteria. We first created a normalized index of all responses to question 11 on forms A and B of the June 2010 Kaiser HTP, which asked if various programs were included in the ACA. This produced a "misinformation index" for all respondents.

We then multiplied the misinformation index by an index measuring whether a respondent would oppose a member of Congress who supported the health care bill. A respondent who answered all questions correctly *or* supported a member of Congress who voted for the ACA received a 0 on the measure of membership in the category of active misinformed. A respondent who answered all questions incorrectly *and* opposed a member of Congress who voted for the ACA received a 1. Those who answered some questions incorrectly *and* would oppose a member of Congress received a score between 0 and 1; the more questions they answered incorrectly, the closer their score was to 1. Actual respondents' scores ranged from the scale's minimum of 0 to its maximum of 1. The survey provided 695 valid cases for this dependent variable.

We repeat our usual caution about causation: cross-sectional survey data do not permit an argument that misinformed individuals are using that misinformation to decide their congressional vote. That seems a reasonable inference but is only that.

13. In both the OLS and tobit regression analyses, with controls the interaction between partisanship and education is neither substantively nor statistically significant. For other evidence that those with more education or political knowledge are more misinformed, see Slothuus and de Vreese (2010), Lodge and Taber (2005), Shani (2006), Achen and Bartels (2006), and Druckman et al. (2010).

14. Some scholars find partisanship to be related to views of health care reform proposals more broadly (Kriner and Reeves 2014). In partial contrast, Michael Tesler (2012: 690) highlights the role of racial attitudes, arguing that views on health care policies "were significantly more racialized when attributed to President Obama than they were when these same proposals were framed as President Clinton's 1993 reform efforts." Partisanship also plays a substantial role in some of his specifications

CHAPTER 5

1. The active misinformed are the targets of Paul Samuelson's (or perhaps John Maynard Keynes's) famous quip: "When events change, I change my mind. What do you do?" (For a discussion of who really said this, see http://quoteinvestigator.com/2011/07/22/keynes-change-mind/.)

2. Zogby International Poll, intermittently from Jan. 4 to Mar. 15, 2003 (two questions, six iterations each); *Newsweek* Poll, intermittently from Oct. 24, 2002, to Mar. 14, 2003 (one question, six iterations). Data are at *PollingReport.com* (www.pollingreport.com/iraq15.htm).

3. The results conform nicely to John Zaller's (1992) Receive-Accept-Sample model when elites present a mostly unified front.

4. CBS/*New York Times*, May 9–12, 2003; Program on International Policy Attitudes (PIPA), May 14–18, June 18–25, July 11–20, Aug. 26–Sept. 3, 2003; NBC/*Wall Street Journal* Poll, Sept. 20–22, 2003; PIPA, Oct. 29–Nov. 10, 2003, Mar. 16–22, 2004, Mar. 1–6, 2006; Harris Poll, Oct. 16–20, 2008; PIPA, Aug. 19–25, 2011.

5. This falsehood was also a reasonable belief given the information that the media and national elites were providing during the

early 2000s. As two analysts put it, "President Bush never publicly blamed Saddam Hussein or Iraq for the events of September 11, but by consistently linking Iraq with terrorism and al Qaeda he provided the context from which such a connection could be made. Bush also never publicly connected Saddam Hussein to Osama bin Laden, the leader of al Qaeda. Nevertheless, . . . the way language and transitions are shaped in his official speeches almost compelled listeners to infer a connection" (Gershkoff and Kushner 2005: 525; see also Zeller 2004).

"Compelled" is too strong, since some Americans did not hold Hussein responsible for 9/11 even at the height of this belief, and the proportion that did hold him responsible declined over several years. Nonetheless, even a milder version of their argument reinforces our claim that believing and using misinformation are dangerous to a democratic polity and its members.

On the association between this false belief and support for the war: as of early 2003, "among those who think Iraq directly supports Al Qaeda, 73 percent favor taking military action to oust Saddam. Among those who don't think he supports Al Qaeda, support for military action drops to 45 percent" (Langer 2003). A poll a month later found the same pattern. Furthermore, "In the postwar period there was also a strong relationship between beliefs about the nature of the connection between al Qaeda and Iraq and support for the war" (Kull et al. 2003–2004: 576, 577). The causal direction here is ambiguous, but the association is not.

6. Untitled PDF file posted by the U.S. Department of Defense, www.defense.gov/NEWS/casualty.pdf.

7. The article was "Ileal-Lymphoid-Nodular Hyperplasia, Non-Specific Colitis, and Pervasive Developmental Disorder in Children." The *Lancet* retracted it after the lead author, Andrew Wakefield, was found to have conflicts of interest and to have falsified some of the data (*Lancet* 2010). Wakefield's license to practice medicine was later revoked.

Refusal to vaccinate one's children can be expensive as well as dangerous. Twelve cases of measles in San Diego in 2008 among the children of vaccine refusers led to a quarantine of forty-eight additional children too young to be vaccinated, at a cost of more than $600,000 in public funds as well as private expenditures (Sugerman et al. 2010). Fourteen cases of measles in Tucson cost local hospitals $800,000 to contain in 2008 (Chen et al. 2011).

8. Some drug research may also be a long-term casualty of the current controversy. "No one is developing a better vaccine to replace the current one. . . . Even discussing the problem [of

ineffective pertussis vaccines] provokes uneasiness: with anti-vaccine sentiments and vaccine refusal at historic highs, nobody wants to impeach one of public health's crucial tools" (McKenna 2013: 34).

9. Poll results are in Pew Research Center and American Association for the Advancement of Science, Apr. 28–May 12, 2009; Harvard School of Public Health, Sept. 14–20, 2009; Gallup/*USA Today*, Nov. 20–22, 2009; CBS News, Nov. 18–21, 2011; Harris Poll 2011.

10. Unlike in Mnookin's case studies, in this survey liberals were less likely than moderates or conservatives to endorse parental choice about vaccination. In the more recent CBS poll of 2011, respondents with lower incomes or less education were most suspicious of vaccination (CBS, Nov. 18–21, 2011).

CHAPTER 6

1. As of September 2012, 39 percent in each category (Kaiser HTP, Sept. 2012). Similarly, two-fifths of ANES respondents in 2012 agreed that the ACA authorizes end-of-life decisions by government panels; three in ten cautiously agreed that the law "probably" does not do so, and only three in ten were sure that death panels are a chimera.

2. Knowing the facts is not the same thing as supporting a particular candidate, so a campaign's effort to hunt where the ducks are is not quite a case of seeking to galvanize the inactive informed. Nevertheless, it is close enough for our purposes, since campaign activists believe that partisan support grows out of knowledge or is itself a correct (not just preferred) stance. So, from the vantage point of a political activist, a supporter's view is the functional equivalent of holding correct information.

3. Labour Thatcherites were working-class, traditionally Labour, voters in the United Kingdom who regularly voted for Margaret Thatcher and the Conservative Party in the 1980s.

4. Constitutionally, a person need not be born within the borders of the United States to be eligible to become president. Residents of U.S. territories that assign U.S. citizenship at birth are also eligible: Puerto Rico (since 1941), Guam, and the U.S. Virgin Islands (also the District of Columbia). A person born outside the United States to parents who are U.S. citizens is also eligible. The Congressional Research Service has written two reports, in 2000 and 2011, affirming these rules through "the weight of legal and historical authority" (Congressional Research Service 2011: 2).

5. Mark Penn sent a memo to Clinton in March 2007, noting that a story about Obama's international connections exposed a weakness—the perception by some voters that his connection with basic American values and culture was shallow. "I cannot imagine Americans electing a president during a time of war who is not at his center fundamentally American in his thinking and his values. . . . Every speech should contain the line that you were born in the middle of America to the middle class in the middle of the last century" (quoted in Green 2012). Penn never implied that Obama was not native born or was anti-American, but he did identify the political advantage of hinting that Obama is somehow not one of us.

6. Fear that political leaders are illegitimately acquiring and using power is an old and powerful trope in American politics, going back to Puritan New England and its own rebellious offspring, the colony of Rhode Island (Bailyn 1967). The "paranoid style" of American electoral politics rises and falls but almost never disappears (Hofstadter 2008; Davis 2008).

7. For example, some survey houses asked those who initially said "don't know" whether they leaned toward thinking that Obama was born in the United States or that he was born elsewhere. We did not include those who reported "elsewhere" after the probe in the totals for figure 6.1.

8. Rove was not alone in this view. Arizona's Republican governor, Jan Brewer, vetoed a bill similar to Louisiana's on the (metaphorically confusing) grounds that it was "a bridge too far" (Apr. 19, 2011). Conservative commentator Glenn Beck dismissed birtherism as "the dumbest thing I've ever heard" (Jan. 4, 2010). Columnist David Frum warned that "Republican credibility—and viability—would not recover from the self-inflicted wounds of a primary season dominated by candidates abandoning the political mainstream and attempting to out-crazy one another on fringe non-issues" (May 1, 2011). After release of Obama's full birth certificate, the Republican National Committee chair finally declared that "my position is that the president was born in the United States" (Apr. 27, 2011). (He could not resist, however, the presumably nonironic statement that Obama's "talk about birth certificates is distracting him from our No. 1 priority—our economy.")

9. "Noting that the Republican candidate has criticized wind energy, saying a windmill can't be put on top of a car to power it, Obama had a zinger. 'I don't know if he's actually tried that,' Obama said. 'I know he's had other things on his car.' Decades ago, Romney put his family's dog, Seamus, in a carrier on the roof

of their station wagon for a trip to Canada" (Epstein 2012). "Dogs Against Romney" became a popular Internet blog and locus for social activism in the 2012 presidential campaign (slogan: "Remember Crate-Gate").

10. During the week in which Obama released the long form of his birth certificate, two-thirds of television news coverage of him—about 8 percent of all news—addressed his birthplace. That was the third week in a row in which birtherism received "significant attention in the mainstream media" (Pew Research Center's Project for Excellence in Journalism 2011).

11. MSNBC's and other liberal media attention to the birther issue may explain why roughly a fifth of Democrats or liberals agreed that Obama was not born in the United States (and another tenth or more of both groups were uncertain).

12. For Democrats and independents, the significant difference lies between those who say that Obama was definitely born in the United States and those who say that he was probably U.S. born, probably foreign born, and definitely foreign born.

13. Equating the racial resentment scale with anti-black sentiment is controversial in some quarters, and we too find it problematic (Hochschild 2011). Nevertheless, it has a well-established association with many measures of racial antagonism.

14. Another issue that deserves further analysis: people who are active but misinformed on one issue may be more likely to hold (and act on?) false information on other issues as well. As an initial example, at every level of education, the more one moves toward the birther end of the four possible response categories in the 2012 ANES, the less likely one is to know the actual unemployment rate. The pattern holds for both Democrats and Republicans.

15. A staff member defended Kyl's comment in response to protests on the grounds that "his remark was not intended to be a factual statement, but rather to illustrate that Planned Parenthood, an organization that receives millions of dollars in taxpayer funding, does subsidize abortions." After further criticism from the opposite partisan direction, Kyl corrected this correction; the same staffer loyally fell on his sword by stating that "Senator Kyl misspoke when he incorrectly cited a statistic on the Senate floor last week regarding Planned Parenthood. Rather than simply state that in response to a media inquiry, I responded that his comment was not intended to be a factual statement; a comment, that, in retrospect, made no sense. Senator Kyl neither saw nor approved that response" (Apr. 8–17, 2011).

16. Committee on House Administration (2009) provides rules on the sending of newsletters. See Cook (1989), Yiannakis (1982), and Lipinski (2004) for other analyses of congressional newsletters. The small amount of research on the subject indicates that legislators' unsolicited direct mail can affect electoral outcomes (Gerber et al. 2011).

17. Examples of partisan appeals include "Under Republican leadership, the foreclosure crisis has reached new heights" and "This session of Congress has been extremely productive." Almost all statements with a first-person reference are personal appeals.

18. "Amy's Story: When Amy's son Antonio became cold and clammy, she thought his fever had finally broken. When her pediatrician told her to rush Antonio to the hospital, she found out how dangerous flu can be and how the vaccine could have helped. Learn More" (American Academy of Pediatrics, 2013).

19. See also Kuklinski et al. (2000) and Nyhan and Reifler (2010). However, Nyhan and Reifler (2013) provide evidence that some actions can be effective in correcting other legislators' use of misinformation.

20. A full video clip of this *Tavis Smiley* episode can be found at www.youtube.com/watch?v=KaIV2SHigJo (accessed Feb. 22, 2013). The show featured similar comments from other prominent black intellectuals including Cornel West and Farah Jasmine Griffin.

21. Polls also show that an increasing number of Americans, both black and white, have come to believe that Hill was telling the truth and Thomas was lying in the October 1991 hearings.

22. We used proportions rather than numerical counts in order to accommodate the wide variance in newsletter length. In 2004 the newsletters contained 7,176 paragraphs; the median number of paragraphs per newsletter was 23, with a range of 3–72 paragraphs. In 2006 the newsletters contained 5,011 paragraphs, with a median of 18 paragraphs per newsletter and a range of 3–60 paragraphs.

23. Actually, George W. Bush in 2000 was the most recent Republican to campaign for and win in an open presidential race. But we did not want to analyze him twice, so we used his most recent predecessor as a Republican candidate for an open office, that is, George H. W. Bush in 1988.

CHAPTER 7

1. For the full document, see *America and the Holocaust* [PBS], "The Film and More," Primary Sources, at *American Experience*,

n.d. www.pbs.org/wgbh/amex/holocaust/filmmore/reference/primary/newsusdept.html.

2. Whether the active use of misinformation was excusable is a different question. In a highly reputed book on the U.S. government's response to German anti-Semitism before and during World War II, David Wyman concludes that, although the growing savagery of Nazi policies toward Jews dismayed Roosevelt, in the end "the era's most prominent symbol of humanitarianism turned away from one of history's most compelling moral challenges" (Wyman 1985: 312–13; see also Katznelson 2013; Larson 2012).

3. Just to keep the record clear: we are not arguing that all American responses to the Holocaust were appropriate, or that all appropriate responses were made. Our point is narrower: individuals and states did eventually move from active misinformation and inactive information into active use of correct information upon coming to grips with the facts of the Nazis' extermination policy.

4. Conversely, there is a positive association between hearing misleading rhetoric from political elites about the imminent bankruptcy of Social Security and agreement with the claim that Social Security is in fact in dire straits (Holbrook 1999).

5. In keeping with this result, a substantial literature finds similarly that scientific literacy is not always associated with support for science or actions in accord with scientists' recommendations (Allum et al. 2008; Evans and Durant 1995).

6. Our use of Thaler and Sunstein's terminology and framework differs somewhat from their own presentation. They focus on the psychological mechanisms that lead people to make poor choices from the perspective of their own interests, whereas we focus on the failure to use facts or the use of pseudo-facts in the public arena. Nonetheless, we build our discussion on theirs and intend it to complement their much more extensive analysis.

7. A 1998 survey found that 70 percent of Americans endorsed fluoridation of community water, 12 percent were unsure, and 18 percent opposed it. The survey is possibly suspect because it was sponsored by the American Dental Association and is reported in CDC (1999a).

8. Martin (1989) provides a broad bibliography as well as a useful caution about assuming that opponents of fluoridation are simply misinformed. He has a point: in response to a relatively high proportion of adolescents with some staining of their teeth (dental fluorosis), the federal government recommended in 2011 a small reduction in the level of fluoride in drinking water. As

a result, communities with high natural levels of fluoride from mineral deposits might stop fluoridating their municipal water supplies.

To our knowledge, there is no good evidence that fluorosis is harmful or that fluoridation at appropriate levels is dangerous. For our analytical purposes, however, the actual value of fluoridation is not centrally important, since we are using this case to explore the strategy of ignoring what is widely agreed to be misinformation. For a good summary of health-related objections, see Committee to Coordinate Environmental Health and Related Programs (1991). On the politics of fluoridation, see Reilly (2007).

The fluoridation controversy is not limited to the United States, and opposition extends well beyond a few idiosyncratic extremists. Many European countries have stopped fluoridating the water supplies in part because toothpaste, in combination with mineral deposits, may now provide enough fluoride. These points too matter greatly for the politics and policy of fluoridation but not for *Do Facts Matter?*

9. The third objection is ideological or normative. In the 1950s and early 1960s, opponents charged that fluoridating the water supply was a plot by an overzealous federal government, the Communist Party, and perhaps the United Nations to weaken Americans and thereby conquer the United States: "The US Public Health Service has been corrupted by the Aluminum Trust. . . . The Soviet General Staff is very happy about it. Anytime they get ready to strike, and their 5th column takes over, there are tons and tons of this poison 'standing by' municipal and military water systems ready to be poured in within 15 minutes" (quoted in Reilly 2004: 138). That argument has disappeared, but some Americans continue to object, on religious or libertarian grounds, that fluoridation is forced mass medication.

10. This is a classic case of the impact of an intense minority on votes that have low visibility and low turnout, as in most referenda or votes for local public officials. Sapolsky (1968), however, argued that many fluoridation supporters become opponents after, or even as a result of, public debate on the topic.

11. That prediction may depend on how the current regulatory contest is resolved; see below in this section.

12. When Javitt et al. (2004) raised concerns, a consumer test cost $350,000; by 2013 it sold, with vastly more information, for $99. See Spector-Bagdady and Pike (2014: 13) for a quick review of criticisms; one expert described a firm's claim as "complete garbage"

(n111). Spector-Bagdady and Pike also provide examples of criticism from government agencies (nn85, 101, 106).

13. One author of *Do Facts Matter?* has 3 percent Neanderthal ancestry, within the normal range of Europeans, who average 2.7 percent Neanderthal genes.

14. Another example, from the *Washington Post:* "False Claims about a Health-Care Memo Persist Even after Testimony" (Kessler 2013). Gottfried et al. (2013) and Nyhan and Reifler (forthcoming), however, argue that fact checking can be effective in some circumstances. One reader of a draft of this book made a concrete suggestion: "Newspapers could usefully print short features—in boxes or sidebars or wherever—headed 'Lie of the day,' 'Dubious claim of the day,' or whatever. Obviously the approach would have to be evenhanded and nonpartisan, but if such items clearly were disinterested they might well be picked up on television, widely read blogs, etc., and disseminated more widely" (Anthony King, communication with authors, Feb. 3, 2014). We concur.

15. For other research on the importance of appealing to professional norms, see Gates and Brehm (1997), Jones-Correa (2008), Ramakrishnan and Lewis (2005), and Marrow (2011). We relegate this work to a footnote because these researchers focus on norms or choices for budgets, practices, or policies rather than on the determination and use of correct information.

16. Despite this sort of earnest effort, however, comparative effectiveness research "got caught up in the wider ideological struggle over national health reform" (Gerber and Patashnik 2011: abstract). As a result, its impact so far is slight.

17. All data in this paragraph are from NORC, May 1944. Additionally, in 1946 more than two-fifths of a national sample concurred that blacks are less intelligent than whites (NORC, May 1946). By 1956 the proportion of concurring whites was just over one-fifth (NORC, Jan., Apr. 21–30, 1956), and by 1999 the proportion was 1 percent, with an additional 4 percent who did not know (PSRA/*Newsweek*, Apr. 16–19, 1999).

18. For a similar result on earning a good living, see "Postwar Problems, Schools, Free Speech" (NORC, Nov. 1943). On Negro blood, see similar results in NORC, May 1946.

19. Myrdal's analysis is the classic statement of the societal importance of the inactive informed. The American dilemma is a

> problem in the heart of the [white] American. . . . It is the ever-raging conflict between, on the one hand, the valuations preserved on the general plane which we shall call the "American Creed," where

the American thinks, talks, and acts under the influence of high national and Christian precepts, and, on the other hand, the valuations on the specific planes of individual and group living, where personal and local interests; economic, social, and sexual jealousies; considerations of community prestige and conformity; group prejudice against particular persons or types of people; and all sorts of miscellaneous wants, impulses, and habits dominate his outlook. . . . The moral struggle goes on within people. (Myrdal 1944: xlvii)

Myrdal also recognized the category of active misinformed: *"People will twist and mutilate their beliefs of how social reality actually is.* In our study we encounter whole systems of firmly entrenched popular beliefs concerning the Negro and his relations to the larger society, which are bluntly false" (xlix). Nonetheless, "Scientific truth-seeking and education are slowly rectifying the beliefs and thereby also the valuations" (xlix). And about a thousand pages later, he insists that Americans know that "caste is wrong and should not be given recognition. . . . What America is constantly reaching for is democracy at home and abroad. The main trend in its history is the gradual realization of the American Creed" (1021).

We are not fully persuaded of this assertion (probably Myrdal was not either). But we offer *An American Dilemma* as the quintessential example of the aspiration to move people into the realm of informed activity through a combination of detailed empirical analysis, shaming, and exhortation.

20. For readers inclined to pursue this subject, current books with rather different views on this question include Hochschild et al. (2012), King and Smith (2011), Haney López (2014), and Glaser and Ryan (2013).

REFERENCES

Abramowitz, Alan. 2010. *The Disappearing Center: Engaged Citizens, Polarization, and American Democracy.* New Haven, Conn.: Yale University Press.
———. 2011. "The Race Factor: White Racial Attitudes and Opinions of Obama." *Sabato's Crystal Ball,* May 12. www.centerfor politics.org/crystalball/articles/AIA2011051201/.
Abravanel, Martin. 2002. "Public Knowledge of Fair Housing Law: Does It Protect against Housing Discrimination?" *Housing Policy Debate* 13 (3): 469–527.
Achen, Christopher, and Larry Bartels. 2006. "It Feels Like We're Thinking: The Rationalizing Voter and Electoral Democracy." Princeton, N.J.: Princeton University, Department of Politics.
Agency for Healthcare Research and Quality. c. 2012. "Evidence-Based Practice Centers (EPC) Program Overview." www.ahrq .gov/research/findings/evidence-based-reports/overview /index.html.
Alba, Richard, et al. 2005. "A Distorted Nation: Perceptions of Racial/Ethnic Group Sizes and Attitudes toward Immigrants and Other Minorities." *Social Forces* 84 (2): 901–19.
Allum, Nick, et al. 2008. "Science Knowledge and Attitudes across Cultures: A Meta-Analysis." *Public Understanding of Science* 17 (1): 35–54.
Alsop, Stewart. 1963. "Can Goldwater Win in '64?" *Saturday Evening Post,* Aug. 24, 19–25.
Althaus, Scott. 1998. "Information Effects in Collective Preferences." *American Political Science Review* 92 (3): 545–58.
———. 2003. *Collective Preferences in Democratic Politics: Opinion Surveys and the Will of the People.* New York: Cambridge University Press.
American Academy of Pediatrics. 2013. "Immunization," May 3. www2.aap.org/immunization/.
American Lung Association. 2010. *Trends in Tobacco Use.* American Lung Association, Epidemiology and Statistics Unit. www.lung

usa.org/finding-cures/our-research/trend-reports/Tobacco
-Trend-Report.pdf.

American Medical Association. c. 2013. "Pediatric Vaccination."
www.ama-assn.org/ama/pub/physician-resources/public
-health/vaccination-resources/pediatric-vaccination.page/.

American National Election Studies. c. 2013. University of Michigan, Survey Research Center. www.electionstudies.org.

Angelou, Maya. 1991. "I Dare to Hope." *New York Times*, Aug. 25.

Ansolabehere, Stephen, and David Konisky. 2012. "The American Public's Energy Choice." *Daedalus* 141 (2): 61–72.

Applebome, Peter. 1991. "Dr. King's Rights Group Backs Court Nominee." *New York Times*, Sept. 27.

Atlantic. 2013 [1963]. "Martin Luther King's 'Letter From Birmingham Jail.'" Apr. 16.

Aukofer, Frank. 1991. "Yale Dean's Support for Thomas Raises Eyebrows." *Milwaukee Journal*, Sept. 18.

Bailyn, Bernard. 1967. *The Ideological Origins of the American Revolution.* Cambridge, Mass.: Harvard University Press.

Balz, Dan. 1998. "The Story So Far: Week 4; All Eyes on Grand Jury, Lewinsky's Mother." *Washington Post*, Feb. 15.

Bartels, Larry. 1996. "Uninformed Votes: Information Effects in Presidential Elections." *American Journal of Political Science* 40 (1): 194–230.

———. 2002. "Beyond the Running Tally: Partisan Bias in Political Perceptions." *Political Behavior* 24 (2): 117–49.

———. 2008. "The Irrational Electorate." *Wilson Quarterly* 28 (4): 44–50.

Baxter, Teri. Forthcoming. "Tort Liability for Parents Who Choose Not to Vaccinate Their Children and Whose Unvaccinated Children Infect Others." *University of Cincinnati Law Review.*

Bechtel, Michael, et al. Forthcoming. "Reality Bites: The Limits of Framing Effects for Salient and Contested Policy Issues." *Political Science Research Methods.*

Bennett, Stephen. 1989. "Trends in Americans' Political Information, 1967–1987." *American Politics Quarterly* 17 (4): 422–35.

———. 1994. "Changing Levels of Political Information in 1988 and 1990." *Political Behavior* 16 (1): 1–20.

Berinsky, Adam. 2005. *Silent Voices: Public Opinion and Political Participation in America.* Princeton. N.J.: Princeton University Press.

———. 2012a. "Public Support for Vaccination Remains Strong," Dec. 5. http://today.yougov.com/news/2012/12/05/public
-support-vaccination-remains-strong.

———. 2012b. "Rumors, Truths, and Reality: A Study of Political Misinformation." Cambridge, Mass.: MIT, Political Science Department.

Berke, Richard, and Janet Elder. 1998. "Testing of a President: The Public; Keep Clinton in Office, Most Say in Poll, but His Image Is Eroding." *New York Times*, Sept. 16.

Bobo, Lawrence, and James Kluegel. 1993. "Opposition to Race Targeting: Self-Interest, Stratification Ideology, or Racial Attitudes?" *American Sociological Review* 58 (4): 443–64.

Booz Allen Hamilton. c. 2012. Market Trends in Genetic Services, www.boozallen.com/media/file/GeneticTesting_VP.pdf.

Borick, Christopher, and Barry Rabe. 2012. "Belief in Global Warming on the Rebound: National Survey of American Public Opinion on Climate Change." *Issues in Governance Studies* 44 (Feb. 28).

Boykoff, Maxwell, and Julia Boykoff. 2004. "Balance as Bias: Global Warming and the US Prestige Press." *Global Environmental Change* 14 (2): 125–36.

Brader, Ted. 2005. "Striking a Responsive Chord: How Political Ads Motivate and Persuade Voters by Appealing to Emotions." *American Journal of Political Science* 49 (2): 388–405.

Braiker, Brian. 2007. "Dunce-Cap Nation." *Newsweek*, June 23.

Bruni, Frank. 2013. "America the Clueless." *New York Times*, May 11.

Bullock, John. 2011. "Elite Influence on Public Opinion in an Informed Electorate." *American Political Science Review* 105 (3): 496–515.

Bullock, John, et al. 2013. "Partisan Bias in Factual Beliefs About Politics." New Haven, Conn.: Yale University, Department of Political Science.

Bureau of Justice Statistics. 1992. "Crime and the Nation's Households, 1991." *Alaska Justice Forum* 9 (2): 2–4.

———. 2013. NCVS Victimization Analysis Tool. www.bjs.gov/index.cfm?ty=nvat.

Burnham, Margaret. 1992. "The Supreme Court Appointment Process and the Politics of Race and Sex." In *Race-ing Justice, En-Gendering Power: Essays on Anita Hill, Clarence Thomas, and the Construction of Social Reality*, ed. Toni Morrison, 290–322. New York: Pantheon Books.

Busby, Robert. 2001. *Defending the American Presidency: Clinton and the Lewinsky Scandal*. New York: Palgrave.

Bush, George. 1991. The President's News Conference in Kennebunkport, Maine, American Presidency Project, July 1. www.presidency.ucsb.edu/ws/index.php?pid=29651#axzz1V9cxvvvt.

Caldeira, Greg, and Charles Smith. 1996. "Campaigning for the Supreme Court: The Dynamics of Public Opinion on the Thomas Nomination." *Journal of Politics* 58 (3): 655–81.

Caldwell, Christopher. 2011. "The Politics of Contempt." *Newsweek*, May 1.

Caplan, Arthur, et al. 2012. "Free to Choose but Liable for the Consequences: Should Non-Vaccinators Be Penalized for the Harm They Do?" *Journal of Law, Medicine, and Ethics* 40 (3): 606–11.

Carney, Dana, et al. 2008. "The Secret Lives of Liberals and Conservatives: Personality Profiles, Interaction Styles, and the Things They Leave Behind." *Political Psychology* 29 (6): 807–40.

Casazza, Krista, et al. 2013. "Myths, Presumptions, and Facts about Obesity." *New England Journal of Medicine* 368 (5): 446–54.

Catalogue of Federal Domestic Assistance. c. 2010. "Affordable Care Act (ACA) Personal Responsibility Education Program." www.cfda.gov/?s=program&mode=form&tab=step1&id=e90 85baafbd785d09c9e4e52f9ec4ac4.

CDC (Centers for Disease Control and Prevention). 1999a. "Achievements in Public Health, 1900–1999: Fluoridation of Drinking Water to Prevent Dental Caries." *MMWR Weekly* 48 (41).

———. 1999b. "Ten Great Public Health Achievements—United States, 1900–1999." *MMWR Weekly* 48 (12): 241–43.

———. 2011. "Measles Imported by Returning U.S. Travelers Aged 6–23 Months, 2001–2011." *MMWR* 60 (13): 397–400.

———. 2013a. "Estimated Vaccination Coverage with Individual Vaccines and Selected Vaccination Series." www.cdc.gov/vaccines/imz-managers/coverage/nis/child/tables/12/tab03_antigen_state_2012.pdf.

———. 2013b. "The School Entry Immunization Assessment Report: Reporting Menu for School Year 2010–2011." *School Vaccination Coverage Reports*, Apr. 11. www2.cdc.gov/nip/school surv/rptgmenu.asp.

———. 2014. "Current Cigarette Smoking among Adults—United States, 2005–2012." *MMWR* 63 (2): 29–34.

Ceaser, James. 2010. "The Great Repudiation." *Claremont Review of Books* 10 (4): 6–9.

Center for Climate Change Communication. 2008. "What Are Americans Thinking and Doing about Global Warming: Results of a National Household Survey." www.climatechange communication.org/report/what-are-americans-thinking -and-doing-about-global-warming-results-national-household -survey.

Chen, Sanny, et al. 2011. "Health Care–Associated Measles Outbreak in the United States after an Importation: Challenges and Economic Impact." *Journal of Infectious Diseases* 203 (11): 1517–25.

Christakis, Nicholas, and James Fowler. 2007. "The Spread of Obesity in a Large Social Network over 32 Years." *New England Journal of Medicine* 357 (4): 370–79.

Climate Silence. 2012. "Obama's Descent into Climate Silence: Data." http://climatesilence.org/data/.

CNN. 1998. "A Chronology: Key Moments in the Clinton-Lewinsky Saga." www.cnn.com/ALLPOLITICS/1998/resources/lewinsky/timeline/.

Committee on House Administration. 2009. "Regulations on the Use of the Congressional Frank by Members of the House of Representatives." http://cha.house.gov/sites/republicans.cha.house.gov/files/documents/franking_docs/franking_manual.pdf.

Committee to Coordinate Environmental Health and Related Programs. 1991. *Review of Fluoride Benefits and Risks: Report of the Ad Hoc Committee on Fluoride.* Washington, D.C.: U.S. Department of Health and Human Services, Public Health Service.

Congressional Research Service. 2011. *Qualifications for President and the "Natural Born" Citizenship Eligibility Requirement.* Washington, D.C.: CRS. www.fas.org/sgp/crs/misc/R42097.pdf.

Cook, Fay Lomax, et al. 2010. "Trusting What You Know: Information, Knowledge, and Confidence in Social Security." *Journal of Politics* 72 (7): 397–412.

Cook, Timothy. 1989. *Making Laws and Making News.* Washington, D.C.: Brookings Institution Press.

Cooper, Joel. 2007. *Cognitive Dissonance: 50 Years of a Classic Theory.* London: Sage.

Cooper, Michael. 2012. "Facts Take a Beating in Acceptance Speeches." *New York Times,* Aug. 31.

Cosgrove, Alexandra. 2009. "A Clinton Timeline." www.cbsnews.com/2100–250_162–262484.html.

CounterPunch Wire. 2003. "Weapons of Mass Destruction: Who Said What When." www.counterpunch.org/2003/05/29/weapons-of-mass-destruction-who-said-what-when/.

CoverMissouri.org. 2011. "The Patient Protection and Affordable Care Act: Health Literacy Provisions." http://covermissouri.org/ACATopics/ACA-Literacy.pdf.

Coyle, Kevin. 1998. "Environmental Myths and Misperceptions." *Polling Report* 14: 2–4.

Crabtree, Steve. 1999. "New Poll Gauges Americans' General Knowledge Levels." *Gallup News Service*. www.gallup.com /poll/3742/new-poll-gauges-americans-general-knowledge -levels.aspx.

Crain, Robert, et al. 1969. *The Politics of Community Conflict: The Fluoridation Decision*. Indianapolis, Ind.: Bobbs-Merrill.

Darr, Joshua, and Matthew Levendusky. 2014. "Relying on the Ground Game: The Placement and Effect of Campaign Field Offices." *American Politics Research* 42 (3): 529–48.

Davis, David Brion, ed. 2008. *The Fear of Conspiracy: Images of Un-American Subversion from the Revolution to the Present*. Ithaca, N.Y.: Cornell University Press.

Dawson, Michael. 1994. *Behind the Mule: Race and Class in African-American Politics*. Princeton, N.J.: Princeton University Press.

Delli Carpini, Michael, and Scott Keeter. 1993. "Measuring Political Knowledge: Putting First Things First." *American Journal of Political Science* 37 (4): 1179–206.

———. 1996. *What Americans Know about Politics and Why It Matters*. New Haven, Conn.: Yale University Press.

Delli Carpini, Michael, et al. 2004. "Public Deliberations, Discursive Participation and Citizen Engagement: A Review of the Empirical Literature." *Annual Review of Political Science* 7: 315–44.

Dempsey, Amanda, et al. 2011. "Alternative Vaccination Schedule Preferences among Parents of Young Children." *Pediatrics* 128 (5): 848–56.

De Osuna, Jennifer, et al. 2004. "Qualitative and Quantitative Effects of Surprise: (Mis)Estimates, Rationales, and Feedback-Induced Preferences while Considering Abortion." In *Proceedings of the Twenty-Sixth Annual Conference of the Cognitive Science Society*, ed. Ken Forbus, et al., 422–27. Mahwah, N.J.: Erlbaum.

DeStefano, Frank. 2007. "Vaccines and Autism: Evidence Does Not Support a Causal Association." *Clinical Pharmacology and Therapeutics* 82 (6): 756–59.

Dickerson, John. 2012. "Why Romney Never Saw It Coming." *Slate.com*, Nov. 9. www.slate.com/articles/news_and_politics /politics/2012/11/why_romney_was_surprised_to_lose_his _campaign_had_the_wrong_numbers_bad.html.

Downs, Anthony. 1957. *An Economic Theory of Democracy*. New York: Harper.

Drew, Elizabeth. 2012. "Determined to Vote!" *New York Review of Books*, Dec. 20, 26–28.

Druckman, James. 2012. "The Politics of Motivation." *Critical Review* 24 (2): 199–216.

Druckman, James, and Toby Bolsen. 2011. "Framing, Motivated Reasoning, and Opinions about Emergent Technologies." *Journal of Communication* 61 (4): 659–88.

Druckman, James, and Thomas Leeper. 2012. "Is Public Opinion Stable? Resolving the Micro/Macro Disconnect in Studies of Public Opinion." *Daedalus* 141: 50–68.

Druckman, James, et al. 2010. "Competing Rhetoric over Time: Frames versus Cues." *Journal of Politics* 72 (1): 136–48.

Druckman, James, et al. 2012. "When and How Party Identification Works." Evanston, Ill.: Northwestern University, Department of Political Science.

Druckman, James, et al. 2013. "How Elite Partisan Polarization Affects Public Opinion Formation." *American Political Science Review* 107 (1): 57–79.

Dugan, Andrew. 2014. "Americans Most Likely to Say Global Warming Is Exaggerated." *Gallup: Politics*, Apr. 22.

Dunlap, Riley, and Aaron McCright. 2008. "A Widening Gap: Republican and Democratic Views on Climate Change." *Environment: Science and Policy for Sustainable Development* 50 (5): 26–35.

Dwyer, Devin. 2012. "Obama Camp Trumpets Massive Ground Game on Election Eve." *ABC News*, Nov. 3.

Economist. 2012. "The Melting North." June 16, 3–5.

———. 2013. "Stubborn Things." Oct. 5, 12.

Edsall, Thomas, and E. J. Dionne. 1991. "Core Democratic Constituencies Split: Support for Nominee Reflects Power of Black Vote in the South." *Washington Post*, Oct. 16, A1.

Eichenwald, Kurt. 2012. *500 Days: Secrets and Lies in the Terror Wars.* New York: Touchstone/Simon and Schuster.

Elkin, Stephen, and Karol Soltan, eds. 1999. *Citizen Competence and Democratic Institutions.* University Park: Pennsylvania State University Press.

Epstein, Jennifer. 2012. "Obama Hits Romney on Seamus." *Politico .com*, Aug. 14. www.politico.com/politico44/2012/08/obama -hits-romney-on-seamus-132081.html.

Erskine, Hazel. 1963. "The Polls: Textbook Knowledge." *Public Opinion Quarterly* 27 (1): 133–41.

Evans, Geoffrey, and John Durant. 1995. "The Relationship between Knowledge and Attitudes in the Public Understanding of Science in Britain." *Public Understanding of Science* 4 (1): 57–74.

FactCheck.org. c. 2012. "About Us." www.factcheck.org/spin detectors/about/.

Fadiman, Anne. 1998. *The Spirit Catches You and You Fall Down: A Hmong Child, Her American Doctors, and the Collision of Two Cultures.* New York: Farrar, Straus and Giroux.

Farrar, Cynthia, et al. 2010. "Disaggregating Deliberation's Effects: An Experiment within a Deliberative Poll." *British Journal of Political Science* 40 (2): 333–47.

Fenno, Richard. 1978. *Home Style: House Members in Their Districts.* Boston: Little, Brown.

Festinger, Leon. 1957. *A Theory of Cognitive Dissonance.* Palo Alto, Calif.: Stanford University Press.

Fiorina, Morris. 1981. *Retrospective Voting in American National Elections.* New Haven, Conn.: Yale University Press.

First Impressions. 2009. "Liability for Exercising Personal Belief Exemptions from Vaccination." *Michigan Law Review* 107 (3).

Fischle, Mark. 2000. "Mass Response to the Lewinsky Scandal: Motivated Reasoning or Bayesian Updating?" *Political Psychology* 21 (1): 135–59.

Fish, Stanley. 1982. *Is There a Text in This Class? The Authority of Interpretive Communities.* Cambridge, Mass.: Harvard University Press.

Fishkin, James. 2009. *When the People Speak: Deliberative Democracy and Public Consultation.* New York: Oxford University Press.

Fong, Christina. 2001. "Social Preferences, Self-Interest, and the Demand for Redistribution." *Journal of Public Economics* 82 (2): 225–46.

Frankenberg, Erica, and Rebecca Jacobsen. 2011. "The Polls—Trends: School Integration Polls." *Public Opinion Quarterly* 75 (4): 788–811.

Frankovic, Kathleen, and Joyce Gelb. 1992. "Public Opinion and the Thomas Nomination." *PS: Political Science and Politics* 25 (3): 481–84.

Freed, Gary, et al. 2011. "Sources and Perceived Credibility of Vaccine-Safety Information for Parents." *Pediatrics* 127 (Supplement 1): S107–S112.

Friedman, Jeffrey. 2006a. "Public Competence in Normative and Positive Theory: Neglected Implications of 'The Nature of Belief Systems in Mass Publics.'" *Critical Review* 18 (1–3): i–xliii.

———. 2006b. "Special Issue on Democratic Competence." *Critical Review* 18 (1–3): 1–360.

Friedman, Jeffrey, and Shterna Friedman, eds. 2012. *Political Knowledge.* New York: Routledge.

Friedman, Lauren. 2014. "Vaccination Rates at Some NYC Private Schools Are Worse Than Those of Developing Countries." *Business Insider*, Mar 31. www.businessinsider.com/vaccination-rates-at-nyc-private-schools-2014-3.

Fung, Archon, et al. 2007. *Full Disclosure: The Perils and Promise of Transparency*. New York: Cambridge University Press.

Gaines, Brian, et al. 2007. "Same Facts, Different Interpretations: Partisan Motivation and Opinion on Iraq." *Journal of Politics* 69 (4): 957–74.

Galewitz, Phil. 2013. "Obamacare 'Navigators' Hit GOP Hurdles: 17 States Try to Restrict Guides to New Health Laws." *USA Today*, Sept. 23.

Gallup Organization. 2007. "Americans Assess What They Can Do to Reduce Global Warming." Mar. 23–25. www.gallup.com/poll/27298/Americans-Assess-What-They-Can-Reduce-Global-Warming.aspx.

Gallup Poll. 2013. "Presidential Approval Ratings—Bill Clinton." www.gallup.com/poll/116584/presidential-approval-ratings-bill-clinton.aspx.

Galston, William. 2001. "Political Knowledge, Political Engagement, and Civic Education." In *Annual Review of Political Science* 4: 217–34.

Gara, Tom. 2013. "The Letter: FDA Orders 23andMe to Halt Sales." *Wall Street Journal*, Nov. 25. http://blogs.wsj.com/corporate-intelligence/2013/11/25/the-letter-fda-orders-23andme-to-halt-sales/.

Garcia Bedolla, Lisa, and Melissa Michelson. 2012. *Mobilizing Inclusion: Transforming the Electorate through Get-out-the-Vote Campaigns*. New Haven, Conn.: Yale University Press.

Gates, Scott, and John Brehm. 1997. *Working, Shirking, and Sabotage: Bureaucratic Response to a Democratic Public*. Ann Arbor: University of Michigan Press.

Gawande, Atul. 2013. "Slow Ideas." *New Yorker*, July 29, 36–45.

Gelman, Andrew. 2009. *Red State, Blue State, Rich State, Poor State: Why Americans Vote the Way They Do*. Princeton, N.J.: Princeton University Press.

Gelman, Andrew, and Gary King. 1993. "Why Are American Presidential Election Campaign Polls So Variable When Votes Are So Predictable?" *British Journal of Political Science* 23 (1): 409–51.

General Social Survey. c. 2013. University of Chicago, National Opinion Research Center. www3.norc.org/gss+website/.

Gerber, Alan, and Donald Green. 1999. "Misperceptions about Perceptual Bias." *Annual Review of Political Science* 2: 189–210.

Gerber, Alan, and Eric Patashnik. 2011. "The Politicization of Evidence-Based Medicine: The Limits of Pragmatic Problem Solving in an Era of Polarization." *California Journal of Politics and Policy* 3 (4).

Gerber, Alan, et al. 2011. "The Persuasive Effects of Direct Mail: A Regression Discontinuity-Based Approach." *Journal of Politics* 73 (1): 140–55.

Gershkoff, Amy, and Shana Kushner. 2005. "Shaping Public Opinion: The 9/11-Iraq Connection in the Bush Administration's Rhetoric." *Perspectives on Politics* 3 (3): 525–37.

Gilbert, Daniel, et al. 1993. "You Can't Not Believe Everything You Read: Attitudes and Social Cognition." *Journal of Personality and Social Psychology* 65 (2): 221–33.

Gilens, Martin. 2001. "Political Ignorance and Collective Policy Preferences." *American Political Science Review* 95 (2): 379–96.

———. 2012. *Affluence and Influence: Economic Inequality and Political Power in America*. Princeton, N.J.: Princeton University Press.

Gilens, Martin, et al. 2007. "The Mass Media and the Public's Assessments of Presidential Candidates, 1952–2000." *Journal of Politics* 69 (4): 1160–75.

Gimpel, James, and Lewis Ringel. 1995. "Understanding Court Nominee Evaluation and Approval: Mass Opinion in the Bork and Thomas Cases." *Political Behavior* 17 (2): 135–53.

Glaser, James, and Timothy Ryan. 2013. *Changing Minds, If Not Hearts: Political Remedies for Racial Conflict*. Philadelphia: University of Pennsylvania Press.

Goren, Paul. 2005. "Party Identification and Core Political Values." *American Journal of Political Science* 49 (4): 881–96.

Gottfried, Jeffrey, et al. 2013. "Did Fact Checking Matter in the 2012 Presidential Campaign?" *American Behavioral Scientist* 57 (11): 1558–67.

Green, Donald, and Alan Gerber. 2008. *Get Out the Vote: How to Increase Voter Turnout*, 2nd ed. Washington, D.C.: Brookings Institution Press.

Green, Donald, et al. 2004. *Partisan Hearts and Minds*. New Haven, Conn.: Yale University Press.

Green, Donald, et al. 2011. "Does Knowledge of Constitutional Principles Increase Support for Civil Liberties? Results from a Randomized Field Experiment." *Journal of Politics* 73 (2): 463–76.

Green, Joshua. 2012. "The Birthers' Blue Beginnings." *Boston Globe*, May 30, A15.

Green Nature. 2011. "Paper Recycling in the United States." http://greennature.com/article14.html.

Gupta, Sanjay. 2011. "Dr. Sanjay Gupta Confronts Autism Study Doctor." *CBS Evening News*, Jan. 6.

Haidt, Jonathan. 2013. *The Righteous Mind: Why Good People Are Divided by Politics and Religion*. New York: Vintage.

Hajnal, Zoltan. 2006. *Changing White Attitudes toward Black Political Leadership*. New York: Cambridge University Press.

Halpern, Diane. 1997. "When Students' Conceptual Grasp Clashes with Their Professors.'" *Chronicle of Higher Education*, Mar. 14.

Haney López, Ian. 2014. *Dog Whistle Politics: How Coded Racial Appeals Have Reinvented Racism and Wrecked the Middle Class*. New York: Oxford University Press.

Hayes, Danny. 2010. "Parties and the Media: Getting Messages to Voters." In *New Directions in American Political Parties*, ed. Jeffrey Stonecash, 44–62. New York: Routledge.

Hayes, Danny, and Matt Guardino. 2013. *Influence from Abroad: Foreign Voices, the Media, and U.S. Public Opinion*. New York: Cambridge University Press.

Health Affairs. 2013. Health Policy Brief: "Navigators and Assisters." Oct. 31. www.healthaffairs.org/healthpolicybriefs/brief.php?brief_id=101.

Hehman, Eric, et al. 2011. "Evaluations of Presidential Performance: Race, Prejudice, and Perceptions." *Journal of Experimental Social Psychology* 47 (2): 430–35.

Heilprin, John. 2011. "Europe, Especially France, Hit by Measles Outbreak." *Associated Press*, Apr. 21.

Henderson, Michael, and D. Sunshine Hillygus. 2011. "The Dynamics of Health Care Attitudes 2008–2010: Partisanship, Self-Interest, and Racial Resentment." *Journal of Health Politics, Policy, and Law* 36 (6): 945–60.

Highton, Benjamin, and Cindy Kam. 2011. "The Long-Term Dynamics of Partisanship and Issue Orientations." *Journal of Politics* 73 (1): 202–15.

Hillygus, D. Sunshine, and Todd Shields. 2009. *The Persuadable Voter: Wedge Issues in Presidential Campaigns*. Princeton, N.J.: Princeton University Press.

Hirsch, E. D., Jr. 1988. *Cultural Literacy: What Every American Needs to Know*. New York: Vintage.

Hochschild, Jennifer. 1984. *The New American Dilemma: Liberal Democracy and School Desegregation.* New Haven, Conn.: Yale University Press.

———. 2011. "How, If at All, Is Racial and Ethnic Stratification Changing, and What Should We Do about It?" In *Race, Reform, and Regulation of the Electoral Process: Recurring Puzzles in American Democracy,* ed. Heather Gerken et al., 7–16. New York: Cambridge University Press.

———. 2012. "Should the Mass Public Follow Elite Opinion? It Depends . . ." [Essay on John Zaller, *The Nature and Origins of Mass Opinion*]. *Critical Review* 24 (4): 527–43.

Hochschild, Jennifer, and Monica Herk. 1990. "'Yes, but . . .': Principles and Caveats in American Racial Attitudes." In *Majorities and Minorities (Nomos 32),* ed. John Chapman and Alan Wertheimer, 308–35. New York: New York University Press.

Hochschild, Jennifer, Vesla Weaver, and Traci Burch. 2012. *Creating a New Racial Order: How Immigration, Multiracialism, Genomics, and the Young Can Remake Race in America.* Princeton, N.J.: Princeton University Press.

Hofstadter, Richard. 2008. *The Paranoid Style in American Politics,* Reprint ed. New York: Vintage.

Holbrook, Thomas. 1999. "Political Learning from Presidential Debates." *Political Behavior* 21 (1): 67–89.

Holliday, Matt. 2009. "Sarah Palin Turning to Facebook to Spread Her Political Views." *InsideFacebook,* Aug. 18.

Holsti, Ole. 2011. *American Public Opinion on the Iraq War.* Ann Arbor: University of Michigan Press.

Hooks, Benjamin, et al. 1991–92. "The NAACP Position on Clarence Thomas." *Black Scholar* 22 (1/2): 144–50.

Howell, William, et al. 2011. "Meeting of the Minds: Results from the Fourth Annual *Education Next*–PEPG Survey." *Education Next* 11 (1): 20–31.

Huckfeldt, Robert, and John Sprague. 1995. *Citizens, Politics, and Social Communication: Information and Influence in an Election Campaign.* New York: Cambridge University Press.

Hulse, Carl. 2013. "Lesson Is Seen in Failure of Law on Medicare in 1989." *New York Times,* Nov. 17.

Hutchings, Vincent. 2003. *Public Opinion and Democratic Accountability: How Citizens Learn about Politics.* Princeton, N.J.: Princeton University Press.

Iraq Body Count. 2013. "The War in Iraq: 10 Years and Counting." Press Release 19, Mar. 19. www.iraqbodycount.org/analysis /numbers/ten-years/.

Issenberg, Sasha. 2012. *The Victory Lab: The Secret Science of Winning Campaigns.* New York: Crown.

Jackson, Jacquelyne. 1991. "'Them against Us': Anita Hill v. Clarence Thomas." *Black Scholar* 22 (1/2): 49–52.

Jacobson, Gary. 2011. "The President, the Tea Party, and Voting Behavior in 2010: Insights from the Cooperative Congressional Election Study." Annual meeting of the American Political Science Association. Seattle, Wash.

Jasanoff, Sheila. 2013. "A Mirror for Science." *Public Understanding of Science* 23 (1): 21–26.

Javitt, Gail, et al. 2004. "Direct-to-Consumer Genetic Tests, Government Oversight, and the First Amendment: What the Government Can (and Can't) Do to Protect the Public's Health." *Oklahoma Law Review* 57(2): 251–302.

Jefferson, Thomas. 1779. "A Bill for the More General Diffusion of Knowledge," in *Public Papers*, Electronic Text Center, University of Virginia Library, Charlottesville.

Jerit, Jennifer, et al. 2006. "Citizens, Knowledge, and the Information Environment." *American Journal of Political Science* 50 (2): 266–82.

Jones-Correa, Michael. 2008. "Immigrant Incorporation in Suburbia: Spatial Sorting, Ethnic Mobilization, and Receiving Institutions." In *Immigration and Integration in Urban Communities: Renegotiating the City*, ed. Lisa Hanley et al., 19–48. Baltimore, Md.: Johns Hopkins University Press.

Just, Marion, and Ann Crigler. 2000. "Leadership Image-Building: After Clinton and Watergate." *Political Psychology* 21 (1): 179–98.

Kadushin, Charles. 2011. *Understanding Social Networks: Theories, Concepts, and Findings.* New York: Oxford University Press.

Kahan, Dan. 2013. "Ideology, Motivated Reasoning, and Cognitive Reflection." *Judgment and Decision Making* 8 (4): 407–24.

Kahan, Dan, et al. 2013. "Motivated Numeracy and Enlightened Self-Government." New Haven, Conn.: Yale University Law School.

Kahlenberg, Richard. 2001. *All Together Now: Creating Middle Class Schools through Public School Choice.* Washington, D.C.: Brookings Institution Press.

Kalb, Marvin. 2001. *One Scandalous Story: Clinton, Lewinsky, and Thirteen Days That Tarnished American Journalism.* New York: Free Press.

Kam, Cindy, and Jennifer Ramos. 2008. "Joining and Leaving the Rally: Understanding the Surge and Decline in Presidential

Approval following 9/11." *Public Opinion Quarterly* 72 (4): 619–50.

Kaplowitz, Stan, et al. 2003. "How Accurate Are Perceptions of Social Statistics about Blacks and Whites? Effects of Race and Education." *Public Opinion Quarterly* 67 (2): 237–43.

Katznelson, Ira. 2013. "The Failure to Rescue." *New Republic,* July 1, 50–55.

Kauffman, Bill. 1987. "Clarence Thomas." *Reason,* Nov. 1.

Keeter, Scott. 1996. "Origins of the Disjuncture of Perception and Reality: The Cases of Racial Equality and Environmental Protection." Richmond: Virginia Commonwealth University, Department of Political Science and Public Administration.

Kessler, Glenn. 2013. "The Fact Checker: False Claims about a Health-Care Memo Persist Even after Testimony." *Washington Post,* Nov. 18.

Keyssar, Alexander. 2000. *The Right to Vote: The Contested History of Democracy in the United States.* New York: Basic Books.

Kilpatrick, James. 1992. "Justice Thomas Is Off to a Good Start after a Solidly Conservative First Term." *Atlanta Journal and Constitution,* July 29.

Kinder, Donald. 1998. "Opinion and Action in the Realm of Politics." In *Handbook of Social Psychology,* 4th ed, ed. Daniel Gilbert et al., 778–867. Boston: McGraw-Hill.

Kinder, Donald, and D. Roderick Kiewiet. 1981. "Sociotropic Politics: The American Case." *British Journal of Political Science* 11 (2): 129–61.

Kinder, Donald, and Lynn Sanders. 1996. *Divided by Color: Racial Politics and Democratic Ideals.* Chicago: University of Chicago Press.

Kinder, Donald, and Nicholas Winter. 2001. "Exploring the Racial Divide: Blacks, Whites, and Opinion on National Policy." *American Journal of Political Science* 45 (2): 439–56.

King, Desmond, and Rogers Smith. 2011. *Still a House Divided: Race and Politics in Obama's America.* Princeton, N.J.: Princeton University Press.

Krauthammer, Charles. 1998. "Clinton Should Resign for 'Low Crimes.'" *Washington Post,* Sept. 21.

Kriner, Douglas, and Andrew Reeves. 2014. "Responsive Partisanship: Public Support for the Clinton and Obama Health Care Plans." *Journal of Health Politics, Policy and Law* 39 (4).

Krosnick, Jon. 2010. "The Climate Majority." *New York Times,* June 8.

Krosnick, Jon, et al. 2006. "The Origins and Consequences of Democratic Citizens' Policy Agendas: A Study of Popular Concern about Global Warming." *Climate Change* 77 (1–2): 7–43.

Krupnikov, Yanna, et al. 2006. "Public Ignorance and Estate Tax Repeal: The Effect of Partisan Differences and Survey Incentives." *National Tax Journal* 59 (3): 345–437.

Kuklinski, James, and Paul Quirk. 2000. "Reconsidering the Rational Public: Cognition, Heuristics, and Mass Opinion." In *Elements of Reason*, ed. Arthur Lupia et al., 153–82. New York: Cambridge University Press.

Kuklinski, James, et al. 2000. "Misinformation and the Currency of Democratic Citizenship." *Journal of Politics* 62 (3): 791–816.

Kull, Steven, et al. 2003–2004. "Misperceptions, the Media, and the Iraq War." *Political Science Quarterly* 118 (4): 569–98.

Kuralt, Charles. 1992a. "Sunday Morning: Rita Braver Discusses the 'New' Supreme Court Appointees; New Decisions on Abortion," CBS News Transcripts, July 5.

———. 1992b. "Sunday Morning: Black Leaders of Today in the US." CBS News Transcripts, July 26.

LaBarre, Suzanne. 2013. "Why We're Shutting Off Our Comments." *PopularScience.com*, Sept. 24. www.popsci.com/science/article/2013–09/why-were-shutting-our-comments.

Lancet. 2010. "Retraction—Ileal-Lymphoid-Nodular Hyperplasia, Non-Specific Colitis, and Pervasive Developmental Disorder in Children," *Lancet* 375 (9713): 445.

Langer, Gary. 2003. "Most Say Bush Made Good Case for War." *ABC News Poll Analysis*, Jan. 29.

———. 2010. "This I Believe." *ABC News Online*, Aug. 30. http://blogs.abcnews.com/thenumbers/2010/08/this-i-believe.html.

Larson, Erik. 2012. *In the Garden of Beasts: Love, Terror, and an American Family in Hitler's Berlin.* New York: Broadway Books.

Lavender, Paige. 2013. "Donald Trump Floats Completely Insane Birther Conspiracy after Health Official's Death." *Huffington Post: Politics*, Dec. 12. www.huffingtonpost.com/2013/12/12/donald-trump-birther_n_4435621.html.

Lawrence, Eric, and John Sides. 2009. "Does What You Think You Know Affect What You Think? Explaining Public Spending Preferences." Annual meeting of the Midwest Political Science Association. Chicago, Ill.

———. 2014. "The Consequences of Political Innumeracy." *Research and Politics* 1 (2).

Lebo, Matthew, and Daniel Cassino. 2007. "The Aggregated Consequences of Motivated Reasoning and the Dynamics of Partisan Presidential Approval." *Political Psychology* 26 (6): 719–46.

Lewandowsky, Stephan, et al. 2013. "NASA Faked the Moon
Landing, Therefore (Climate) Science Is a Hoax: An Anatomy
of the Motivated Rejection of Science." *Psychological Science* 24
(5): 622–33.

Lewis-Beck, Michael, et al. 2008. *The American Voter Revisited.* Ann
Arbor: University of Michigan Press.

Lipinski, Daniel. 2001. "The Effect of Messages Communicated by
Members of Congress: The Impact of Publicizing Votes." *Legislative Studies Quarterly* 26 (1): 81–100.

————. 2004. *Congressional Communications: Content and Consequences.* Ann Arbor: University of Michigan Press.

Lippmann, Walter. 1955. *Essays in the Public Philosophy.* Boston:
Little, Brown.

Lipset, Seymour. 1997. *American Exceptionalism: A Double-Edged
Sword.* New York: Norton.

Lodge, Milton, and Charles Taber. 2005. "The Automaticity of Affect for Political Leaders, Groups, and Issues: An Experimental
Test of the Hot Cognition Hypothesis." *Political Psychology* 26
(3): 455–82.

————. 2013. *The Rationalizing Voter.* New York: Cambridge University Press.

Los Angeles Times. 1991. "Confirmation Is Justifiable: Withdrawal Is
the Wiser Course." *Los Angeles Times,* Oct. 15.

Lupia, Arthur. 2006. "How Elitism Undermines the Study of Voter
Competence." *Critical Review* 18 (1–3): 217–32.

Lupia, Arthur, and Matthew McCubbins. 1998. *The Democratic Dilemma: Can Citizens Learn What They Need to Know?* New York:
Cambridge University Press.

Lupia, Arthur, et al. 2007. "Were Bush Tax Cut Supporters 'Simply Ignorant'? A Second Look at Conservatives and Liberals in
'Homer Gets a Tax Cut.'" *Perspectives on Politics* 5 (4): 773–84.

Luskin, Robert, and John Bullock. 2011. "'Don't Know' Means
'Don't Know': DK Responses and the Public's Level of Political
Knowledge." *Journal of Politics* 73 (2): 547–57.

Lyotard, Jean-François. 1984. *The Postmodern Condition: A Report on
Knowledge.* Minneapolis: University of Minnesota Press.

Malthus, Thomas. 2008 [1798]. *An Essay on the Principle of Population.* New York: Oxford University Press.

Mann, Thomas, and Norman Ornstein. 2013. *It's Even Worse Than It Looks: How the American Constitutional System Collided with the New Politics of Extremism.* New York: Basic Books.

Marable, Manning. 1992. "Clarence Thomas and the Crisis of Black Political Culture." In *Race-ing Justice, En-Gendering Power: Essays on Anita Hill, Clarence Thomas, and the Construction of Social Reality,* ed. Toni Morrison, 61–85. New York: Pantheon Books.

Marcus, George, et al. 2000. *Affective Intelligence and Political Judgment.* Chicago: University of Chicago.

Marrow, Helen. 2011. *New Destination Dreaming: Immigration, Race, and Legal Status in the Rural American South.* Stanford, Calif.: Stanford University Press.

Marsden, Peter, ed. 2012. *Social Trends in American Life: Findings from the General Social Survey since 1972.* Princeton, N.J.: Princeton University Press.

Martin, Brian. 1989. "The Sociology of the Fluoridation Controversy: A Reexamination." *Sociological Quarterly* 30 (1): 59–76.

Masket, Seth. 2009. "Did Obama's Ground Game Matter? The Influence of Local Field Offices during the 2008 Presidential Election." *Public Opinion Quarterly* 73 (5): 1023–39.

Mayhew, David. 1974. *Congress: The Electoral Connection.* New Haven, Conn.: Yale University Press.

McCarthy, J. J., et al. 2001. *Climate Change 2001: Impacts, Adaptation, and Vulnerability.* Cambridge, U.K.: Cambridge University Press.

McCright, Aaron, and Riley Dunlap. 2011. "The Politicization of Climate Change and Polarization in the American Public's Views of Global Warming, 2001–2010." *Sociological Quarterly* 52 (2): 155–94.

McDonnell, Lorraine. 2004. *Politics, Persuasion, and Educational Testing.* Cambridge, Mass.: Harvard University Press.

McGhee, Eric. 2010. "How Much Does the Public Know about the State Budget, and Does It Matter?" *California Journal of Politics and Policy* 2 (3): 1–21.

McKenna, Maryn. 2013. "The Pertussis Parable." *Scientific American* 309, 34–36.

McMillan, James B. 1981. Statement to Senate Judiciary Committee, Subcommittee on Separation of Powers. *Hearings on Court-Ordered School Busing,* 97th Cong., 1st Sess.: 511–17.

Melillo, Jerry, Terese Richmond, and Gary Yohe, eds. 2014. *Climate Change Impacts in the United States: The Third National Climate*

Assessment. Washington, D.C.: U.S. Global Change Research Program.

Mendelberg, Tali. 2001. *The Race Card: Campaign Strategy, Implicit Messages, and the Norm of Equality.* Princeton, N.J.: Princeton University Press.

Miller, Arthur H. 1999. "Sex, Politics, and Public Opinion: What Political Scientists Really Learned from the Clinton-Lewinsky Scandal." *PS: Political Science and Politics* 32 (4): 721–29.

Miller, Joanne, and Jon Krosnick. 2000. "News Media Impact on the Ingredients of Presidential Evaluations: Politically Knowledgeable Citizens Are Guided by a Trusted Source." *American Journal of Political Science* 44 (2): 301–15.

Miller, Lisa, and Joni Reynolds. 2009. "Autism and Vaccination: The Current Evidence." *Journal for Specialists in Pediatric Nursing* 14 (3): 166–72.

Miller, Melissa, and Shannon Orr. 2008. "Experimenting with a 'Third Way' in Political Knowledge Estimation." *Public Opinion Quarterly* 72 (4): 768–80.

Mirkinson, Jack. 2013. "'60 Minutes' Briefly Apologizes for Benghazi Report: 'We Are Very Sorry.'" *Huffington Post: Media,* Nov. 10. www.huffingtonpost.com/2013/11/10/60-minutes-apology-benghazi-lara-logan_n_4252253.html.

Mnookin, Seth. 2011. *The Panic Virus: A True Story of Medicine, Science, and Fear.* New York: Simon and Schuster.

Mondak, Jeffery. 1999. "Reconsidering the Measurement of Political Knowledge." *Political Analysis* 8 (1): 57–82.

Mondak, Jeffery, and Belinda Davis. 2001. "Asked and Answered: Knowledge Levels When We Will Not Take 'Don't Know' for an Answer." *Political Behavior* 23 (3): 199–224.

Monroe, Bill. 1991. "Anita Hill Explosion Also Hit the Press." *American Journalism Review,* Dec.

Musto, Richard. 1987. "Fluoridation: Why Is It Not More Widely Adopted?" *Canadian Medical Association Journal* 137: 705–708.

Mutz, Diana. 2006. *Hearing the Other Side: Deliberative versus Participatory Democracy.* New York: Cambridge University Press.

Myrdal, Gunnar. 1944. *An American Dilemma.* New York: Harper and Brothers.

Nadeau, Richard, et al. 2008. "Election Campaigns as Information Campaigns: Who Learns What and Does It Matter?" *Political Communication* 25 (3): 229–48.

National Academy of Sciences Committee on the Science of Climate Change. 2001. *Climate Change Science: An Analysis of Some Key Questions.* Washington, D.C.: National Academy Press.

Newman, Brian. 2002. "Bill Clinton's Approval Ratings: The More Things Change, the More They Stay the Same." *Political Research Quarterly* 55 (4): 781–804.

Nie, Norman, et al. 1996. *Education and Democratic Citizenship in America*. Chicago: University of Chicago Press.

Nisbet, Matthew, and Teresa Myers. 2007. "The Polls—Trends: Twenty Years of Public Opinion about Global Warming." *Public Opinion Quarterly* 71 (3): 444–70.

Nordhaus, William. 2013. *The Climate Casino: Risk, Uncertainty, and Economics for a Warming World*. New Haven, Conn.: Yale University Press.

Nyhan, Brendan, and Jason Reifler. 2010. "When Corrections Fail: The Persistence of Political Misperceptions." *Political Behavior* 32 (2): 303–30.

———. Forthcoming. "The Effect of Fact-Checking on Elites: A Field Experiment on U.S. State Legislators." *American Journal of Political Science*.

———. 2013. *Which Corrections Work? Research Results and Practice Recommendations*. Washington, D.C.: New America Foundation, Media Policy Initiative.

Nyhan, Brendan, et al. 2013. "The Hazards of Correcting Myths about Health Care Reform." *Medical Care* 51 (2): 127–32.

Nyhan, Brendan, et al. 2014. "Effective Messages in Vaccine Promotion: A Randomized Trial." *Pediatrics* 133 (4): e835–e842.

O'Leary, Sean, et al. 2010. *Risk Factors for Non-receipt of Hepatitis B Vaccine in the Newborn Nursery*. Arlington, Va.: Infectious Diseases Society of America.

Oliver. J. Eric. 2001. *Democracy in Suburbia*. Princeton N.J.: Princeton University Press.

Omer, Saad, et al. 2012. "Vaccination Policies and Rates of Exemption from Immunization, 2005–2011." *New England Journal of Medicine* 367 (12): 1170–71.

Opinion Business Research. 2008. "New Analysis 'Confirms' 1 Million+ Iraq Casualties." Jan. 28. www.opinion.co.uk.

Oprah Winfrey Show. 2007. "Mothers Battle Autism: Jenny Mccarthy and Holly Robinson Peete Fight to Save Their Autistic Sons." Sept. 18. www.oprah.com/oprahshow/Mothers-Battle-Autism/1.

Overby, L. Marvin, et al. 1992. "Courting Constituents? An Analysis of the Senate Confirmation Vote on Justice Clarence Thomas." *American Political Science Review* 86 (4): 997–1003.

Owen, Diana. 2000. "Popular Politics and the Clinton/Lewinsky Affair: The Implications for Leadership." *Political Psychology* 21 (1): 161–77.

Page, Susan. 2011. "Poll: What Kind of President Would Donald Trump Make?" *USA Today*, Apr. 26.

Partin, Randall. 2001. "Campaign Intensity and Voter Information: A Look at Gubernatorial Contests." *American Politics Research* 29 (2): 115–40.

Patterson, Matt. 2011. "Second Thoughts about That Birth Certificate." *Washington Examiner*, Apr. 4.

Patterson, Thomas. 2013. *Informing the News: The Need for Knowledge-Based Journalism.* New York: Vintage Books.

Paumgarten, Nick. 2011. "Anyone? Anyone?" *New Yorker*, June 27.

Pear, Robert. 2014. "Missouri Obstructing Health Law, Judge Rules." *New York Times*, Jan. 24.

Pennock, Pamela. 2007. *Advertising Sin and Sickness: The Politics of Alcohol and Tobacco Marketing, 1950–1990.* DeKalb: Northern Illinois University Press.

Peterson, Merrill. 1966. *Democracy, Liberty and Property: The State Constitutional Conventions of the 1820s.* Indianapolis: Bobbs-Merrill.

Pew Research Center's Project for Excellence in Journalism. 2011. *Tornadoes Lead News in Days before Bin Laden Death: PEJ News Coverage Index: April 25–May 1, 2011.* Washington, D.C.: Pew Research Center for People and the Press.

Pew Research Center. 2010. *Increasing Partisan Divide on Energy Policies: Little Change in Opinions about Global Warming.* Washington, D.C.: Pew Research Center for People and the Press.

———. 2011. *Modest Rise in Number Saying There Is "Solid Evidence" of Global Warming.* Washington, D.C.: Pew Research Center for People and the Press.

———. 2012. *More Say There Is Solid Evidence of Global Warming.* Washington, D.C.: Pew Research Center for People and the Press.

———. 2013a. *As Health Care Law Proceeds, Opposition and Uncertainty Persist.* Washington, D.C.: Pew Research Center for People and the Press.

———. 2013b. *King's Dream Remains an Elusive Goal: Many Americans See Racial Disparities.* Washington, D.C.: Pew Research Center for People and the Press.

———. 2013c. *"What the Public Knows—in Pictures, Maps, Graphs, and Symbols.* Washington, D.C.: Pew Research Center for People and the Press.

Pew Research Center and American Association for the Advancement of Science. 2009. *Public Praises Science: Scientists Fault Public, Media.* Washington, D.C.: Pew Research Center for People and the Press.

Phelps, Timothy, and Helen Winternitz. 1992. *Capitol Games: Clarence Thomas, Anita Hill, and the Story of a Supreme Court Nomination.* New York: Hyperion.

Pierce, J. P., et al. 2011. "Prevalence of Heavy Smoking in California and the United States, 1965–2007." *Journal of the American Medical Association* 305 (11): 1106.

Pinderhughes, Dianne. 1992. "Divisions in the Civil Rights Community." *PS: Political Science and Politics* 25 (3): 485–87.

Plait, Phil. 2013. "Still Not Vaccinated? U.S. Measles Cases in 2013 Spike to *Three Times* Normal." *Slate*, Dec. 6. www.slate.com/blogs/bad_astronomy/2013/12/06/measles_2013_us_cases_triple.html.

Poland, Gregory, and Robert Jacobson. 2011. "The Age-Old Struggle against the Antivaccinationists." *New England Journal of Medicine* 364 (21): 97–99.

Popkin, Samuel. 1993. "Information Shortcuts and the Reasoning Voter." In *Information, Participation, and Choice*, ed. Bernard Grofman, 17–35. Ann Arbor: University of Michigan Press.

Popkin, Samuel, et al. 1999. "Political Knowledge and Citizen Competence." In *Citizen Competence and Democratic Institutions*, ed. Steven Elkin and Karol Soltan, 117–46. University Park: Pennsylvania State University Press.

Powell, James Lawrence. 2012. *The Inquisition of Climate Science* New York: Columbia University Press.

Prasad, Monica, et al. 2009. "'There Must Be a Reason': Osama, Saddam, and Inferred Justification." *Sociological Inquiry* 79 (2): 142–62.

Prior, Markus, and Arthur Lupia. 2008. "Money, Time, and Political Knowledge: Distinguishing Quick Recall and Political Learning." *American Journal of Political Science* 52 (1): 169–83.

Public Policy Polling. 2012a. "Obama's Lead up to 5 in Ohio." Sept. 9. www.publicpolicypolling.com/main/2012/09/obamas-lead-up-to-5-in-ohio.html.

———. 2012b. "North Carolina Remains a Toss-up." Sept. 10. www.publicpolicypolling.com/main/2012/09/north-carolina-remains-a-toss-up.html.

Putnam, Robert. 2007. "E Pluribus Unum: Diversity and Community in the Twenty-First Century." *Scandinavian Political Studies* 30 (2): 137–74.

Putnam, Robert, and David Campbell. 2012. *American Grace: How Religion Divides and Unites Us.* New York: Simon and Schuster.

Raab, Earl. 1988. "High Anxiety." *Present Tense* 15: 46–49.

Ramakrishnan, S. Karthick, and Paul Lewis. 2005. *Immigrants and Local Governance: The View from City Hall.* San Francisco: Public Policy Institute of California.

Ravitch, Diane, and Chester Finn. 1988. *What Do Our 17-Year-Olds Know? A Report on the First National Assessment of History and Literature.* New York: Harper and Row.

Redlawsk, David, et al. 2010. "The Affective Tipping Point: Do Motivated Reasoners Ever 'Get It'?" *Political Psychology* 31 (4): 563–93.

Rees, Laurence, et al. 2004. *Auschwitz: The Nazis and the "Final Solution."* Video, six episodes. BBC.

Rehmeyer, Julie. 2010. "'Discounting' the Future Cost of Climate Change." *Science News,* May 21. https://www.sciencenews.org/article/discounting-future-cost-climate-change.

Reilly, Gretchen. 2004. "'Not a So-Called Democracy': Anti-fluoridationists and the Fight over Drinking Water." In *The Politics of Healing: Histories of Alternative Medicine in Twentieth-Century North America,* ed. Robert Johnston, 131–50. New York: Routledge.

———. 2007. "The Task Is a Political One: The Promotion of Fluoridation." In *Silent Victories: The History and Practice of Public Health in Twentieth-Century America,* ed. John Ward and Christian Warren, 323–40. New York: Oxford University Press.

Reuters. 1991. "Thomas Given 'Qualified' Rating by ABA." *Christian Science Monitor,* Aug. 29. www.csmonitor.com/1991/0829/29083.html.

Rodriguez, Lori. 1992. "Electing Minority Isn't Always Best." *Houston Chronicle,* Aug. 8.

Rolfe-Redding, Justin, et al. 2012. "Republicans and Climate Change: An Audience Analysis of Predictors for Belief and Policy Preferences." Annual meeting of the International Communication Association, Phoenix, Ariz., May 24.

Ross, Oakland. 2011. "Andrew Wakefield's Fraudulent Vaccine Research." *Toronto Star,* Jan. 7.

Rowley, James. 1991. "Senate Confirms Thomas, 52–48, to High Court." *Memphis Commercial Appeal,* Oct. 16.

Rucinski, Dianne. 1993. "Rush to Judgment? Fast Reaction Polls in the Anita Hill–Clarence Thomas Controversy." *Public Opinion Quarterly* 57 (4): 575–92.

Saad, Lydia. 2013. "Republican Skepticism toward Global Warming Eases Concern among Republicans Back to Pre-2009 Levels." *Gallup: Politics*, Apr. 9. www.gallup.com/poll/161714/republican-skepticism-global-warming-eases.aspx.

Sapiro, Virginia, and Joe Soss. 1999. "Spectacular Politics, Dramatic Interpretations: Multiple Meanings in the Thomas/Hill Hearings." *Political Communication* 16 (3): 285–314.

Sapolsky, Harvey. 1968. "Science, Voters, and the Fluoridation Controversy." *Science* 162 (3852): 427–33.

Scalia, Laura. 1999. *America's Jeffersonian Experiment: Remaking State Constitutions, 1820–1850*. DeKalb: Northern Illinois University Press.

Schwarz, Norbert, et al. 2007. "Metacognitive Experiences and the Intricacies of Setting People Straight: Implications for Debiasing and Public Information Campaigns." In *Advances in Experimental Social Psychology* 39, ed. Mark Zanna, 127–61. New York: Academic Press.

Scruggs, Lyle, and Salil Benegal. 2012. "Declining Public Concern about Climate Change: Can We Blame the Great Recession?" *Global Environmental Change* 22 (2): 505–15.

Sears, David, and Carolyn Funk. 1990. "Self-Interest in Americans' Political Opinions." In *Beyond Self-Interest*, ed. Jane Mansbridge, 147–70. Chicago: University of Chicago Press.

Sears, David, et al. 1979. "Whites' Opposition to 'Busing': Self-Interest or Symbolic Politics?" *American Political Science Review* 73 (2): 369–84.

Seitz-Wald, Alex. 2013. "The Fight of Obamacare's 'Navigators' against Republican Hurdles." *National Journal*, Oct. 30.

Sentencing Project. 2003. "The Thinking Advocate's List of Mitigating Factors." Jan. http://sentencingproject.org/detail/publication.cfm?publication_id=110.

Shah, Dhavan, et al. 2002. "News Framing and Cueing of Issue Regimes: Explaining Clinton's Public Approval in Spite of Scandal." *Public Opinion Quarterly* 66 (3): 339–70.

Shambaugh, George. 2013. "Perceptions of Threat, Trust in Government, and Policy Support for the War in Iraq." In *The Political Psychology of Terrorism Fears*, ed. Samuel Justin Sinclair and Daniel Antonius, 20–50. New York: Oxford University Press.

Shani, Danielle. 2006. "Knowing Your Colors: Can Knowledge Correct for Partisan Bias in Political Perceptions?" Annual meeting of the Midwest Political Science Association, Chicago, Ill.

Shapiro, Nina. 2013. "With Fewer Vaccinations, Is Your Child's School Safe?" *Los Angeles Times*, Aug. 10.

Shapiro, Robert, and Yaeli Bloch-Elkon. 2008. "Do the Facts Speak for Themselves? Partisan Disagreement as a Challenge to Democratic Competence." *Critical Review* 20 (1–2): 115–39.

Sharp, Elaine. 1996. "Culture Wars and City Politics: Local Government's Role in Social Conflict." *Urban Affairs Review* 31 (6): 738–58.

Shoemaker, Pamela, et al. 2002. "Item Nonresponse: Distinguishing between Don't Know and Refuse." *International Journal of Public Opinion Research* 114 (2): 193–201.

Sides, John. 2009. "Crime: The Striking Gap between Perceptions and Reality." *The Monkey Cage*, Oct. 14. http://themonkeycage .org/2009/10/14/crime_the_striking_gap_between/.

———. 2011. "Stories, Science, and Public Opinion about the Estate Tax." Washington, D.C.: George Washington University, Department of Political Science.

Sides, John, and Jack Citrin. 2007. "European Opinion about Immigration: The Role of Identities, Interests and Information." *British Journal of Political Science* 37 (3): 477–504.

Sides, John, and Lynn Vavreck. 2013. *The Gamble: Choice and Chance in the 2012 Presidential Election.* Princeton, N.J.: Princeton University Press.

Sigelman, Lee, and Richard Niemi. 2001. "Innumeracy about Minority Populations: African Americans and Whites Compared." *Public Opinion Quarterly* 65 (1): 86–94.

60 Minutes. 2012. "Unaired Excerpts from the Obama, Romney Interviews." www.cbsnews.com/media/unaired-excerpts-from -the-obama-romney-interviews/10/.

Skocpol, Theda, and Vanessa Williamson. 2012. *The Tea Party and the Remaking of Republican Conservatism.* New York: Oxford University Press.

Slothuus, Rune, and Claes de Vreese. 2010. "Political Parties, Motivated Reasoning, and Issue Framing Effects." *Journal of Politics* 72 (3): 630–45.

Smith, Tom. 1995. *Holocaust Denial: What the Survey Data Reveal.* New York: American Jewish Committee.

Somin, Ilya. 1998. "Voter Ignorance and the Democratic Ideal." *Critical Review* 12 (4): 413–58.

Sonner, Molly, and Clyde Wilcox. 1999. "Forgiving and Forgetting: Public Support for Bill Clinton during the Lewinsky Scandal." *PS: Political Science and Politics* 32 (3): 554–57.

Sourcebook of Criminal Justice Statistics. Various years. Albany, N.Y.: University at Albany, School of Criminal Justice.

Spector-Bagdady, Kayte, and Elizabeth Pike. Forthcoming. "Consuming Genomics: Regulating Direct-to-Consumer Genomic Interpretation." *Nebraska Law Review* 92 (4): 677–745.

Starr Commission and Kenneth Starr. 1998. *The Starr Report: The Official Report of the Independent Counsel's Investigation of the President.* Roseville, Calif.: Prima Lifestyles.

Stelter, Brian. 2011. "In Trying to Debunk a Theory, the News Media Extended Its Life." *New York Times,* Apr. 28, A16.

Stimson, James. 2004. *Tides of Consent: How Public Opinion Shapes American Politics.* New York: Cambridge University Press.

St. Louis Post-Dispatch. 1992. "Rookie Justice Thomas Pleased Conservatives." *St. Louis Post-Dispatch,* July 29, 3B.

Sturgis, Patrick, et al. 2007. "An Experiment on the Measurement of Political Knowledge in Surveys." *Public Opinion Quarterly* 85 (1): 90–102.

Sugerman, David, et al. 2010. "Measles Outbreak in a Highly Vaccinated Population, San Diego, 2008: Role of the Intentionally Undervaccinated." *Pediatrics* 125 (4): 747–55.

Sunstein, Cass. 2011. *Going to Extremes: How Like Minds Unite and Divide.* New York: Oxford University Press.

———. 2013. *Simpler: The Future of Government.* New York: Simon and Schuster.

SurveyUSA. 2011. "Results of SurveyUSA News Poll #18161." Apr. 28. www.surveyusa.com/client/PollReport.aspx?g=826a 5884-2d30-4d86-90bc-13e3fc9df7f9&c=12.

Taber, Charles, et al. 2009. "The Motivated Processing of Political Arguments." *Political Behavior* 31 (2): 137–55.

Talbot, David. 1998. "The Salon Report on Kenneth Starr." *Salon,* Sept. 10.

Tate, Katherine. 1993. *From Protest to Politics: The New Black Voters in American Elections.* New York: Russell Sage Foundation.

———. 2002. "Invisible Woman." *American Prospect,* Nov. 30.

Tesler, Michael. 2012. "The Spillover of Racialization into Health Care: How President Obama Polarized Public Opinion by Racial Attitudes and Race." *American Journal of Political Science* 56 (3): 690–704.

Tesler, Michael, and David Sears. 2010. "Is the Obama Presidency Post Racial? Evidence from His First Year in Office." Annual meeting of the Midwest Political Science Association. Chicago, Ill.

Thaler, Richard, and Cass Sunstein. 2009. *Nudge: Improving Decisions about Health, Wealth, and Happiness.* New York: Penguin Books.

Theodoridis, Alexander. 2012. "Party Identity in Political Cognition." Ph.D. dissertation, Berkeley: University of California, Department of Political Science.

Tomasky, Michael. 2011. "Birthers and the Persistence of Racial Paranoia." *Guardian.co.uk*, Apr. 27. www.guardian.co.uk /commentisfree/michaeltomasky/2011/apr/27/barack-obama -obama-administration.

Toobin, Jeffrey. 2011. "Partners: Will Clarence and Virginia Thomas Succeed in Killing Obama's Health-Care Plan?" *New Yorker,* Aug. 29.

United States Holocaust Memorial Museum. n.d. "A Changed World: The Continuing Impact of the Holocaust." www.ushmm .org/museum/exhibit/focus/aftermath/pdf/brochure.pdf.

United States Senate. 1991. *Nomination of Judge Clarence Thomas to Be Associate Justice of the United States Supreme Court.* Committee on the Judiciary. Washington, D.C.: U.S. Government Printing Office.

U.S. Congressman Joe Wilson. 2009. "Congressmen Announce Amendment to Strengthen Enforcement Mechanisms in Pelosi's Health Care Takeover." Nov. 5. http://joewilson.house.gov /News/DocumentSingle.aspx?DocumentID=219735.

Valentino, Nicholas, et al. 2008. "Is a Worried Citizen a Good Citizen? Emotions, Political Information Seeking, and Learning via the Internet." *Political Psychology* 29 (2): 247–73.

Verba, Sidney, et al. 1995. *Voice and Equality: Civic Voluntarism in American Politics.* Cambridge, Mass.: Harvard University Press.

Voteview. 2013. "An Update on Political Polarization through the 112th Congress." *voteview.blog,* Jan. 16. http://voteview.com /blog/?p=726.

Wallance, Gregory. 2012. *America's Soul in Balance: The Holocaust, FDR's State Department, and the Moral Disgrace of an American Aristocracy.* Austin, Tex.: Greenleaf Book Group.

Walton, Alice. 2013. "Should Companies Have the Right to Refuse to Hire Smokers?" *Forbes,* Mar. 28.

Washington Post. 1991a. "The Thomas Hearings." *Washington Post,* Sept. 15, C6.

———. 1991b. "The Thomas Nomination." *Washington Post,* Oct. 15.

Washington Post et al. 1995. *The Four Americas: Government and Social Policy through the Eyes of America's Multi-racial and Multi-ethnic Society*. Washington, D.C.: Washington Post.

Weingarten, Gene. 1996. "Read It and Veep." *Washington Post*, Feb. 4.

Westen, Drew. 2008. *The Political Brain: The Role of Emotion in Deciding the Fate of the Nation*. New York: Public Affairs.

Williams, Linda. 1995. "Anita Hill, Clarence Thomas, and the Crisis of Black Political Leadership." In *African American Women Speak Out on Anita Hill-Clarence Thomas*, ed. Geneva Smitherman, 243–65. Detroit, Mich.: Wayne State University Press.

Wong, Cara. 2007. "'Little' and 'Big' Pictures in Our Heads." *Public Opinion Quarterly* 71 (3): 392–412.

Working Group I. 2013. *Climate Change 2013: The Physical Science Basis*. Geneva, Switzerland: Intergovernmental Panel on Climate Change.

Working Group II. 2014. *Climate Change 2014: Impacts, Adaptation, and Vulnerability*. Geneva, Switzerland: Intergovernmental Panel on Climate Change.

Working Group III. 2014. *Climate Change 2014: Mitigation of Climate Change*. Geneva, Switzerland: Intergovernmental Panel on Climate Change.

WorldPublicOpinion.Org. 2010. "Misinformation and the 2010 Election: A Study of the American Electorate." College Park: University of Maryland, Program on International Policy Attitudes.

Wright, Caroline. 2010. "Size of the Direct-to-Consumer Genomic Testing Market." *Genetics in Medicine* 12 (9): 594.

Wyman, David. 1985. *The Abandonment of the Jews: America and the Holocaust, 1941–1945*. New York: Pantheon Books.

Xu, Xiaowen, et al. 2013. "Does Cultural Exposure Partially Explain the Association between Personality and Political Orientation?" *Personality and Social Psychology Bulletin* 39 (11): 1497–517.

Yeager, David, et al. 2011. "Measuring Americans' Issue Priorities: A New Version of the Most Important Problem Question Reveals More Concern about Global Warming and the Environment." *Public Opinion Quarterly* 75 (1): 125–38.

Yiannakis, Diana. 1982. "House Members' Communication Styles: Newsletters and Press Releases." *Journal of Politics* 4 (2): 1049–71.

Zaller, John. 1985. "Pre-testing Information Items on the 1986 NES Pilot Study. Report to the National Election Study Board

of Overseers." Ann Arbor: University of Michigan, Survey Research Center.

———. 1992. *The Nature and Origins of Mass Opinion.* New York:
Cambridge University Press.

———. 1998. "Monica Lewinsky's Contribution to Political Science." *PS: Political Science and Politics* 31 (2): 182–89.

Zeller, Tom. 2004. "The Iraq-Qaeda Link: A Short History." *New
York Times,* June 20.

INDEX

Italicized references indicate figures.

voter turnout, 106, 185n10
voting rights, 4

Walgreens, 154
Washington, Harold, 30
Washington Post, 77–78, 110
Watergate scandal, 30
weapons of mass destruction,
    alleged to be in Iraq, 89–91,
    92, 93, 95, 97, 122–23, 136
Weingarten, Gene, 17
Welles, Sumner, 146

West, Cornel, 183n20
Wilder, Douglas, 77
Wilson, Joe, 69
Winfrey, Oprah, 128
World Health Organization,
    97
World Jewish Congress, 145
World Meteorological
    Organization, 46
Wyman, David, 184n2

Zaller, John, 42, 50, 64, 109